THE STORY WE LIVE BY

Text copyright © R. Alastair Campbell 2004
The author asserts the moral right
to be identified as the author of this work

Published by
The Bible Reading Fellowship
First Floor, Elsfield Hall
15–17 Elsfield Way, Oxford OX2 8FG
ISBN 1 84101 359 7

First published 2004
1 3 5 7 9 10 8 6 4 2 0

Acknowledgments
Unless otherwise stated, scripture quotations are taken from the Holy Bible, New
International Version, copyright © 1973, 1978, 1984 by International Bible Society, and
are used by permission of Hodder & Stoughton Limited. All rights reserved. 'NIV' is a
registered trademark of International Bible Society. UK trademark number 1448790.

Scripture quotations taken from The New Revised Standard Version of the Bible, Anglicized
Edition, copyright © 1989, 1995 by the Division of Christian Education of the National Council
of the Churches of Christ in the USA, are used by permission. All rights reserved.

Scriptures quoted from the Good News Bible published by The Bible
Societies/HarperCollins Publishers Ltd, UK © American Bible Society 1966, 1971,
1976, 1992, used with permission.

Revised English Bible with the Apocrypha copyright © 1989 by Oxford University Press
and Cambridge University Press.

Extracts from The Book of Common Prayer of 1662, the rights of which are vested in
the Crown in perpetuity within the United Kingdom, are reproduced by permission of
Cambridge University Press, Her Majesty's Printers.

A catalogue record for this book is available from the British Library

Printed and bound in Finland

THE STORY WE LIVE BY

A READER'S GUIDE TO THE NEW TESTAMENT

R. ALASTAIR CAMPBELL

For Dotha

PREFACE

When my friend, Joe Davis, at that time one of the ministers at West Croydon Baptist Church, asked me to give a series of midweek lectures to church members on the New Testament, I was dubious. Would anyone turn up? I wondered.

'How many people would you need to make it worthwhile?' he asked.

I said I would do it for six.

'Oh,' he said, 'I'll get you at least twenty.'

In the event we opened with 65 and kept that number more or less intact through the series of six talks on the Gospels that followed. Seemingly there was a 'market' among thoughtful Christians for the kind of information about the Bible that ministers meet in their training but which they rarely feel able to share with their congregations. Later this was confirmed when, as minister of the International Church in Kathmandu, I repeated the series and added talks on Paul and his letters and on Revelation.

What is a 'Reader's Guide to the New Testament'? Think of visiting a historic building, rich in history and full of treasures. You may be allowed to wander round on your own, but you will probably get more out of your visit if you have a guide, someone who knows something of the history and will point out some of the treasures. The New Testament may be compared to such a building. It has many rooms, each with its own history, and contains far more treasures of wisdom and knowledge than you can hope to take in at one visit. The present book is intended to be such a guide. As we go from room to room, I shall tell you something about their stories and point out what seems to me of greatest interest or importance in them. My hope is that you will have a New Testament open beside you as you read, so that you can see the things I point to, and that when we have been round this great building together you will be able to go round on your own and make other discoveries for yourself.

The purpose of this book, then, like the talks from which it sprang, is to offer a readable and satisfying answer to such questions as 'What are these writings? How did they come to be written? What do they say to us today?' and to do so in such a way that the reader is able to see the New Testament as a whole and not in the fragmentary form it often takes in Sunday sermons.

There is little here that is original. Nearly all of it has been learned from others and may be found in longer and more technical books. At the same time this is a personal interpretation of the New Testament. Where scholars differ, I have not always given you the majority view, but felt free to follow my own instincts and adopt less widely held opinions when I think they are right. I have been privileged to study the New Testament for many years and during this time I have learned from many other scholars. Some of my more recent debts are acknowledged in the notes, but other insights have become so much part of my thinking that I no longer know from whom I first learnt them. To all my teachers I am very grateful.

I would also like to express thanks to the Bible Reading Fellowship for agreeing to publish this book, especially to Naomi Starkey as Commissioning Editor, and Lisa Cherrett for seeing the book through to publication, and to those friends who encouraged me to write it in the first place. My prayer is that, as you read it, it will help you to grasp the message of the New Testament writings and the witness they bear to the great story, the life, death and resurrection of Jesus Christ, the story Christians live by.

Alastair Campbell
Feast of the Epiphany, 2004

CONTENTS

THE STORY BEHIND THE STORY[1]

'Why is this night different from all other nights?' asks the youngest son at the Jewish Passover, and the answer is a story—the story of slavery in Egypt and of the great escape (or Exodus). Nations and peoples live by the stories they tell. Jews do not tell that story to pass the time, but to define who they themselves are: 'this is *our* story, and *we* are the people who came out of Egypt'. Americans do the same thing every year at Thanksgiving. They tell the story of the first settlers, their hardships and eventual triumph, and other stories too that tell of the birth of the nation and invite the hearers to say, 'This is our story. This is who we are.' English people tell the story of Magna Carta or the defeat of the Spanish Armada; Protestants tell the story of Martin Luther ('Here I stand...'); Methodists tell the story of John Wesley ('I felt my heart strangely warmed...'). Whatever country or movement you belong to, you probably have such stories, stories you tell your children to give them a sense of who they are and where they belong. We may note in passing that these stories are often highly simplified versions of the events they describe. The 'reality', as the historian will tell you, was generally much messier and more ambiguous, but then history, as Sellar and Yeatman famously remarked, is not so much what happened as what you can remember![2]

At the heart of Christianity is not a code or a creed but a story, the story of Jesus. Even the most widely recited Christian creed makes this plain, being not so much a list of doctrines to be believed as a story to be told. 'I believe in Jesus Christ, God's only Son, our Lord, who was conceived... born... suffered... descended... rose...'—and there's your story! Christians have lived by it for centuries and we come back to it again and again to renew our faith and get our bearings. As often as fresh challenges to Christian belief or behaviour arise, as they do in every generation, it is to the story of Jesus, rather than to proof texts, that we return to seek a fresh understanding and obedience 'for the living of these days'.[3]

It shouldn't surprise us, then, that something like half of both the Old and New Testaments consists of story, and the story is what gives coherence to all the rest. The New Testament begins with the story of Jesus, told in four different ways, and continues with the story of the first years of the Church. The rest of the New Testament—the letters and the book of Revelation—is simply commentary on that story, presupposing the story, drawing out its implications, and making little sense without it. I make no apology, therefore, for calling the whole New Testament 'the story we live by'.

Yet the story of Jesus cannot be understood apart from another story, the story of Israel. The very first words of the New Testament make this plain, for the book begins (rather unpromisingly, we might think), 'A record of the genealogy of Jesus Christ the son of David, the son of Abraham' (Matthew 1:1). To understand Jesus, says Matthew, you have to see him as the fulfilment of a story that goes all the way back to David (who lived a thousand years before) and behind him to Abraham (several hundred years before that). There is a story behind the story, without which the story of Jesus will make little sense.

The Old Testament is a long book, or rather a large collection of books, that together witness to the story of Israel over many centuries. It contains many different kinds of literature—story, law, poetry, wisdom and prophecy. All of it is important and worth studying, but to expect people to read it all before they embark on the New Testament would be unrealistic. Fortunately, it is possible to be selective (as Matthew shows in his genealogy) and to pick out certain key stories within the story that are of special importance, and which together form a thread that will lead us through the maze, all the way from Abraham to Jesus. These stories are:

- the story of Abraham and the promise
- the story of Moses and the great escape
- the story of David and the kingdom
- the story of the exile and the Servant of the Lord
- the story of the Maccabean persecution and the Son of Man

ABRAHAM AND THE PROMISE

The story of Israel begins with the promise of God to Abraham, but to see the significance of that, we need to observe where the biblical writer has placed the story. The first eleven chapters of the book of Genesis form an introduction to the Bible as a whole. They tell the story of how God created the world and how, through human sin and disobedience, that world was spoilt; and they finish with the sad story of the tower of Babel, symbol of human arrogance and failed dreams (Gen. 11:1–9). God and humanity are now far away from each other, the human race is divided and scattered in mutual suspicion and incomprehension... and God started again!

Now the Lord said to Abram, 'Go from your country and your kindred and your father's house to the land that I will show you. I will make of you a great nation, and I will bless you, and make your name great, so that you will be a blessing. I will bless those who bless you, and the one who curses you I will curse; and in you all the families of the earth shall be blessed.'
GEN. 12:1–3 (NRSV)

God starts again by calling a man, calling him out of his homeland and culture to live in dependence on God's word of promise. From this man and his descendants will come a great nation, and this nation will be a blessing to all the other peoples on earth. It is as if Abraham were to be a second Adam, the progenitor of a nation—the people of Israel—that will be a light to the nations, a witness to God's word and will, until those very nations, at present scattered and alienated, are brought home to God to form a new humanity.[4]

When Matthew calls Jesus the son of Abraham, he is saying that, in Jesus, God has taken a decisive step towards fulfilling this ancient promise. Luke begins his Gospel with scenes in which pious Israelites hail the birth of Jesus as the fulfilment of God's promise to Abraham (Luke 1:54–55, 72–73; 2:32). There is much more to the story of Abraham, of course, but we shall leave him and move forward several hundred years to the story of Moses.

MOSES AND THE GREAT ESCAPE

The family of Abraham has grown in numbers, but its members are still a long way from enjoying the land promised them. They are in Egypt and they are slaves—and God calls another man, a man providentially preserved in infancy, prepared (though he does not know it) by long years in obscurity and exile.

The Lord said, 'I have indeed seen the misery of my people in Egypt. I have heard them crying out because of their slave drivers, and I am concerned about their suffering. So I have come down to rescue them... So now, go. I am sending you to Pharaoh to bring my people the Israelites out of Egypt.'
EX. 3:7–8a, 10

'I have *seen*, I have *heard*, I am *concerned* and I have *come down*,' God says. The answer is that someone must be sent to save, and that man is Moses. It is a pattern repeated many times in the Bible, culminating in the coming of Jesus himself, and it all happened as God had said. Moses did confront Pharaoh and tell him to 'let my people go'. He did lead the people out of Egypt and through the Red Sea to freedom, and he also gave his people God's laws so that they could be a great nation (just as God had promised Abraham) and a light to the world.

The New Testament never calls Jesus 'the son of Moses', any more than the people of Israel are thought of in the Old Testament as Moses' descendants, but some New Testament writers clearly think of Jesus as a second Moses. Matthew tells us how the child Jesus was threatened by an evil king, as Moses had been, and how he sought refuge in Egypt (Matt. 2:13–15), so that, like Moses and Israel, he came 'out of Egypt' to bring his people a new and fuller statement of God's law on the mountain (Matt. 5—7). Luke remembers how Moses had said that God would raise up a prophet like himself—a new Moses in fact, not so much a law-giver as a saviour and leader—and how in Jesus people had recognized the advent of such a prophet (Luke 7:16; Acts 7:37), someone who would accomplish a new exodus or escape for his people (Luke 9:31).

DAVID AND THE KINGDOM

It is time for us to leave Moses and jump forward more than two centuries to the story of David, who lived around 1000BC. The Israelites are living in the land promised to them, but they are not really in possession of it. They have been pushed out of much of the most fertile land and are reduced to clinging to the hill-tops, subject to raids from the desert tribes, and paying tribute to the militarily superior Philistines. They are 'in office but not in power', as one of our politicians famously remarked of a singularly ineffective administration. They need a king—someone who will 'go out before us and fight our battles' (1 Sam. 8:20). This is exactly what David does. In the famous story of David and Goliath, David (who has already been secretly anointed as Israel's king) goes out in front of all Israel as their representative and overcomes the Philistine champion on their behalf. His victory is the victory of the whole people.

David went on to become a great king, and made Israel a great nation (the promise to Abraham again). In Israel's memory, his reign became a sort of golden age, but after his death it all began to go wrong. His son Solomon is an ambiguous figure: he was remembered as a truly wise man, but his reign was marred by oppression and extravagance. David's kingdom broke apart under the strain, Israel assimilated their faith to the religion of the surrounding nations (instead of being a light to them, as God had intended) and, in the end, lost their king and their independence. In the centuries that followed, people longed for God to give them a new king, a new David, to be their champion and fight their enemies. Their hopes were kept alive by the promise God made to David towards the end of his life.

When your days are fulfilled and you lie down with your ancestors, I will raise up your offspring after you, who shall come forth from your body, and I will establish his kingdom. He shall build a house for my name, and I will establish the throne of his kingdom forever. I will be a father to him, and he shall be a son to me.

2 SAM. 7:12–14 (NRSV)

When the New Testament writers call Jesus the son of David, they are saying that, in Jesus, this promise has been fulfilled. The word 'Christ' means 'anointed', and anointed as Israel's king. 'Son of God' was originally a royal title, however much it may have acquired a deeper meaning. When Jesus was born, the angel said to Mary, 'He will be great and will be called the Son of the Most High. The Lord God will give him the throne of his father David' (Luke 1:32).

The New Testament presents Jesus as God's anointed king, not just of Israel but of the nations too, and also as our champion and representative who has engaged a greater enemy than Goliath in single combat and won the victory for all of us.

THE SERVANT OF THE LORD

We move forward another few hundred years to the middle of the sixth century BC. It is obvious to people of spiritual insight that God's plan to rescue the world through Israel is not on track. The laws given through Moses are not being obeyed. The land given through Moses' successor Joshua is no longer theirs. The kingdom of David is no more, its temple destroyed and its leaders deported. Israel is in exile in Babylon.

Into this desperate situation, Isaiah speaks a message of hope. God is in charge of the nations, as he always has been. Kingdoms rise and fall at his command. There is a new world order coming and a new emperor who will end Israel's exile and make it possible for them to return. Isaiah is talking about the Persian emperor, Cyrus, who in 539BC overthrew the Babylonian empire and issued a decree per-mitting the Jews to return to their homeland (Ezra 6:3–5). Yet it is plain that the really significant figure in God's sight is not the all-conquering Persian emperor, but someone whom God, speaking through Isaiah, calls 'my servant'.

Here is my servant, whom I uphold, my chosen, in whom my soul delights; I have put my spirit upon him; he will bring forth justice to the nations. He will not cry or lift up his voice, or make it heard in the street; a bruised reed he will not break, and a dimly burning wick he will not quench; he will faithfully bring forth justice. He will not grow faint or be crushed until he has established justice in the earth; and the coastlands wait for his teaching.
IS. 42:1–4 (NRSV)

The Ethiopian pilgrim was not the last person to ask, 'Who is the prophet talking about?' (Acts 8:34). In fact, it is plain that the prophet is talking about Israel, who is addressed by name as God's servant at least seven times in these chapters of Isaiah. It was through Israel that the nations were to be blessed (Gen. 12:3), and it is the servant's task to 'establish justice in the earth' (Is. 42:4) and to be 'a light for the nations' (42:6).

This is still Israel's task, as the prophet makes plain: 'And he said to me, "You are my servant, Israel, in whom I will be glorified"' (Is. 49:3, NRSV). Yet the sad truth is that the Israelites are quite unable to carry out their task. They are blind and deaf, unable to see what God is doing, unable to hear his word or believe it (Is. 42:19). It becomes plain that there will have to be a mission *to* Israel before there can be a mission *through* Israel. Someone will have to do for Israel what they cannot do for themselves, 'to bring Jacob back to him and gather Israel to himself' (Is. 49:5). Only so will God's purpose for the whole world be fulfilled: '[God] says, "It is too light a thing that you should be my servant to raise up the tribes of Jacob and to restore the survivors of Israel; I will give you as a light to the nations, that my salvation may reach to the end of the earth"' (Is. 49:6, NRSV).

As before, God will call a man, as he called Abraham or Moses or David, to rescue his people and his plan for the world, to stand in for his people as representative and champion. But unlike David, this person will fight not with Israel's enemies but with sin itself, and conquer not with a sling or a sword but through his own sufferings.

Surely he has borne our infirmities and carried our diseases; yet we accounted him stricken, struck down by God, and afflicted. But he was wounded for our transgressions, crushed for our iniquities; upon him was the punishment that made us whole, and by his bruises we are healed. All we like sheep have gone astray; we have all turned to our own way, and the Lord has laid on him the iniquity of us all.
IS. 53:4–6 (NRSV)

Isaiah's picture of God's servant has been likened to an advertisement: 'WANTED! Someone who will be born within Israel, to represent Israel, to bear her sins and sorrows, so that she in turn can bear the sins and sorrows of the world, so that the world can have light and all the nations of the world may be blessed.' In the end, of course, there was only one successful applicant![5]

THE SON OF MAN

There is one other story that you need to know in order to make sense of the New Testament. Once again we have to scroll forward through the history book another 400 years, to the year 167BC. Israel is again in trouble. The glowing promises of Isaiah still await their fulfillment. Empire has succeeded empire: Israel is now part of the Greek empire, and the new king Antiochus has adopted a militantly anti-Jewish policy. Here is what happened according to the Jewish history known as 1 Maccabees.

Now on the fifteenth day of Chislev, in the one hundred and forty-fifth year, they erected a desolating sacrilege upon the altar of burnt offering. They also built altars in the surrounding cities of Judah and burnt incense at the doors of the houses and in the streets. The books of the law which they found they tore to pieces and burnt with fire. Where the book of the covenant was found in the possession of anyone, or if anyone adhered to the law, the decree of the king condemned him to death. They kept using violence against Israel, against those found month after month in the cities. And on the twenty-fifth day of the month they offered sacrifice on the altar which was upon the altar of burnt offering. According to the decree, they put to death the women who had their children circumcised, and their families and those who circumcised them; and they hung the infants from the mothers' necks. But many in Israel stood firm and were resolved in their hearts not to eat unclean food. They chose to die rather than to be defiled by food or to profane the holy covenant; and they did die.

1 MACC. 1:54–63 (NRSV)

If you wonder why you need to know about these things, given that they are not in the canon of Scripture recognized by most of our churches, the answer is that it helps to make sense of things we do find in the New Testament. In the first place, you'll have noticed that Jesus himself refers to this passage with his reference to the 'desolating sacrilege' (Matt. 24:15, NRSV). More generally, when we remember that faithful Israelites had been willing to die rather than break the laws regarding clean and unclean food (and had died rather than fight on the Sabbath), we begin to understand the passions that were aroused when Jesus appeared to sit loose to those laws, and Paul disregarded those boundary markers of Jewish identity. But there is more.

In these dark days of persecution, the wise men of Israel recalled the stories of how Daniel had been faithful to God during the Babylonian exile centuries before, and they brought out a fresh edition of his exploits to encourage the people of God in their resistance. This is our book of Daniel, and in this book Daniel has a dream in which he sees four great monsters coming up out of the sea (Daniel 7:1–8). (In 7:17, we are told that these monsters represent the successive pagan empires that have oppressed Israel, climaxing with the current savage regime.) Then Daniel sees God himself, 'the Ancient of Days', taking his seat. 'The court sat in judgment and the books were opened' (v. 10, NRSV), and the evil empires are condemned by God. Next Daniel sees a human figure, 'one like a son of man', being presented before God and being given the kingdom (vv. 13–14). This human figure, we are told, represents the faithful people of God, 'the saints of the Most High' (vv. 17–18).

Although there are obscurities, the central message of this dream is fairly clear. The phrase 'son of man' simply means 'human being', but in the dream this human figure represents Israel. In contrast to the pagan empires, which are bestial, Israel is called to model true humanity. The pagan empires are allowed to oppress Israel for a time, but the dream declares that, after they have suffered, God will vindicate his own. We saw earlier that God called Abraham as a kind of second Adam, so it is no surprise if Abraham's descendants, the true Israel, are also the true humanity. It has even been suggested that the victory of this true humanity over the beasts hints at the final restoration of Adam's sovereignty over the animals.

All this throws a flood of light on what Jesus may have meant by referring to himself as the Son of Man, suggesting that he saw his own career represented by this figure. Three points are of importance: the Son of Man is collective, a symbol for Israel; the Son of Man suffers; and the Son of Man is then vindicated. This suggests that, in calling himself the Son of Man, Jesus was making a claim to be the true representative of Israel, standing in for Israel like a new David. Second, he was accepting a destiny—to suffer and die on behalf of his people, like the Servant of the Lord. Third, he was issuing an invitation to faithful Israelites to form a new people of God, a true Israel, around himself. This true Israel would become the nucleus of a new humanity, a second Adam. We shall return to these points when we encounter the Son of Man on the lips of Jesus in the Gospels.[6]

CONCLUSION

We have traced a line from Adam to Jesus through key figures of Israel's story, to show that there is a 'story behind the story' which we need to have in mind if we are to understand the story of Jesus in the New Testament. Jesus came into a world that was looking for a saviour. In particular, he came to a people who were looking for the kingdom of God (Luke 23:51) to come in ways that would be 'the consolation of Israel' (Luke 2:25) and 'the redemption of Jerusalem' (Luke 2:38). Their hope is nicely expressed by the old Advent hymn that Christians still sing:

> *O come, O come, Immanuel, and ransom captive Israel,*
> *that mourns in lonely exile here until the Son of God appear.*
> *Rejoice! Rejoice! Immanuel shall come to thee, O Israel.*

Jesus' contemporaries were looking for a new David, a new Moses, who would bring to fulfilment the original promise to Abraham. When Jesus came, he fulfilled these hopes, but in an unexpected way, drawing on a different strand of Israel's hopes and dreams. He embraced the vocation of the Servant of the Lord, who wins the victory for his people not by fighting their battles but by bearing their griefs and carrying their sorrows. In giving his life as a ransom for many (Mark 10:45), he was also accepting the destiny of the Son of Man who comes to his throne only after suffering.

PART ONE

THE STORY OF JESUS

CHAPTER I

WHAT ARE THE GOSPELS?

COMING TO TERMS WITH DIVERSITY

The story of Jesus has come down to us in four different forms, the four biographical memoirs we call the Gospels.[1] While these Gospels are broadly similar in length and structure, with many stories and sayings of Jesus in common, they also differ from one another in significant ways, both in what they include or omit, and also in the way the stories and teaching of Jesus are reported. This can be disturbing if you approach them as you might four police officers' notebooks, trying to piece together 'what really happened', but such an approach may do violence to the kind of writing the Gospels actually are and the kind of purpose they are designed to serve. After all, a pathologist's report on a person who has died and a eulogy at his or her funeral are both accounts of the same person and both may be true, but they are different kinds of truth. Or again, a passport photo will not be the same as a portrait painted by an artist, which may sacrifice a certain kind of accuracy in the interests of conveying an idea of the subject's character.

Portrait painter's truth is not the same as pathologist's truth. Two pathologists examining the same corpse are expected to come up with identical findings. Two portrait painters are not expected to produce identical portraits, because a portrait is not just a record of what a person looked like. It is an interpretation of that person's character, which conveys a message about them. Think for a moment of the late Diana, Princess of Wales. Hundreds of portraits of her must exist (especially in photographic form), and some of them stick in the mind. While some portrayed her as the fairytale princess, others saw the compassionate friend of AIDS sufferers, or the intrepid campaigner against landmines, the devoted mother or the deserted wife. Each picture captures a part of truth, and each is also an interpretation in which the insight and intention of the photographer contributes to what we see. This helps to explain the way the Gospels differ from each other. They should be thought of as portraits, different interpretations of the same subject, as Richard Burridge makes clear in his helpful book, *Four Gospels, One Jesus?*[2]

Mark portrays Jesus as the suffering Servant of God, yet also as a strong and demanding leader, one who goes ahead of his disciples and leads them on. It is a harsh portrait with strong lines and bold colours, an enigmatic portrait that leaves us with many unresolved questions. Matthew portrays Jesus as the new Moses, the teacher of Israel, who is also the Lord of the whole world. In contrast to Mark, he explains everything and smooths away the rough edges. Luke portrays Jesus as prophet and saviour, a man full of the Spirit, who as the Son of God brings salvation to the weak and sinful. This is a polished and attractive portrait designed to appeal to an educated public. As George Bernard Shaw said, 'It is Luke's Jesus who has won our hearts.'[3] Finally, John sees Jesus as the man from heaven who acts as both witness and advocate in God's lawsuit against the world. This is a highly distinctive portrait using a largely different selection of stories to make its impact.

The Gospels do not differ only in overall presentation; they also differ in detail when they are telling the same story. There is nothing surprising about this. It happens with all great men and women. Stories about them are told and retold, and in the process the details get confused or are changed to suit the lesson being drawn by the storyteller. A revealing example is provided by the great 19th-century preacher, Charles Haddon Spurgeon. A famous story is told about his encounter with a lamplighter, but it exists in at least two forms. Compare the two versions of the story printed overleaf. The first comes from a book about Spurgeon; the second is taken from Spurgeon's autobiography.[4]

A	B
He was walking one day up Norwood Hill with a friend. Some distance ahead of them, moving up the hill, they could see a lamplighter, lighting lamp after lamp until he disappeared over the brow of the hill. Turning to his friend, Spurgeon said, *'I hope my life will be just like that. I should like to think that when I've gone over the brow of the hill I shall leave lights shining behind me.'* Spurgeon left many lights behind him. More than any other great preacher he fashioned and moulded others after his own model. His influence will not leave the earth until they have left it; perhaps not then. That is the greatest of tributes to his ministry. Ronald W. Thompson	Coming one Thursday in the late Autumn from an engagement beyond Dulwich, my way lay up to the top of the Herne Hill ridge. I came along the level out of which rises a steep hill I had to ascend. While I was on the lower ground, riding in a hansom cab, I saw a light before me, and when I came near the hill I marked that light gradually go up the hill, leaving a train of stars behind it. This line of new-born stars remained in the form of one lamp, and then another and then another. It reached from the foot of the hill to the summit. I did not see the lamplighter. I do not know his name, nor his residence; but I saw the lights which he had kindled, and these remained when he himself had gone away. As I rode along I thought to myself, *'How earnestly do I wish that my life may be spent in lighting one soul after another with the sacred flame of eternal life! I would myself be as much as possible unseen while at my work, and would vanish into the eternal brilliance above when my work is done.'*

It is without doubt the same incident. Spurgeon will often have seen lamplighters at work, but he will not often have had the same moment of revelation, or gone round boring his friends by pretending to do so. Yet the story differs in both incidental details and also in the lesson being drawn. The point of the story in each case lies in the 'saying' of Spurgeon, but even this is remembered somewhat differently. This is exactly what we find in the Gospels. The incidental details may vary, though the saying of Jesus remains the same, or the saying itself may be preserved in a different form to make a different point, while the details of the incident itself remain constant.

Traditionally, we have responded to the differences between the Gospels by trying to harmonize them, telling a composite story that takes a bit from here and a bit from there, but there are good reasons for avoiding this approach. In the first place, it can't always be done without grotesque improbability. Mark says that Jesus healed the blind man as he was leaving Jericho (Mark 10:46); Luke says that it happened as they were approaching the city (Luke 18:35). Or, to give another example to which we shall return, compare the way in which Mark and Matthew each finish the story of Jesus walking on the water. Mark says, 'Then he got into the boat with them and the wind ceased. And they were utterly astounded, for they did not understand about the loaves, but their hearts were hardened' (Mark 6:51–52, NRSV). Matthew says, 'When they got into the boat, the wind ceased. And those in the boat worshipped him, saying, "Truly you are the Son of God"' (Matthew 14:32–33, NRSV).

The difference is all the more striking when we remember, as I shall argue, that Matthew wrote with Mark's Gospel in front of him, so that the difference is due to Matthew's intention, not simply to his having got hold of a different story. Yet the way each writer has ended his story fits perfectly into the rest of the portrait he has painted. Mark often shows the disciples as uncomprehending, and likes to leave the reader with unanswered questions. Matthew's portrait is much smoother and the truth is made explicit. It is impossible to harmonize these two accounts satisfactorily, but why should we want to? After all, that is not how we treat portraits! We do not think of taking bits from different portraits to make a composite picture, and to do so would be entirely to miss the message that each painter wished to convey to us. We shall find that it is best to sit and listen to each Gospel writer in turn if we are to hear the unique message that each writer brings, and all the more so if, as Christian readers, we believe that it is God who has inspired this diversity. In trying to hear all of them at once, we may end up not hearing any of them at all.

In studying a portrait, it is revealing to notice not just what effect the painter is seeking to produce but also how he or she goes about producing it—in other words, their technique. In the case of the Gospels, we find that the technique used is more like collage than watercolour. The portrait is assembled by sticking together a different selection of the materials available. To change the analogy, the Gospels tell the story of Jesus by selecting and arranging separate stories, like a person putting together a collection of snapshots, which capture different moments and characteristic actions of the subject. It is characteristic of the stories that make up our Gospels that they are generally self-contained. Each story is complete in itself and is linked only loosely to the stories on either side of it. The stories could be put in a different order without spoiling the sense, and we do, in fact, find them differently arranged in different Gospels. In this way they resemble snapshots.

No doubt there were hundreds of stories of Jesus circulating in the years after his resurrection—John says as much (John 21:25)—but the Gospel writers have selected those they thought of special importance, and they differ from one another in the selection they make. John in particular has given us a quite different selection of stories that only occasionally overlaps with that of the other Gospels, but even Matthew and Luke differ widely from each other and from Mark. For example, the parable of the good Samaritan, or the story of Zacchaeus, are found only in Luke, while the parable of the un-forgiving servant is found only in Matthew. Even where they include the same stories, the Gospel writers sometimes place them in a different order. John has Jesus clearing the temple at the start of his ministry, while the other Gospels place it in the last week of his life. We can argue about which is more likely to have been historical, but if we attend to what each writer is saying, we shall find that the story fits perfectly in its place.

Yet we should not exaggerate the problem. For all their differences, all the Gospels tell the story of the man who was baptized by John, who called Israel by word and deed to make way for the coming of

God's kingdom, clashed with the Jewish authorities, died on a Roman cross and rose from the dead two days later. In every Gospel the story of Jesus' public ministry begins with John the Baptist, moves between Galilee and Jerusalem and climaxes with the trial, crucifixion and resurrection of Jesus. The Gospels agree far more than they differ. To recognize the differences between them should not be thought to call into question the truth or the divine inspiration of these documents. Belief in the inspiration of scripture will not tell us what kind of writing the Gospels are; examination of what the Gospels are will tell us what it is that God has inspired.

HOW WERE THE GOSPELS WRITTEN?

Jesus himself wrote nothing, but his teaching was remembered and passed on. Stories about Jesus were preserved and repeated endlessly by Christian teachers and evangelists. In the thirty years or so after Jesus' ascension, these teachings and stories came to form the young Church's 'memory bank', and all the writers have drawn on this bank in putting their Gospels together. This in itself goes a long way to explaining the similarities between them. But in many places there is close word-for-word agreement that goes beyond anything that could be expected from two writers drawing on the same collective memory—the sort of agreement that happens only when one writer has copied from another. Even when two stories differ in significant respects, there is often word-for-word agreement in the incidental details, exactly the opposite of what you would expect if two eyewitnesses were reporting the same event. In the case of two eyewitnesses, you would expect them to describe the same events but to do so in their own words. The Gospel writers sometimes differ in what they relate, yet agree in the words they use, which means either that one writer has copied another or that both have drawn on a common source. This is particularly true of the first three Gospels, usually called the synoptic Gospels. Over the last 200 years, scholars have subjected the Greek text of the Gospels to intense scrutiny in an effort to determine which writer has copied from another, and the following conclusions are widely, but not universally, held today.

Mark is probably the earliest Gospel. There are three reasons for thinking so. First, it is much shorter than Matthew or Luke, and it is much more likely that Matthew and Luke improved Mark's account by adding material than that Mark, with Matthew and Luke in front of him, deliberately left out large parts of their accounts. Mark contains no story of Jesus' birth, little of Jesus' teaching and only a brief account of his resurrection. He has neither Matthew's great discourses (for example, the Sermon on the Mount) nor Luke's distinctive parables (for example, the prodigal son). If Mark was using Matthew and Luke, is it likely that he would have left these things out?

Second, although Mark is shorter than the other two synoptic Gospels, when they have a story in common Mark's version is generally longer, with more colourful detail. You can see this by comparing the story of the healing of the demon-possessed man in Gadara in Mark 5:1–20 with the account in Matthew 8:28–34, or the story of the paralysed man let down through the roof in Mark 2:1–12 with Matthew 9:1–7. If Mark set out to write a summary of Matthew and Luke, as is sometimes suggested, why would he want to lengthen some stories while leaving out so much other material?

Third, Mark's style is rougher and simpler (though you need to be able to read Greek to appreciate this point fully). It is easier to believe that Matthew and Luke have improved Mark's style than that Mark deliberately coarsened theirs.

Matthew is the closest of the other Gospels to Mark and can best be seen as an expanded version of it. Almost all of Mark is found in Matthew, with the exception of a few 'odd' stories (for example, Mark 7:31–37; 8:22–26; 14:51–52) and obscure sayings (for example, Mark 9:50), and is for the most part in the same order. Matthew has added the story of Jesus' birth and large amounts of Jesus' teaching, which he has grouped together in five long discourses. He also has a much fuller account of Jesus' resurrection. Much of this material is unique to Matthew, and we may suppose that he drew independently on the Church's memory bank. Some of it, however, is very close in wording and content to material also found in Luke (but not in Mark), which raises the question of the relationship of Matthew and Luke.

A large amount of Mark is also found in Luke, and in the same words, and Luke has preserved Mark's basic framework. Jesus teaches in Galilee, journeys to Jerusalem and is there put to death by the

WHAT ARE THE GOSPELS?

authorities. But Luke has added a large amount of material not found anywhere else—the story of Jesus' birth, told from a quite different point of view to Matthew's; stories of Jesus encountering individuals (see Luke 7:36–50; 19:1–10), and stories told by Jesus (such as the good Samaritan or the prodigal son, Luke 10:30–37; 15:11–32). Presumably this is the product of his own research, which he tells us he carried out (Luke 1:1–4). There are also about 235 of Luke's 1151 verses that are more or less identical with verses found in Matthew, mostly in the form of sayings and teachings of Jesus. Have Matthew and Luke each drawn on a now-lost collection of Jesus' teaching (as most scholars believe), or has Luke taken up and adapted material that he found in Matthew (a significant minority opinion)?

The view that Matthew and Luke have used a lost document (conventionally called 'Q') has long been popular in Gospel studies, not least because, if correct, it offers us the possibility of an additional and distinctive early source for studying the life and teaching of Jesus, and great efforts have been made to determine its shape and theology. The view I take in this book is that Luke has used and adapted Matthew. Admittedly, this means that Luke has used Matthew very freely, breaking up his long discourses and retelling some of Matthew's stories with a different emphasis—but why should he not have done so? The attraction of this view is that we confine our attention to the Gospels we actually have, rather than chasing after hypothetical documents about whose scope and contents there is no agreement.[5]

John's Gospel is quite different from the other three. It still tells the story of Jesus' public ministry followed by his arrest, trial, death and resurrection, but John has given us a different selection of stories. Much of the action takes place in Judea, in or around Jerusalem, as opposed to Galilee. John's account features a number of miracles or signs, most of which are absent from the synoptic Gospels. Instead of short sayings, we find long discourses, and whereas in the synoptic Gospels Jesus mainly teaches about the kingdom of God, in John's Gospel he mainly teaches about himself, who he is and what he has come into the world to do. Most scholars think that John was written later than the other Gospels. In places, John seems to presuppose a knowledge of Mark, but he doesn't use Mark as a source in the way that Matthew and Luke have done.

WHO WROTE THE GOSPELS?

It is not known for certain who actually wrote the Gospels. The authors do not identify themselves in the body of the text, and the traditional ascriptions, 'according to Mark', 'according to Matthew' and so on, were added at a later date—but not much later! It has been convincingly argued that the practice of naming the Gospels as 'according to Mark' or 'according to Matthew' became a necessity as soon as more than one Gospel was in existence and the different Gospels were kept in church libraries for use in worship.[6] The fact that there was never any dispute about the titles of the Gospels suggests that they were added very early by people who were in a position to know who had written them.

Nevertheless, the titles are not part of the sacred text, and so the Gospels are strictly anonymous and contain few other clues as to their date of writing. It is easier to relate them to each other than to date them in relation to other events in history. One of the key dates is the destruction of Jerusalem by the Romans in AD70. From the space given to Jesus' prediction of it in the synoptic Gospels, it is likely that this event was a catalyst in the production of the Gospels and had probably occurred in the recent past.

'Mark' is presumably the John Mark mentioned as a companion of Paul and Barnabas in Acts 13:13; 15:37–39 and 2 Timothy 4:11, and of Peter in 1 Peter 5:13 (if this is the same person). An early tradition says that the author was Peter's secretary and companion in prison, and so the Gospel is usually thought to have been written in Rome, either just before or just after the destruction of Jerusalem. Judging by the fact that Mark needs to explain Jewish customs (7:3) it is likely that he wrote for Gentile readers, and the emphasis on suffering makes it likely that they were experiencing or expecting persecution for their faith.

'Matthew' is traditionally the tax collector of that name mentioned in Matthew 9:9—one of the Twelve, and, if so, an eyewitness of the events he describes. This is possible, but we need to recognize that the author never writes as an eyewitness. He never speaks in the first person singular or plural (contrast the 'we' passages in Acts) or supports his account by saying, 'I was there, and it happened like this.' Moreover, as we have seen, much of his account is borrowed from

Mark and, in contrast to Mark, is actually less fresh and vivid, which is strange if he writes as an eyewitness. Matthew's readers are clearly expected to be familiar with the Jewish scriptures and Jewish customs. At the same time, the way in which Matthew can talk of 'their synagogues' (see 12:9) suggests that his readers are alienated from the Jewish community, which would fit well with a date after AD70. They probably lived in Syria, perhaps in the great city of Antioch.

'Luke' is probably the companion of Paul of that name (Col. 4:14), since the same person also wrote Acts and there speaks of himself as a participant in some of Paul's adventures. He was not, however, an eyewitness of Jesus' ministry (Luke 1:2), and acknowledges his debt both to such eyewitnesses and to other written sources. He has often been thought of as a Gentile writing for Gentiles (represented by the Theophilus of 1:3, whoever he may have been), but we should not overlook Luke's strong interest in showing the new Christian movement to be the fulfilment of 'all that the prophets have spoken' (24:25). This suggests that Luke may well have been a Greek-speaking Jew writing for the same sort of people that Paul addresses in his letters.

Traditionally, the author of the fourth Gospel was John son of Zebedee, and many people still believe this. However, the Gospel itself points to the author as a person unknown to us (though presumably known to the readers) simply called 'the disciple whom Jesus loved'. This person was an eyewitness of the events described or, at least, of Jesus' death (19:26–27, 35), but has apparently died at the time of the Gospel's final edition. So the fourth Gospel rests on the testimony of the beloved disciple, but in its present form it has been presented by a later author, or group of people, simply identified as 'we' (21:24). The first readers are usually thought to have lived in Ephesus around AD90.[7]

In the end, we do not know who actually wrote the four Gospels, but does it matter? Their authors evidently did not think so. They have not written memoirs to draw attention to themselves (*'Jesus of Nazareth: My Part in His Victory'*). All their attention is on Jesus himself, and that is where they would want ours to be too. This brings us to the final section of this Introduction.

THE SUBJECT OF THE GOSPELS

In *Four Gospels, One Jesus?*, to which reference has already been made, Richard Burridge likens the diverse portraits of Jesus to the many different portraits of Winston Churchill that can be seen at Chartwell, for many years Churchill's country home and now a museum to his memory. Let's pursue that idea a little. People go to Chartwell because they already know something of Churchill's life, and their appreciation of the portraits is enhanced by this knowledge. They do not look at the portraits in order to learn whether he was a great man or what he did. Rather, they look at the portraits in order to gain an insight into the character of the great man whose life in outline they already know. The same is true of Jesus. The first readers of the Gospels knew the main facts of Jesus' career, and the Gospel writers wrote so that they would understand him better. Today, however, many people are ignorant of the facts of Jesus' life and, as a result, often miss the significance of the stories they read.

When I was planning this book, I had intended to follow the four chapters on the Gospels with a chapter on Jesus, the man behind the portrait, but I came to see that this would be misleading. It would suggest that, after reading the different Gospel accounts, we would then be ready for 'the truth', as revealed by the historian who had sifted the Gospels' evidence and was prepared, like Sherlock Holmes or Hercule Poirot, to tell the assembled company 'what really happened'. I make no such claim! If this were a book about the 'historical Jesus' we might examine the Gospels as a preliminary to forming a satisfying hypothesis about his life. As it is a book about the Gospels (and the other New Testament writings) and how to read them, it seems better to begin by offering a short summary of Jesus' career, as pieced together by reliable scholars, so that we can better appreciate the Gospel portraits.

A person who wanted to appreciate the portraits at Chartwell would need to know the main facts of Churchill's life—that he was born into an upper-class English family; that he was for many years a mercurial and controversial politician; that he came quite late to the leadership of his nation, at a time when it was facing defeat in war; that he rallied the nation by his oratory and force of personality and led it to a famous victory; and that he was subsequently rejected by the electorate and never again enjoyed the same success, either in opposition or in government. This is the man whose character the portrait painters have tried to capture.

A person who wants to appreciate the portraits of Jesus in the Gospels needs to know certain things about him which are often forgotten or misunderstood. He was born into a devout Jewish family in or around what we now call 4BC and grew up believing in one God, the maker of heaven and earth and judge of all people, who had chosen Israel as his own people and given them the law so that they could be the means of bringing healing to the whole world. He grew up among people seething with resentment against the Roman occupation, longing for God to establish his promised reign of justice and peace, bitterly divided among themselves over how to prepare for that event. Jesus grieved over his people's subjection and shared their hope of God's kingdom. While still a young man, he felt himself called and empowered by God to launch out as a prophet, announcing that God was about to act and calling Israel to prepare for this event by practising love and mercy. He demonstrated the nearness of God's reign by the exercise of healing power, and the character of God's reign by banqueting with the poor and outcast. He condemned the violence and separatism characteristic of popular nationalist sentiment, and warned that these would lead to the destruction of the nation at the hands of Roman armies. God's coming would then be for judgment rather than salvation.

Born into the family of David, Jesus knew himself to have been anointed king of Israel by the Spirit of God. This, indeed, is the meaning of the term 'Christ' or 'Messiah', which Jesus did not refuse, even though, because of its nationalist overtones, he preferred other titles. 'Son of God', which in the Old Testament had been given to the nation of Israel as a whole and especially to the king, also served to express Jesus' sense of calling, although the full implications of this title would not become plain until after the resurrection. Jesus himself seems to have preferred to speak of himself as the Son of Man. While this could mean no more than 'I' or 'someone like me', on the lips of Jesus it constitutes a claim to fulfil the role of the human figure in Daniel's dream. Representing faithful Israel, that figure comes to royal dignity only after great suffering, making him a specially suitable symbol for Jesus' understanding of his own role as king of Israel.

However expressed, Jesus' claim to be the anointed king through whom God's kingdom would come is the answer to the question of why he died as he did. On the one hand, he was put to death by the authorities as a messianic pretender. As the Jewish leaders put it in John's Gospel, 'Anyone who claims to be a king opposes Caesar' (John 19:12), and those who were seen to oppose Caesar ended up on a Roman cross, as many others before Jesus had done. On the other hand, it explains why Jesus might have seen it as his duty and calling to die for his people. Already, in Isaiah 52:13—53:12, we have the idea that the death of the righteous atones for the guilt of the nation as a whole, an idea which had been invoked to explain the deaths of the Maccabean martyrs 200 years before Jesus. As we have seen, Jesus warned the nation against provoking the wrath of God in the form of Roman armies (or the wrath of Rome in which God's judgment would be expressed). Now Jesus, knowing himself to be the king and representative of his people, instead of avoiding the retribution of the Roman authorities, voluntarily stands in for his people and takes that retribution on himself so that they will not have to suffer it.

Following the death of Jesus, three things happened that changed the history of the world. First, Jesus' grave was found empty. There seems no reason to doubt this, partly because Christian belief in his resurrection could never have got off the ground otherwise, and partly because if Jesus' grave were not empty it is hard to see why the authorities did not advertise the fact instead trying to explain it away. Second, Jesus' closest followers were convinced that they had seen him alive. Third, the Christian movement enjoyed phenomenal success. Even if, as a recent study has concluded, there were no more than 10,000 Christians by the end of the first century, the wonder is that there were any![8]

Jewish messianic movements normally fizzled out when their leader was executed. This one didn't. Instead it grew and spread, so that 30 to 50 years after Jesus' death there was a demand for the portraits of him that we know as the four Gospels. The empty tomb, the conviction of Jesus' followers and the rise of Christianity are facts, explain them how you will. The Christians' explanation was that God had raised Jesus from the dead. For those who believed it, this meant, first, that Jesus was vindicated in his claim to be the Son of God and king of Israel. It meant, second, that the kingdom of God had come in power. It meant, third, that the restoration of God's people was a reality, and that with Jesus the resurrection of the last day had begun.

CHAPTER 2

MARK'S STORY

The first Christians were people with a story to tell. They called their story 'gospel', or 'good news', a word associated in Jewish minds with Isaiah's announcement of God's coming victory and in Greek minds with the announcement of the birth or accession of an emperor. 'Gospel' was thus a good word for the story of how God had acted decisively to bring salvation to the world through the man Jesus, whom God raised from the dead and announced to be his true Son, king of Israel and Lord of the world. When Mark begins his work, 'The beginning of the gospel of Jesus Christ, the Son of God' (1:1, NRSV), he is referring to the Christian message, and that message is a story, the story of Jesus.

The story is nicely summarized for us in a passage from the Acts of the Apostles, where Peter is preaching to the household of Cornelius:

'You know the message God sent to the people of Israel, telling the good news of peace through Jesus Christ, who is Lord of all. You know what has happened throughout Judea, beginning in Galilee after the baptism that John preached —how God anointed Jesus of Nazareth with the Holy Spirit and power, and how he went around doing good and healing all who were under the power of the devil, for God was with him.

'We are witnesses of everything he did in the country of the Jews and in Jerusalem. They killed him by hanging him on a tree, but God raised him from the dead on the third day and caused him to be seen. He was not seen by all the people, but by witnesses whom God had already chosen—by us who ate and drank with him after he rose from the dead. He commanded us to preach to the people and to testify that he is the one whom God appointed as judge of the living and the dead. All the prophets testify about him that everyone who believes in him receives forgiveness of sins through his name.'
ACTS 10:36–43

According to Peter in Acts 10:36, the message is a message from God —and Mark also calls it the gospel of God (1:15). It was addressed in the first place to Israel, in fulfilment of prophecy—and Mark also begins with the words of the prophet (1:2–3)—and it is a message of peace and forgiveness through Jesus Christ. Then Peter proceeds to tell the story of Jesus, highlighting the following facts:

- He was empowered by the Spirit (Acts 10:38; Mark 1:1–15).
- He went about doing good and healing (Acts 10:38; Mark 1:16— 10:52).
- He started in Galilee but finished in Jerusalem (Acts 10:39; Mark 11—13).
- He was put to death on a cross (Acts 10:39; Mark 14—15).
- He was raised from the dead (Acts 10:40; Mark 16:1–8).
- He was seen alive by chosen witnesses (Acts 10:41; Mark 16:7).

As the above points show, Peter's sermon corresponds almost exactly to the story Mark has to tell. It is a story in two parts, beginning in Galilee and finishing in Jerusalem. The first half deals with Jesus' healing ministry and the second with his death. The climax of the story is the resurrection of Jesus from the dead, but 'the beginning of the gospel' is the empowering of Jesus following his baptism by John, and this is where Mark begins.

THE STORY IN OUTLINE

There is widespread agreement on the broad outline of Mark's story. It divides into two roughly equal halves, with Peter's confession of Jesus as the Christ forming the hinge. Up to that point Mark has told us about Jesus' powerful public ministry in Galilee. From then on, Jesus for the most part teaches his disciples in private and the story moves inexorably towards his death in Jerusalem. In addition to this basic division of the Gospel into two, many people have seen the opening verses as a kind of prologue that tells the reader who Jesus is before his public ministry begins; and the closing verses dealing with the resurrection as an epilogue to the main story—the climax to the main story being the centurion's confession, 'Surely this man was the Son of God!' (15:39). A further possibility is to see each of the main parts of the story as divided into three roughly equal sections, perhaps reflecting the need to divide up the Gospel for reading aloud to its first audience.

When we look at the detailed analyses proposed by different scholars, however, we find little agreement among them. For example, does the prologue end with 1:13 or 1:15? Is Jesus' announcement of the nearness of the kingdom the end of this opening section, or the start of the next? And where does the second half of the Gospel actually begin? Is the story of Peter's confession (8:27–30) the climax of the first half, or the start of the second—or both?

The ancient manuscripts contained no chapter divisions or headings, and Mark has left no clue as to how he intended to structure his narrative. This reminds us that such structural analyses are something brought to the text by the modern reader.[1] The fact that no two people agree over where to draw the lines might suggest that the quest for Mark's structure is hopeless, but while the results of such a quest can never be final, the quest itself can still be fruitful. Constructing an outline forces us to pay attention to the text. When we do that, we find recurring patterns and evidence that the Gospel is not just a random collection of stories but the work of a careful and purposeful author who cannot have been unaware of what he was doing. In what follows, I have had the help of other scholars in forming my analysis of Mark, but since they do not always agree with each other I have often had to make up my own mind, and in doing so I have gained a deeper understanding of the Gospel. I hope you will find my analysis helpful, but you are not bound to accept it! You should feel quite free to improve on it, if you can, and you will certainly learn more about Mark's Gospel in the attempt.

'ANOINTED WITH THE HOLY SPIRIT AND POWER' (MARK 1:1–15)

The central event in this section is the empowering of Jesus. This, for Mark, is where the Gospel begins. The ministry of John points forward to it, and the ministry of Jesus flows from it. John the Baptist was a major figure in recent Jewish history, but John's work in itself is of no interest to Mark. Its function in the narrative is to set up a contrast between the admittedly prestigious ministry of John and the far greater achievement of Jesus. Unlike John, who only baptizes in water, Jesus will baptize in the Holy Spirit (v. 8). This does not refer to anything that happens in the story Mark is about to tell (Jesus did not go around baptizing people in Spirit), but refers to the new life that Mark and his readers enjoy because of the life, death and resurrection of the Messiah.

Jesus is baptized by John, but it is not from John or through baptism that he receives the Holy Spirit. This is the direct gift of God, who declares Jesus to be his Son (v. 11). The title 'Son of God', for Mark, does not have all the connotations of divinity that it would acquire in later Christian reflection: it means rather that Jesus is the true king of Israel (see Ps. 2:7). The words that follow ('with you I am well pleased') recall the suffering servant of Isaiah (Is. 42:1) and warn us that Jesus is a king who will come to his kingdom only through service and suffering.

Thus empowered, Jesus declares that the kingdom of God is near (v. 15). The phrase 'kingdom of God' expresses the ancient Jewish hope that God would one day become king over everything that contradicts his reign. This would involve the liberation and restoration of Israel and ultimately the destruction of death itself (1 Cor. 15:26). Jesus saw his own ministry of power as a sign that the kingdom was near, but he knew that it would not come apart from his death. When God raised him from the dead, the kingdom arrived in power (Mark 9:1), but it would be completed only with the resurrection of all God's people and the 'restoration of all things' (Acts 3:21).

'HE WENT AROUND DOING GOOD...' (MARK 1:16—3:7)

Two themes intertwine and dominate this opening section about Jesus' ministry. The first is the *authority* of Jesus. This is seen in various ways: he calls men to follow him and they obey; he silences evil spirits and drives them out; he heals the fever-stricken with a simple gesture. As the man with leprosy puts it, 'If you are willing, you can make me clean' (1:40), and Jesus proves him right, but his authority is not confined to healing. He not only heals the paralysed man who is so dramatically lowered through the roof; he also forgives sins, to the consternation of the orthodox (2:1–10).

This brings us to the second theme—*controversy*. Starting with the story of the paralysed man, it becomes increasingly clear that Jesus' 'doing good' does not please everybody. The teachers of the law challenge his right to pronounce sins forgiven. The Pharisees object to his eating with sinners after Jesus has called Levi the tax collector to follow him and has enjoyed Levi's hospitality (2:15–16). People are offended by his failure to fast (2:18). Above all, he breaks the Sabbath, allowing his disciples to pluck ears of corn and healing a man in the synagogue on the Sabbath day (2:23–24; 3:2–5). Jesus is unrepentant. He is the doctor and it is right for him to spend time with the sick and sinful. He is the bridegroom and this is his big day (2:19). He is Lord even of the Sabbath, because he is the 'Son of Man'.

Although this phrase 'the Son of Man' could mean simply 'I' or 'a person like me' (as in the colloquial English 'Can't a guy even get a drink here?' meaning '*I* can't get a drink', or 'they refuse to serve *me*'), it is widely held that Jesus intended to refer to the 'son of man' in Daniel's dream. As we saw in the Prologue (page 16), this human figure is a symbol for Israel, who suffers and is then given authority by God. So Jesus is claiming to embody the people of God, accepting a destiny in which triumph comes only after suffering, and inviting others to join him on his destined path. This makes plain the nature of Jesus' authority. It is not the result of self-assertion but an authority received from God in answer to prayer and as a result of obedient suffering on behalf of all God's people. So it is not a title for the Messiah as such, but it is a covert claim to be and do what the Messiah as representative of Israel would be and do. It does not simply make the (uninteresting) claim that Jesus is a human being; rather, it permits us to think of him, like the Israel he represents, as the true Human Being, or, in Paul's phrase, 'the last Adam' (1 Cor. 15:45).

It is noteworthy that this section of the Gospel begins with Jesus calling his first disciples and ends with unbelief and rejection in the synagogue. It is a pattern that will be repeated. The Son of Man is not a lonely figure but the figurehead of a new people. Jesus is calling a new Israel into being around himself in the face of rejection by the leaders of the old.

'... AND HEALING ALL WHO WERE UNDER THE POWER
OF THE DEVIL...' (MARK 3:7—6:6)

Mark's summary statement of Jesus' widening influence (3:7–12) is a good example of a passage that could be seen (like 1:14–15) either as the conclusion of one section or the beginning of the next. It leads directly to the appointment of the Twelve, an inner circle of disciples to be with Jesus and to be sent out to preach and drive out demons (3:13–19).

The same two themes occupy this section as the last—opposition and works of power—and both are intensified. First, Jesus' own family say that he is out of his mind (3:20–21). While they are on their way to take charge of him, Mark inserts the accusation of the teachers of the law that Jesus' power is due to demon-possession (3:22–30). Then the family turn up but, significantly, they stand 'outside', to be replaced as Jesus' true family by those who respond to God's call through him (3:31–35). This is the setting for one of Jesus' most famous parables, the parable of the sower, in which it is made plain that opposition and unbelief are only to be expected (4:1–8). The mystery of the kingdom of God is the paradox of Jesus' own person and ministry, powerful in its effects yet seemingly unimpressive, like seed. Those on the 'outside', who include the religious leaders and Jesus' own family, cannot fathom it. Faith is the gift of God, yet those who refuse to accept it must bear their loss (4:10–12).

At the same time, a series of vivid stories makes the truth plain to Mark's readers. Jesus calms a storm, prompting the disciples to ask, 'Who is this?' (4:41). We, the readers, already know the answer, because we have heard the voice at Jesus' baptism declaring him to be the Son of God. Throughout the Gospel, we watch the disciples slowly coming to the conclusion that we have known all along.

Jesus then encounters a man with a legion of demons. Jesus drives them out and the man becomes a model disciple, sitting at Jesus' feet, and the first evangelist, telling his own people how much God has done for him (5:1–20). The most dramatic manifestation of Jesus' power is then seen in the raising of a twelve-year-old girl from death. Sandwiched into this story is the story of the woman with chronic bleeding who touches Jesus' clothes as he is on his way to heal the sick girl, who by this time has died (5:21–43). The two stories are closely linked. The girl is twelve years old and the woman has been ill for twelve years. Jesus commends the woman for her faith, and demands similar faith of Jairus. Both stories are parables of the kingdom of God whose power is seen in bringing in the outcast (the woman's illness would have cut her off from contact with the community), and in raising the dead. Nevertheless, back in the synagogue in his home town, Jesus is the subject of wondering unbelief (6:1–6). The section that began with the call of the Twelve ends with the rejection of the prophet by his own neighbours and relatives.

'... BECAUSE GOD WAS WITH HIM' (MARK 6:7—8:30)

For those with eyes to see, the healing miracles of Jesus point to only one conclusion: God is with him. Accordingly, this section leads us to the first great climax of the Gospel as Peter declares that Jesus is the Christ. It begins as the previous two sections have done, with a story about the disciples. Jesus sends out the Twelve on a mission. The story of Herod's concern, and the flashback to the death of John the Baptist, make clear that the message of the kingdom poses a serious threat to the guardians of the old order and the rulers of this world. It is bad enough if Jesus is John the Baptist risen from the dead, but what if he is more? What if he is the real king? What if it proves impossible to silence him by death?

Mark leads us to this conclusion by a sequence of four stories that is repeated for emphasis. The table below makes the point clear.

	1st sequence	2nd sequence
Jesus feeds the crowd	6:30–44	8:1–10
The disciples fail to understand	6:45–56	8:14–21
The Pharisees are blind	7:1–30	8:11–15
Jesus opens ears and eyes	7:31–37	8:22–26
At last, Peter gets the point		8:27–30

The stories of Jesus feeding the crowd in the desert should not be seen as a gratuitous exercise of power (the sort of temptation that Jesus on another occasion famously refused: Matt. 4:3–4); nor are they mainly about the relief of hunger. They spring from Jesus' compassion, certainly, but that compassion is prompted by the sight of people without proper guidance, like sheep without a shepherd (6:34). They remind us of Moses giving the people manna in the wilderness, but already in Jewish thinking the manna had come to be understood as a symbol for the law, so these stories mean that Jesus is the true teacher who brings the true bread to his people. (The account in John 6:25–40 only makes explicit what is implied by the other Gospels.) Together, the stories are saying to us that Jesus is the Christ.

Yet even the disciples are slow to get the point. The first feeding miracle is followed by the story of Jesus walking on the water, which, like the similar story of Jesus stilling the storm (4:35–41), prompts the question, 'Who is this?' But Mark has bolted this story tightly to the preceding one. The disciples are unable to answer the question raised by the walking on the water because 'they had not understood *about the loaves*' (6:52)! The conversation between Jesus and the disciples after the second feeding miracle shows this clearly. Jesus warns them to beware of the 'yeast' of the Pharisees and Herod—that is, their teaching and mindset. The disciples suppose he is talking about bread, but Jesus reminds them of the feeding miracles, and says in exasperation, 'Do you still not understand?' (8:14–21). What they are supposed to understand is that God is with Jesus and he is the true teacher and ruler of his people.

The blindness of the official teachers is made plain in the dispute over clean and unclean hands and food. Cleanness, and hence acceptability to God, is not a matter of outward observance but of heart attitudes. The evil things that come from the heart, not the food that enters a person from outside, are what make a person unclean (7:1–23). The story of the Syro-Phoenician woman and her demonized daughter provides the contrast (7:25–30). On the one hand we have the law-observant Pharisees with their concern for purity, who find themselves left outside, and on the other hand we have a foreigner, rendered doubly unclean by her sick daughter, whose faith prevails with Jesus and with God and is counted to her for righteousness. The blindness of the Pharisees is further illustrated by their request for a sign (8:11–13).

Meanwhile, Jesus is shown to be the one who opens the ears of the deaf and the eyes of the blind with two stories that appear only in Mark's Gospel. Both of them show Jesus struggling to overcome the afflicted person's ailment (which is perhaps why Matthew left these stories out). In the first we are told in detail how Jesus put his fingers in the man's ears, spat and touched his tongue, and uttered 'a deep groan' (7:34, GNB). We gain the impression that Jesus is engaged in a battle, not just with illness in the man but with unbelief in those around him. In the second story, the healing of the blind man, Jesus actually has to touch him twice before he is able to see properly (8:22–36). This miracle, coming immediately before Peter's confession, is usually thought to symbolize not just the power of Jesus but the disciples' slowness to believe. Like the blind man, they see, but not clearly, and they will need a second touch from Jesus before everything is plain to them.

Finally Jesus challenges the disciples, 'Who do you say I am?' and Peter says simply, 'You are the Christ' (8:27–30). It is the right answer, as the readers have known since the first sentence of the Gospel (1:1), but what does it mean exactly? What sort of a Christ? Surprisingly, instead of congratulating Peter on his insight, Jesus, in this Gospel, tells the disciples to tell no one. As the next section of the Gospel shows, they still have much to learn, and so perhaps have we.

'WE ARE WITNESSES...' (MARK 8:31—10:52)

If the first half of the Gospel has concentrated on the mighty deeds of Jesus through which he is seen to be the Christ, the second half concentrates on the suffering and death of Jesus through which he is seen to be the Son of God (15:39), something that is then confirmed by his resurrection.

The present section shows Jesus teaching the men who will be his witnesses and preparing them for his death. In contrast to the first half of the Gospel, most of this teaching takes place in private. The section divides into three and each part has a similar pattern, as follows:

	1st sequence	2nd sequence	3rd sequence
Jesus predicts his death and resurrection	8:31	9:31	10:33
Disciples are rebuked	8:32—9:13	9:33–50	10:35–45
Lessons in discipleship	9:14–29	10:1–31	10:46–52

The agenda for this section is set by Jesus' solemn threefold prediction of his forthcoming death and resurrection. It is particularly striking the way the first of these predictions follows immediately on from Peter's confession, as if Jesus, like a teacher, no sooner sees that the pupils have grasped the first lesson than he moves them on to the second. 'He then began to teach them that the Son of Man must suffer...' (8:31). There have been intimations of the cross before (for example, 2:20), but this is a new topic. From this point on, the cross will rarely be out of sight. Four things should be noted. First, Jesus' suffering and death are a necessity. He must suffer because this is God's plan set out in Scripture. Second, it is as the Son of Man that Jesus suffers. Like the human figure in Daniel's dream, he will undergo suffering as the representative of God's people. Third, where Daniel's Son of Man suffered at the hands of the pagan nations, Jesus will be handed over to them by the leaders of his own people. Fourth, Jesus' suffering may not be seen apart from his resurrection. The Son of Man will be vindicated by God.

Three times in this section, the disciples are found guilty of thinking 'as men think, not as God thinks' (8:33, REB). First Peter tries to deflect Jesus from his chosen path. Jesus sees him as the mouthpiece of Satan, who has from the beginning tried to tempt Jesus away from God's will (1:13). Peter is given a dressing-down in the hearing of all the disciples, and the disciples are then solemnly warned in the presence of the crowds of the necessity of suffering for anyone who wants to follow Jesus. Yet suffering will not have the last word, and no one will have to suffer as a Christian before they have seen Jesus risen from the dead. This is the most probable meaning of 'before they see the kingdom of God come with power' (9:1). The saying is linked to the transfiguration by the time-note 'after six days' (9:2), but the transfiguration hardly exhausts the meaning of the saying. Rather, it confirms the saying by pointing forward to the glory that Jesus will enjoy when he is raised from the dead. Meanwhile, the voice from heaven reinforces the lesson just given by repeating what was said to Jesus at his baptism and calling on the disciples (and the readers) to listen to him.

In the second sequence, the disciples are rebuked for arguing about which of them is the greatest (9:33–36), and in the third, James and John are rebuked for wanting the best seats in the kingdom (10:35–37). They are told that they will share Jesus' baptism and drink his cup (that is, they will share his suffering), but the places at his right and left are already reserved for others (15:27). In contrast to earthly kingdoms, lowly service is the law of the kingdom of God, 'for even the Son of Man did not come to be served, but to serve, and to give his life as a ransom for many' (10:45).

The remaining stories in this section are best seen as lessons in discipleship also. In the healing of the epileptic boy (9:14–29), the accent is not so much on the power of Jesus as on the failure of the disciples (vv. 18, 28). They are told that they need to pray more. The teaching on divorce comes where it does (10:1–12) because it teaches the radical nature of Jesus' demand, as does the case of the rich man who fails to follow Jesus because he cannot let go of his possessions (10:17–27). Such demands might easily induce pride in those who can claim to fulfil them, so each story has a tailpiece that makes it clear that the kingdom is open to children, not ascetics (10:13–16), and 'many who are first will be last, and the last first' (10:28–31). The healing of blind Bartimaeus is also clearly a lesson in discipleship. Here is a man who cries out to Jesus for mercy, who refuses to be silenced, who asks only to be able to see, and who then follows Jesus 'on the way' (10:52, NRSV). As such, he serves to summarize the teaching of the whole section. The story recalls the healing of the other blind man at the end of the first part of the Gospel (8:22–26). Only if God opens our eyes will we be able to see Jesus for who he is and understand the 'upside down kingdom' to which he calls us. The way on which the healed man follows Jesus is clearly the way of the cross.

'... AND IN JERUSALEM...' (MARK 11:1—13:37)

The events of the next chapters will make sense only if we remember that Jesus was not just what we would think of as a religious teacher going about 'doing good' and teaching people to love their neighbours. He did that, certainly, but it was part of what we would call a political programme aimed at capturing the heart of the nation. He was concerned neither with helping people to get to heaven nor with enabling them to lead more satisfying lives on earth. When he spoke of the kingdom of God, he was using language that many other people were using as they looked to God to end the oppression under which they lived. When he said that the kingdom of God was near, he was articulating the hopes and dreams of many other Israelites. When he spoke of loving enemies, showing mercy to sinners and welcoming outcasts, he was putting forward a new way of being Israel in opposition to the narrow nationalism that aimed to restore the kingdom to Israel by violence and exclusion.

Jesus believed and taught that God was offering Israel a choice. They could continue to take the way of violence and nationalism, which would lead inevitably to the judgment of God in the form of Roman armies, or they could follow God's way as represented by himself and his teaching, which would lead to life and peace and to Israel's being restored to their role as the light of the world. Jesus' ministry in Galilee, outlined in the previous sections of the Gospel, can be seen as a time for gathering support. Now it is time for Jesus to go up to Jerusalem, to the heart of the nation, and confront the rulers on their own territory.[2]

The section falls into three parts. In the first, Jesus rides into Jerusalem as king and stages a demonstration against the temple and what it has come to stand for (11:1–26). Everything about the story of the triumphal entry—his decision to ride a donkey, the response of the crowd, spreading their cloaks in the road and waving palm branches in the accepted manner of those who salute a king— declares Jesus to be the true king. This is very much a political demonstration, and the same is true of Jesus' action in the temple. The temple was the heart of the national life, not just religiously but politically as well. The high priest was recognized by the Romans as the ruler of the Jews, and his council effectively governed the country.

So what was Jesus doing when he overturned the tables of the money changers?

The traditional title of this incident, 'the cleansing of the temple', tends to suggest that Jesus saw the temple as being defiled by commerce, and perhaps by the extortionate prices charged by the money changers and merchants, and that he was instituting a reform. It is more likely, however, that he was staging a demonstration and pronouncing judgment. In the first place, as an attempt to reform the temple, his action could hardly be called effective. He was in no position to police the temple or keep the money changers out permanently, and in fact they were probably back the next morning. Then the words of Jesus suggest that what he found offensive about the temple was not its commerce but the way it served as a symbol for the violent nationalism that he had come to denounce. It was supposed to be 'a house of prayer for all nations', but excluded more people than it let in. As in Jeremiah's day, it had become 'a den of robbers' (Jer. 7:11), but the word 'robbers' was used not for extortionate traders but for freedom fighters (like Barabbas in John 18:40)—the people who were seeking to restore the kingdom by force with the covert support of many of the leading Jews. Finally, Mark has set this incident in the context of Jesus' cursing of the fig tree, which itself makes sense only as an acted parable of judgment against a nation that was no longer bearing fruit for God. Like the fig tree, the temple was barren, and by interrupting its sacrifices, however briefly, Jesus was pronouncing God's judgment on the temple and all that it had come to stand for. The discourse of chapter 13 will confirm the point.

The second part of this section sees Jesus in dispute with various sections of the Jerusalem elite, who are shown to be defaulting tenants of God's vineyard (11:27—12:44). It is 'the chief priests, the teachers of the law and the elders' (11:27) who challenge Jesus' authority to act as king of Israel. The Pharisees and Herodians try to trap him over the issue of paying Roman taxes. The Sadducees attack him over the resurrection of the dead. The teachers of the law are condemned for their ostentation and extortion, even though one of their number is presented in a better light (12:28–34). In the middle of these debates, Jesus tells a parable in which he adapts Isaiah's song of the vineyard (Is. 5:1–7) to portray the nation's rulers as murderous tenants with a long history of killing God's messengers and withholding the honour due to him. The parable points forward both to the killing of Jesus himself, here referred to as a beloved son (12:6, 35–37), and to the ultimate destruction of Jerusalem which the rulers will bring on themselves (12:9). What is wrong with the Jerusalem establishment is pinpointed by the story of the widow's mite (12:41–44). The poor woman is forced to put in all she has to live on, but there is no suggestion that it was right that she should do so. She is usually taken as a model of generosity, but is probably intended as a glaring example of the greed of the authorities 'who devour widows' houses' (12:40). The pomp and circumstance of the temple rests on such extortionate demands, and its judgment cannot be long delayed.

This leads directly to the third part of the section, in which Jesus pronounces judgment on the city and temple within a generation (13:1–37). Chapter 13 begins with Jesus predicting the temple's destruction (v. 2). The disciples ask when this will happen and how they will know (v. 4). Jesus says that it will happen within a generation (v. 30), and Mark, of course, knows that he was right. But before this happens, there will be terrible times of war and upheaval when the disciples of Jesus will be hated and persecuted. This is 'business as usual' for the Church and does not betoken any special time (vv. 5–13). But a day will come when Jerusalem itself will be surrounded by armies, just as in the days of Antiochus Epiphanes spoken of by Daniel (v. 14; compare Dan. 9:16). That will be the time to flee, because God's judgment will be about to fall on the city and temple with terrifying finality and Jesus himself will be vindicated against the nation that rejected him. This is the event described by Jesus in apocalyptic imagery taken from the Old Testament prophets, who often used 'end-of-the-world language' to describe earth-shattering events expected to happen within their own world (13:24–25; compare Isaiah 13:10; 34:4).[3]

Just as in Daniel's vision, the human figure who represents the people of God comes to God in clouds of glory to be vindicated and given authority, so this terrible event will vindicate Jesus and confirm him as Israel's true king, and in this sense 'men will see the Son of Man coming in clouds with great power and glory' (v. 26).

Of course, the destruction of Jerusalem was not the last such disaster. God's judgment has been expressed in the destruction of many cruel or idolatrous societies and empires, and all of these are dress-rehearsals for Jesus' final coming to judge the world. So the command to watch, originally addressed to the disciples, applies to us all, for none of us knows the day or hour of the end—whether of the world or of our corrupt society, or of our own little lives!

'THEY KILLED HIM BY HANGING HIM ON A TREE...'
(MARK 14:1—15:47)

It has long been recognized that the Passion narrative is the heart and climax of Mark's narrative. Here, for the first time in Mark, we have a connected narrative, the separate parts being linked together with indications of the time. The pace of the narrative gets slower and slower until, by the end, we are made aware of the passing hours as Jesus hangs on the cross. Everything in the story builds towards this as the climax of the Gospel.

Mark's story divides into seven scenes, distinguished from one another by the place where they occur. The first scene takes place in the house of Simon the leper, where a woman anoints Jesus with expensive perfume, and Jesus says that she has anointed him before-hand for his burial (14:1–11). The second scene takes place in a friend's guest room, where Jesus, in the context of Passover, takes bread and wine and makes them into prophetic pointers to his death (14:12–26). The third scene occurs on the Mount of Olives. Jesus warns the disciples and Peter of their coming failure, a warning that is immediately fulfilled as the disciples first fall asleep while Jesus is praying in the garden of Gethsemane and then run away as Jesus is arrested (14:27–52). The fourth scene takes place at the palace of the high priest, and on two levels. On the upper level, Jesus is examined before the high priest's council and, put on oath, confesses himself to be the Christ (14:55–65). On the lower level, Peter sits with the guards and denies all knowledge of Jesus (14:53–54, 66–72). The scene then moves to Pilate's residence, and there is a brief account of Jesus' trial before the governor, the main point of which is to show how the crowd prefers the murderer, Barabbas, to Jesus, ironically described as the king of the Jews (15:1–20).

The sixth scene takes place at Golgotha, the place of execution (15:21–41). Mark divides this scene into two periods of three hours.

From nine o'clock until midday, Jesus suffers the mockery of passers-by, chief priests and even of his fellow victims. From midday until three o'clock, there is darkness and silence, broken at last by Jesus' terrible cry, 'My God, my God, why have you forsaken me?' (15:34). Then, seemingly immediately afterwards, Jesus gives a loud cry. Mark does not explain this cry, but it is probably right to see it as a cry of strength—as if Jesus, like a wrestler, with his last gasp throws his opponent. Jesus dies, and two remarkable things follow. The curtain of the temple is torn in two—whether as a sign that the temple is finished or as a sign that the way to God is now open through the death of Jesus, Mark does not explain. Lastly, the centurion in charge of the execution squad, who saw how he died, becomes the first human being to recognize Jesus for who he is and declares, 'Surely this man was the Son of God!' (15:39). It is the high point of the drama, which even the resurrection can hardly match.

The seventh and last scene takes place at the tomb of Joseph of Arimathea, where the body of Jesus is laid to rest.

We are struck by the restraint with which Mark tells his story. He does little to work on our emotions. He describes the most horrific tortures with an economy of words: 'He had Jesus flogged... and they crucified him' (15:15, 24). In a real sense, he allows the events to speak for themselves. He also resists the temptation to preach. Mark believes that the death of Jesus achieved salvation for the whole world (10:45), but he records the death of Jesus almost without theological explanation of any kind. Jesus himself is also notably silent, speaking only twice from the arrest in the garden until his death, once to tell the high priest of his coming vindication (14:62), and once to express his own utter desolation. No fine speeches or beautiful words here! Even the cry of desolation is left without explanation. It is left to the Roman soldier to tell us the meaning of what we have witnessed.

'... BUT GOD RAISED HIM FROM THE DEAD' (MARK 16:1–8).

It is well known that there is a mystery about the ending of Mark's Gospel. Only the first eight verses of chapter 16 are by the author of the rest of the Gospel. The remaining verses that appear in our Bibles are by a different hand. They are not in the best and oldest manuscripts and look like an attempt to provide the Gospel with a more satisfactory ending. For us, the Gospel ends with the words, 'They said nothing to anyone, because they were afraid' (v. 8). But did Mark mean to end it there? Did he leave his work unfinished? Or did he write more and has the original ending been lost? There are problems with each solution, and scholars are not agreed. To some it is obvious that Mark must have intended to fulfil the promise made over and over again in his Gospel to show us Jesus risen from the dead. To others, such a curiously understated ending is exactly what we might expect of this enigmatic writer.

Whatever may be the case, the story of the visit of the women to the tomb is all we have from Mark's pen, but its contribution is not negligible. Although we do not see Jesus, we are met by a young man, certainly to be understood as an angel, who tells us that Jesus is alive. This means that the resurrection has begun, the age to come has broken in and the kingdom of God has come in power (9:1)! The angel says, 'But go, tell his disciples and Peter, "He is going ahead of you into Galilee. There you will see him, just as he told you"' (16:7). Since the angel is quoting a prediction previously made by Jesus, we may be certain that it was fulfilled. Although we are not allowed to see it, Mark certainly believes that there was a reunion between Jesus and his disciples, and this is significant for another reason. It tells us that the disciples were restored to faith and forgiven their treachery and all their slowness to understand, which has been such a feature of Mark's portrayal of them. Jesus is still ahead of them, as always, but he has not left them behind.

KEY THEMES IN MARK'S GOSPEL

Whether or not the author of this Gospel is the Mark mentioned in 1 Peter 5:13, it is likely that he would have agreed with the sentiment expressed in that letter: 'Beloved, do not be surprised at the fiery ordeal that is taking place among you to test you, as though something strange were happening to you. But rejoice insofar as you are sharing Christ's sufferings, so that you may also be glad and shout for joy when his glory is revealed' (1 Peter 4:12–13, NRSV).

The references to persecution in Mark's Gospel strongly suggest that he too was writing for a Christian Church under severe pressure and wanted the believers to know that such persecution is the normal lot of Christians, having been the experience of Jesus himself. Accordingly, two key themes in Mark's Gospel are what it means to be the Christ, and what it means to be a Christian.

WHAT IT MEANS TO BE THE CHRIST

All Christians by definition believed Jesus to be the Christ, but what did that mean exactly? Was he the Christ in spite of, or because of, the fact that he died on the cross? Mark is at pains to tell us that Jesus is the Son of God. He is declared to be such by God at his baptism (1:11) and at the transfiguration (9:7), but he is especially recognized as such by the centurion at the moment of his death (15:39). Being the Son of God is, above all, a matter of obedience to the will of God. Jesus' preferred title for himself is the Son of Man, and, as we have seen, this is a title in which suffering and glory combine. Accordingly, the Son of Man 'must' suffer (8:31) before he sits 'at the right hand of the Mighty One' and comes 'on the clouds of heaven' (14:62).

Titles only take us so far, though, in our search for what it means to be the Christ. Although the term is not used, the figure Jesus most closely resembles is the suffering servant of Isaiah who 'bore the sin of many, and made intercession for the transgressors' (Is. 53:12). In a key statement, Jesus says that, as Son of Man, he 'did not come to be served, but to serve, and to give his life as a ransom for many' (10:45). Yet Jesus is not a pathetic figure. On the contrary, he is the 'more powerful one' pointed to by John the Baptist (1:7), able to bind the strong man and carry off his possessions (3:27)—the strong leader who strides ahead of his disciples (10:32) and is still going ahead of them at the end (16:7). This leads us to the second theme.

WHAT IT MEANS TO BE A CHRISTIAN

The disciples occupy a prominent place in this Gospel. Jesus' first public action is to call disciples (1:16–20). Each of the early sections of the Gospel begins with a story about the disciples, and the central section of the Gospel is devoted to their instruction (8:31—10:52). From first to last, Jesus calls people to follow him and take up the cross (8:34), and it is made very clear that being a disciple will involve suffering and public disgrace. By contrast, the disciples are portrayed as slow to understand (6:52; 8:14–21), unready to suffer (8:32–33), and anxious for status and fame (10:35). As such, they represent us, the readers. We are meant to identify with them and learn from their mistakes. There is plenty here to make us uncomfortable, but at the same time there are grounds for hope. For if the disciples came good in the end—and the words of the angel to the women at the tomb suggest that they did (16:7)—then so, by God's grace, may we!

CHAPTER 3

MATTHEW'S STORY

On the wall of the dining hall of a theological college I know hang the portraits of former principals of the college. One recent principal elected to be painted wearing his robes as a university professor. His successor is portrayed wearing the collar and bands of a Free Church minister. Both men were ordained ministers, both were academics, but each portrait is making a statement about its subject. The Gospel writers have made similarly distinctive statements about Jesus. Although all the Gospels record Jesus teaching, it is Matthew who paints Jesus as the new Moses, the teacher of Israel. He achieves this by the space he gives to Jesus' teaching and by showing how, in his life, Jesus fulfils the words of the prophets and recapitulates the experience of Moses. Matthew's Jesus wears the rabbi's shawl.

Matthew, we believe, had Mark's Gospel in front of him when he wrote, and sometimes he followed Mark very closely. He adopted Mark's structure, from the Jordan to Galilee, and from Galilee to Jerusalem. Almost all of Mark is also found in Matthew, often in the same words and in the same order, but a great deal of Matthew is not found in Mark. Matthew has added whole chapters of material, so that his Gospel may be thought of as an expanded version of Mark. You can see this from the table overleaf.

A. Markan material		B. Mixed material		C. Matthean material	
				1—2	Birth of Jesus
3—4	Baptism & temptation				
				5—7	Sermon on the Mount
		8—9	Miracles in Galilee		
				10	Mission discourse
		11—12	Who is Jesus?		
		13—15	Mixed response		
		16—17	Peter's confession		
				18	Community discourse
19—20	Teaching on the road				
21—22	Jesus in Jerusalem				
				23	Leaders denounced
24	Fall of Jerusalem predicted				
				25	Parables of judgment
26—27	Trial and death of Jesus				
				28	Risen Lord appears to his disciples

The numbers 1–28 refer to chapters of Matthew's Gospel as we have it in our Bibles. In the chapters in column 'A', Matthew has followed Mark very closely. In the chapters in column 'B', Markan material is mixed with non-Markan material. The chapters in column 'C' consist of material not found in Mark at all. The divisions are only approximate. You might want to label a chapter as 'B' rather than 'A', for example, but as it stands the table makes its point well enough.

Take the 'A' and 'B' chapters first. We start with the baptism of Jesus and go on to his temptation and the call of the first disciples (chs. 3—4). Then we have a number of miracles and stories about discipleship, almost all found in Mark, though not in the same order (chs. 8—9). Matthew then records the mixed response to Jesus, controversies over the Sabbath, accusations that he was in league with Beelzebub, the parable of the sower, the feeding miracles and disputes with the Pharisees over purity, all the way to Peter's confession and the transfiguration (chs. 12—17). Jesus travels to Jerusalem, stages a demonstration in the temple, argues with the religious leaders and predicts the destruction of Jerusalem (chs. 19—22; 24). He is arrested, tried and put to death on the cross, with the same words said by him and about him. His tomb is then found to be empty (26:1—28:8). Now that is Mark's story, from the baptism to the empty tomb, from Galilee to Jerusalem. So what has Matthew added?

Look at the 'C' chapters. We have two chapters on the birth of Jesus (chs. 1—2). Then there are three chapters given to the Messiah's teaching, the Sermon on the Mount (chs. 5—7). Matthew has added a chapter of teaching to the disciples on their mission (ch. 10), and John the Baptist's question and Jesus' great self-disclosure and invitation (ch. 11). Chapter 18 gives teaching about the Christian community. Chapter 23 denounces the religious leaders. Chapter 25 adds a number of parables of judgment to the discourse about the destruction of Jerusalem, and chapter 28 recounts the meeting of the risen Jesus with his disciples. The majority of this new material is in the form of teaching (chs. 5; 6; 7; 10; 11; 18; 23; 25), and the rest gives the Gospel a less abrupt beginning and ending.

Several other characteristics of Matthew's 'brushwork' can be listed. This Gospel has a profound Jewish interest, both positively and negatively. Positively, Matthew is at pains to show that the story of

Jesus is the fulfilment of the story of Israel. This is most obvious in the genealogy with which the Gospel begins, but is continued in the distinctive use of scriptural quotations, each beginning, 'This was to fulfil what was spoken by the prophet...' (for example, 1:22). Negatively, we see Matthew's Jewish interest in the harsh treatment of the Pharisees and other leaders, which probably reflects the ongoing tensions between the Christians for whom Matthew wrote and the synagogues from which they had recently been expelled. This emphasis is not absent from the other Gospels, but it is specially pronounced in Matthew.

As a teacher and storyteller, Matthew omits many of the 'odd' features of Mark's stories. The story of the blind man who needed a second touch, for example, is omitted altogether. This tends to result in shorter stories. Compare the story of the paralysed man (9:1–8) with the same story in Mark 2:1–12. The words of Jesus are the same but the memorable picture of the man being let down through the roof is completely missing. Again, Mark's story of the healing of the Gadarene demoniac (5:1–20) has been reduced to a mere seven verses in Matthew 8:28–34, and there is no mention of 'Legion' at all! At the same time, in some places we find a heightened interest in the supernatural as evidence of God's presence, especially around the death of Jesus: note the earthquake and the resurrection of the saints (27:52–53) and the appearance of the angel at the tomb of Jesus (28:2–4). Perhaps we should include here Matthew's odd tendency to double the number of those receiving healing, so that the Gadarene demoniac becomes two men (8:28), as does blind Bartimaeus (20:30). Finally, like a good teacher, Matthew explains things, most notably in the Lord's Prayer. Where Luke will be content with 'Your kingdom come', Matthew adds, '... your will be done on earth as it is in heaven'. Where Luke has 'And lead us not into temptation', Matthew adds, '... but deliver us from evil' (6:10, 13). In line with this, his picture of the disciples is kinder: they *do* understand. Compare Matthew 16:12 with the ending of the same story in Mark (8:21), and study the following exchange.

'Have you understood all these things?' Jesus asked.

 'Yes,' they replied.

 He said to them, 'Therefore every teacher of the law who has been

instructed about the kingdom of heaven is like the owner of a house who
brings out of his storeroom new treasures as well as old.'
MATTHEW 13:51–52

Matthew's Jesus is a successful teacher, as Matthew himself aspires to be, bringing out the new but making clear its continuity with the old.

THE STORY IN OUTLINE

As with Mark, there is no agreement about the structure of Matthew's Gospel. Some people see the key to Matthew's intention in the five discourses he has added to his Markan outline (chs. 5—7; 10; 13; 18; 24—25), each followed by words such as, 'When Jesus had finished saying these things...', but this relegates the Passion story to a sort of epilogue, whereas most people think it is meant to be the climax of the book. Other people draw attention to the words, 'From that time on Jesus began...' in 4:17 and 16:21, and think that the book should be divided into three sections dealing respectively with the person of Jesus, the ministry of Jesus and the death and resurrection of Jesus. This is attractive, but it cannot be said that the 'signposts' are very obvious.

Rather than looking for such structural markers, it seems best simply to divide up the Gospel in terms of the story it tells. First, Jesus is introduced as Son of David and Son of God. Then he announces the kingdom to Israel in word and deed. When this receives a mixed response, Jesus concentrates his attention on the disciples who will be the nucleus of a renewed Israel. Finally he goes up to Jerusalem, challenges the nation, and triumphs through his death. The plan of Matthew's Gospel as I see it looks like this:

- The birth and empowering of Jesus the Messiah (1:1—4:22)
- The proclamation of the kingdom to Israel (4:23—13:58)
- The birth of a new community (14:1—18:35)
- The coming of the Son of Man (19:1—28:20)

THE BIRTH AND EMPOWERING OF JESUS THE MESSIAH
(MATTHEW 1:1—4:22)

The first followers of Jesus believed and declared to their Jewish neighbours that Jesus of Nazareth was the promised Messiah, the king of Israel. They were met with scepticism. How could he be, given the doubts surrounding his birth and the shameful manner of his death? The Christians replied that, as to the first, he was a true son of David and therefore qualified to be the Christ, and, as to the second, he was a true son of God—in fact *the* true Son of God, commissioned by God at his baptism, obedient to God in life and death and vindicated by God in resurrection. These two claims provide Matthew with the agenda for his Gospel, and especially the first part of it. The first two chapters set out to show that Jesus was the son of David and the next two that he was the Son of God.

First, Matthew begins his Gospel with a genealogy whose purpose is to show that Jesus' mother was married to a son of David. He traces the ancestry of Joseph from Abraham to David, from David to the exile in Babylon and from the exile down to the birth of Jesus. This long story is centred on David, as the emphasis on the number fourteen shows (1:17; the letters of David's name in Hebrew add up to fourteen). Mary married into the family and so made this the heritage of her son.

Then Matthew tells the story of Jesus' birth in such a way as to show that this son of David, Joseph, named Jesus and so claimed him as his own son (1:21, 25). Naming a baby in the ancient world was not just a matter of attaching a convenient label to the child to distinguish it from others. It was an act of adoption by which the father owned the child and incorporated him or her into the family. Joseph the son of David had done this, so making Jesus a son of David too. Next, the story of the magi shows that Jesus was born in David's city (2:5–6), and, if his early life was shrouded in obscurity—first in Egypt and then Nazareth—that fits the Old Testament pattern too. Had not God called Israel out of Egypt in the first place? This had not prevented Israel from being God's son (2:15).

But what about the virgin birth? The exact circumstances of Jesus' birth were clearly a matter of controversy, and Jewish critics had their own unflattering explanation, just as they had of that other mystery, the empty tomb of Jesus (28:11–15). Matthew of course has a different explanation. He has prepared the way for this by including four women in his genealogy—Tamar, Rahab, Ruth and Bathsheba—all of whom were involved in irregular unions in one way or another, through which God's purpose was worked out nevertheless. Then he tells how Joseph was persuaded that God's hand was similarly at work in the unexpected conception of Jesus. Finally he shows that Scripture itself would lead you to expect that God would intervene in a special way to set his people free, just as he had in the days of Isaiah (1:22–23). But all this is of secondary importance to Matthew, whose main interest was to show that Jesus was a true son of David. He never refers to the virginal conception or birth of Jesus again, and never suggests that it is this that makes Jesus the Son of God.

Having shown that Jesus' birth makes him the son of David, Matthew goes on to show that his empowering by the Holy Spirit marks him out as the Son of God (3:1—4:21). Matthew is following Mark here, so our focus will be on what Matthew has added. Of greatest importance are his additions to the stories of Jesus' baptism and temptation. As in Mark, Jesus comes to be baptized by John, but in Matthew John questions the need for this and is told by Jesus, 'It is proper for us to do this to fulfil all righteousness' (3:15). This heightens the sense that Jesus is to be baptized as a sign of his obedience to God, and explains what it means that Jesus is then proclaimed to be God's Son.

This theme is continued in the story of the temptation that immediately follows (4:1–11). In Mark, the temptation of Jesus is mentioned only in passing, but Matthew expands the story so that it becomes a full examination of what it means to be the Son of God. Twice the devil challenges Jesus, 'If you are the Son of God…', proposing that Jesus should exploit his status for his own comfort and glory, and gain a following by the exercise of supernatural power. Jesus' reply makes plain that, as God's Son, he will live by God's word and not presume on God's faithfulness. The same cry, 'If you are the Son of God…' is heard again as Jesus hangs on the cross (27:40), challenging Jesus to prove his sonship by coming down from the cross, although to do so would have been the very opposite of filial obedience. The third temptation, in which the devil offers Jesus all the kingdoms of the world in return for his allegiance, anticipates the conclusion of the Gospel, where Jesus says that all authority in heaven and earth has been given to him (28:18). This conclusion, of course, comes after his suffering and death, making plain that the way to the kingdom is by obedience and not by self-assertion. In this way, by showing Jesus to be the obedient Son of God, Matthew shows how it is possible for him to be the Christ despite his shameful death or, indeed, precisely because of it.

Matthew's other additions to Mark in these chapters introduce another important theme of this Gospel—the emergence of a mixed Jewish and Gentile Church in place of the old, exclusive people of God. On the one hand, John the Baptist delivers a stinging attack on the Pharisees and Sadducees for presuming on their status as children of Abraham while failing to produce fruit for God (3:7–10); on the other hand, after his temptation, Jesus goes to live in Galilee of the Gentiles, for whom the coming of Jesus is the coming of a great light (4:12–16).

THE PROCLAMATION OF THE KINGDOM TO ISRAEL
(MATTHEW 4:23—13:58)

This long section of the Gospel dealing with Jesus' public ministry in Galilee can be divided into three parts. Part 1 consists of the Sermon on the Mount in which Jesus proclaims the kingdom in word (chs. 5—7). In Part 2 he proclaims the kingdom in deed, first through his own miracles and then as he sends out the Twelve (chs. 8–10). Part 3 then makes clear that this proclamation has met with a very mixed response (chs. 11–13).

Proclamation in word (chs. 5—7)

Jesus was not a sage or guru holed up somewhere in Galilee offering enlightenment to those who came to him for teaching. Matthew makes it plain that Jesus embarked on a nationwide campaign, like a politician taking his message to the people, and he was very successful. 'News about him spread all over Syria… Large crowds… followed him' (4:24–25). The reason they did so was that Jesus had news from God that faithful Israelites had been waiting to hear for centuries. The kingdom of God (or heaven, as Matthew has it) was never meant to be understood as a place we go to when we die, nor as an institution like the Church, nor as an ethical ideal like love or brotherhood. It was the hope that God would come to set his people free—free from oppression by their enemies, free from injustice and divisions among themselves, free from sin and from death, which is the penalty for sin. The good news that Jesus proclaimed was that this long-awaited day was near (4:17).

At the same time, the coming of God called for a new obedience on the part of his people. Everybody agreed with that. The Pharisees called for purity in all areas of life, and Jesus too called for a thorough-going obedience to God, though he had a different idea of God's priorities and the attitudes and behaviour that holiness required. Without it, the coming of God would bring judgment rather than salvation. The word that sums up this new obedience is 'repent', and the content of repentance is set out in the summary of Jesus' teaching that we call the Sermon on the Mount.

The Sermon begins with a royal proclamation: 'Blessed are the poor in spirit, for theirs is the kingdom of heaven' and so on. The word 'blessed' does not refer to feelings of happiness, nor are the Beatitudes good advice. Rather, it is the king who speaks and these are his people. As earthly kings reward the great and the good with special marks of favour, so these are the people whom this king delights to honour. They are a strange bunch! They are not the people who would be on Herod's list of those who have rendered great service to the state, and not those who would be on the Pharisees' list of people who have kept the law without deviation. Instead, we find those who know how much they need to be forgiven, and those whose loyalty to Israel engenders mercy and peace rather than censoriousness and violence. These are the people who will fulfil the historic calling of Israel to be the light of the world and the city set on a hill to which the nations would turn, and all who hear are invited to enrol in their number.

This gracious invitation does not betoken any relaxation of the king's requirements. On the contrary, he is looking for perfect obedience, not an obedience made manageable by regulation. The central section of the Sermon is marked out as such by the reference to 'the Law and the Prophets' with which it begins and ends (5:17; 7:12). In it we learn the meaning of 'righteousness', helpfully paraphrased by the Good News Bible as 'doing what God requires' (5:20). This is explained first in a series of six contrasts between an obedience that confines itself to the bare letter of the law, which people might pride themselves on having kept (see 19:20), and one that opens itself to the true intent of the law in the infinite demand and mercy of God. So the law against murder requires that we avoid angry and abusive speech. The law against adultery requires us to avoid lust. The law regulating divorce does not confer divine approval on marital unfaithfulness. The law against oath breaking is not to be evaded by casuistry.

It is probable that most of Jesus' hearers would have agreed with all of this, but the next two contrasts, calling on people to renounce retaliation and to love their enemies, will have been more controversial, since they stand conventional morality on its head. (The command to hate your enemy can be found in the Apocrypha, Sirach 12:1–7.) Uttered in a context of enemy occupation, they define Jesus' programme for the new Israel in contrast to the nationalist sentiment of his day. Whether or not he knew this teaching of Jesus, Paul summarizes it nicely when he says, 'Do not be overcome by evil, but overcome evil with good' (Rom. 12:21).

The same word 'righteousness' that is used for keeping the law is used also for religious observance (6:1). God requires both and he rewards both, but only if they are offered in the right spirit. If obedience is to be offered without limitation, worship is to be offered without ostentation, whether it be almsgiving, prayer or fasting (6:1–18).

Interrupting this series of three beautifully balanced snapshots of the spiritual life is the Lord's Prayer. More than a formula to recite or even a list of topics for prayer, these words depict a whole approach to life that is ambitious for God's honour and kingdom, modest in what it seeks or claims for itself. As the centrepiece of the central section of the Sermon on the Mount, the Lord's Prayer provides a summary of what it means to live under the reign of God.

Jesus famously summed up the requirement of the law with the two commands 'Love the Lord your God with all your heart and with all your soul and with all your mind' and 'Love your neighbour as yourself' (22:37–40), and this double command provides the key to the final part of the central section of the Sermon (6:19—7:12), which might otherwise appear rather disjointed. Loving God with all your heart means seeking first the kingdom of God and his righteousness, and this is contrasted with storing up treasures on earth, trying to serve God *and* money and worrying about life (6:19–34). Loving your neighbour as yourself means doing to others what you would have them do to you, and this is contrasted with passing unfair judgment on them (7:1–12). As the worship of Mammon denies our claim to love God, so our tendency to unfair criticism undermines our claim to love our neighbour. Yet we may notice how grace is mingled with demand in the teaching of Jesus. In relation to both demands, we are assured that God is a generous God who gives 'all these things', and hears and answers the prayers of his children with 'good gifts'. The demands of the Sermon are steep, but God enables us to do what he requires.

The Sermon ends with a solemn warning (7:13–27). For Israel in Jesus' day, as for many a society since, this is the hour of crisis. The popular path of violence and nationalism will lead only to the destruction of the very thing it seeks to preserve. It has many impressive advocates, but they will turn out to be false prophets. Those who seek to build the city of God must do so on the foundation of Jesus' teaching. Only so will their work survive the storms to come. Even the crowds can recognize that this is not just one teacher among many. So who is this who brings God's law to his people from the mountain-top? It is the new Moses (though in truth 'something greater' than Moses is here), calling Israel back to God. And who is this teaching for? It is directed to disciples—Christians, if you will—but it is no secret teaching. It is delivered in the hearing of the crowd, and, as such, it is an invitation to membership of the new people of God for all who will listen to it, then or now.

The table below gives a summary of the structure of the Sermon on the Mount.

A. The people of the kingdom (5:1–16)

	a. True obedience (5:17–48)
B. The law of the kingdom (5:17—7:12)	b. True worship (6:1–18)
	c. True love (6:19—7:12)

C. The challenge of the kingdom (7:13–27)

Proclamation in deed (chs. 8—10)

In the next section, we see something of the careful way in which Matthew has put his Gospel together. Following his summary of the Messiah's teaching, he gives us an account of his mighty works, which he later (11:2) refers to in words that literally mean 'the deeds of the Christ'. He has assembled a sequence of nine miracle stories, arranging them in three groups of three, with teaching about discipleship separating the groups. Thus we have the healing of the leper, the centurion's servant and Peter's mother-in-law followed by the story of the would-be disciples. This leads to the stilling of the storm (which, for Matthew, is also a lesson in discipleship), the healing of the Gadarene demoniacs and the healing of the paralysed man, followed by the call of Matthew and a question on fasting. Finally we have the raising of Jairus' daughter (with which Matthew, following Mark, has linked the healing of the woman with the haemorrhage), two blind men receiving their sight and a dumb man also being healed. Matthew tells us that some people are amazed and others suspicious, anticipating a theme that he will take up more fully later.

With the exception of the centurion's servant and the dumb demoniac, all these miracle stories are found in Mark, but not in the same order, showing that Matthew has selected and arranged them as he thought best. Matthew then tells us of the call and mission of the Twelve as a prelude to a discourse in which instructions to the Twelve shade off into instructions for the mission of the Church in Matthew's time. This leads us to think that the miracle stories also are not merely of historical interest but are intended as lessons for the reader.

We have seen that Jesus' distinctive message was that the kingdom of God was near, and the function of his works of power was to demonstrate the truth of his claim. The prophets pictured a time when God would come to save his people: 'Then will the eyes of the blind be opened and the ears of the deaf unstopped. Then will the lame leap like a deer, and the mute tongue shout for joy' (Is. 35:5–6).

The Jewish people looked forward to a coming age when these things would happen and God would overcome sin and death. When Jesus healed the sick, it was as if the powers of the age to come were invading this age and God's future was throwing its shadow into the present. Of course, everyone could see that the kingdom had not actually arrived. Only a limited number of people were being healed, the dead were still in their graves and the powers of evil were still firmly on their thrones. But Jesus said that it was *near* and the miracles gave substance to his claim. The kingdom, understood as resurrection, would not arrive apart from the cross and not until Jesus was raised from the dead. Even for us it has only been inaugurated. Miracles in the life of the Church have the same function as they did in the ministry of Jesus: they are signs of the coming kingdom, reminders of its nearness and its character.

The character of the kingdom is made plain by the first group of miracles. The first person to be healed is a leper, the second is a Gentile and the third is a woman—demonstrating the inclusive, compassionate character of the kingdom. Like Mark, Matthew brings out the authority of Jesus—first through the words of the leper, who says, 'Lord, if you are willing, you can make me clean' (8:2); then through the centurion, who recognizes in Jesus the same sort of authority as he himself exercises, where to speak the word is to be instantly obeyed (8:9). Finally, Matthew follows Mark's account of the healing of the sick in the evening, but he adds, 'He drove out the spirits *with a word*' (8:16). Matthew then concludes the section by quoting Isaiah 53:4: 'He took up our infirmities and carried our diseases.' Isaiah, of course, was using the language of sickness and healing as a metaphor for sin and forgiveness, and Matthew is hinting at the same thing. From the very beginning, the miracles of Jesus were seen as parables of salvation, so that the stilling of the storm becomes a lesson in discipleship, and the healing of the paralysed man, which is his forgiveness, is closely linked with the call of a tax collector, which is his healing.

The deeds of Jesus are continued in his disciples and through the Church that grew from his ministry. Matthew conveys this by bringing together at this point the call of the Twelve and the mission of the Twelve (which he found in different places in Mark),[1] and adding a substantial discourse on mission, some of which is found in Mark in other contexts but much of which is new. It starts with instructions that clearly belong to the original Galilean mission (10:5–16). The disciples are to confine themselves to 'the lost sheep of the house of Israel' and ignore the Gentiles, taking no money or spare clothing. But then the scene changes: the disciples are faded out and we see the later Church arraigned before councils, flogged in synagogues and brought before governors and kings 'as witnesses to them and to the Gentiles' (10:17–18). Jesus goes on to address the persecutions and family tensions that had become normal for the Church of Matthew's day, and which Mark had seen as a sign of the last days of Jerusalem. The central message of the discourse is 'Do not be afraid' (10:26–30).

We wonder why, if Matthew is writing for the Church of his own day, he has left in words that clearly no longer apply to that Church, which has been told to make disciples of all nations (10:5–6, 23; compare 28:19). The answer perhaps is that he wishes to assure his Jewish readers that Israel had their chance when the Messiah came, even if they rejected it. Matthew concludes with a word of assurance: 'And if anyone gives even a cup of cold water to one of these little ones because he is my disciple, I tell you the truth, he will certainly not lose his reward' (10:42). Jesus is the Lord, and he will look after his own and reward all those who show their faith in *him* by their kindness to *them*. It is a theme to which Matthew will return more fully in the parable of the sheep and the goats.

Mixed response (chs. 11—13)

Like Mark, Matthew knows that Jesus' proclamation of the kingdom in word and deed met with a mixed response, but he devotes much more space to making this point. The section begins with the question of John the Baptist, who is in prison. 'Are you the one who was to come, or should we expect someone else?' (11:3). Jesus points to the things he has been doing, 'the deeds of the Christ' (11:2), and the readers also are challenged to make up their minds. If John has doubts about Jesus, others are more hostile, and Jesus goes on to denounce towns of Galilee who have seen what he has been doing and have failed to respond (11:20–24). Some, however, have responded—not the wise and learned, but little children—simple, ordinary people who have somehow grasped the truth that is simultaneously revealed and concealed by Jesus' ministry, that he is the Son of God (11:25–27). Jesus thanks God for their faith and issues an invitation to all who are 'weary and burdened' to take his yoke and find his rest. In the Jewish tradition it is Wisdom that calls to people, 'Come to me...'; the yoke she offers is the yoke of the law; and it is God who offers rest to those who obey him (Sirach 51:23, 26). Jesus here stands in the place of God, calls people to himself and presents his interpretation of the law as an easy yoke, in contrast presumably to the burdens imposed by Pharisaic teaching (11:28–30).

Matthew then follows Mark in recording how Jesus provoked controversy by allowing his disciples to pluck ears of corn on the Sabbath and by healing a man in the synagogue on the Sabbath, and how the Pharisees accused him of sorcery, attributing his power over demons to Satan. There are significant additions, however. After the Sabbath controversies, Matthew inserts his longest Old Testament quotation identifying Jesus with the Servant of the Lord (12:18–21; cf. Is. 42:1–14). Like the servant, Jesus is anointed with the Spirit of God, and, like him, he accomplishes God's work in gentleness and conceals his power in apparent weakness. Then, in dispute with the Pharisees, who ask for a sign, Jesus three times says that he is greater than a series of Old Testament figures they would have appealed to: greater than the temple—and, by implication David, its founder (12:6); greater than Jonah and the prophets (12:41); greater than Solomon and all the sages of Israel (12:42). We remember that Jesus said that he did not come to abolish the law and the prophets but to fulfil them (5:17).

The chapter ends with Jesus' family standing outside (although Matthew omits the detail that they thought him mad), while Jesus finds his true family in those who do the will of God as taught by himself.

John has doubts about him, the towns of Galilee reject him, the religious leaders accuse him of sorcery, his own family stand outside; and 'that same day' (13:1) Jesus tells the parable of the sower, whose original purpose, as in Mark, was to explain the mixed response to his message (13:3–9). If he is 'the one who was to come', if the kingdom of God is near, why is it not more obvious? Why does everyone not see it? The situation, Jesus says, is like what happens when a person sows seed. Seeds are unimpressive to look at, slow to germinate and, above all, vulnerable to all sorts of hazards. Yet seeds are also very powerful and, at harvest time, people will be amazed at what they have produced. Faith and unbelief are a mystery known only to God, yet everyone is responsible for how they hear the message and what they do with it (13:10–23).

Matthew reinforces this message with another similar parable—the parable of the weeds (13:24–30, 36–43). Once again there is a mixed situation—wheat and weeds together in the field—representative of the mixed response to Jesus' message in the world of his day. Why doesn't God sort it all out, make it more obvious that Jesus is the Christ? Well, he will, but not yet. Time must be given for people to respond to the message and for the true nature of each person to be made clear. The kingdom is near and already its effects can be felt, but it is hidden, like yeast in a batch of dough (13:33), like treasure in a field (13:44). Like finding the treasure, however, it calls for faith and vigorous action before the judgment, when there will be a final sorting out (13:47–50).

The oft-repeated suggestion that the parable of the weeds depicts the mixed nature of the Church may be correct inasmuch as it shows that history repeats itself and that our response to Jesus may be as mixed as was that of his first hearers, but this will hardly have been the original meaning of the parable, and that state of affairs in the Church is certainly not legitimated by it.

Fittingly, the chapter ends with the rejection of Jesus in his home town.

THE BIRTH OF A NEW COMMUNITY (MATTHEW 14:1—18:35)

In the middle of the last chapter, Matthew told us that Jesus left the crowd and went into the house, and his disciples came to him (13:36). It is a symbolic moment. From now on, Jesus will concentrate his efforts on the 'little ones' whom the Father has given him. Accordingly, in this next section we find Jesus spending more time with the disciples. Most of the stories are in Mark, but the changes and additions that Matthew has introduced make it much clearer that this is the birth of a new community.

For example, like Mark before him, Matthew reports the death of John the Baptist, the feeding of the five thousand and Jesus walking on the water, but whereas Mark has Jesus seek solitude because the disciples were tired, Matthew tells us that Jesus withdrew privately to a solitary place in response to the news of John's death (14:13). The kingdom of heaven suffers violence in this world but Jesus will gather and feed his people in the desert. Similarly with Jesus on the water: the sea in the Old Testament is often a symbol for all that is chaotic and hostile to God's purpose, for the power of death itself—and here Jesus plants his feet on it! The miracle is also a response to John's untimely death and looks forward to the resurrection of Jesus himself, but in Matthew there is something else. Peter walks on the water too. Jesus will share his victory with his people. In the hour of death, he will come to them and call for them, and when they cry out in fear and their faith falters, he will catch them and keep them safe and bring them into the company of those who worship him and say, 'Truly you are the Son of God' (14:33).

The next few stories are linked together by the theme of eating bread. First the Pharisees criticize the disciples for not observing the tradition of the elders when they eat, and Jesus pronounces sentence of excommunication on them (15:13), although Matthew stops short of saying that Jesus declared all foods clean (cf. Mark 7:19). In contrast, a pagan woman gets to eat the children's bread. Then Jesus feeds another crowd with bread. When, in response to the Pharisees' request for a sign, Jesus tells the disciples to be on their guard against the yeast of the Pharisees and Sadducees, they think he is talking about ordinary bread, but it is explained that he is talking about their teaching. So bread stands for teaching, and there is true bread and false bread; there are those who get to eat the bread of God even though they are born outside his family, and those who miss out even though they are leaders of God's people. All these stories are in Mark too, but Matthew makes it clearer that the crowd whom Jesus heals and feeds are Gentiles, since they praise the God of Israel (15:31); and, in contrast to Mark, the disciples *understand* the reference to the yeast of the Pharisees (16:12). In response to the failure of the old leaders, Jesus is gathering the people of God into a new community around himself.

Peter's confession of Jesus as the Christ no longer plays the same role in Matthew that it did in Mark. There it marked a significant stage in the disciples' coming to faith; here it marks the birth of the Church. In Matthew, Jesus has been publicly declared as the Son of God at his baptism (3:17). He has already given thanks that there are those who recognize him as such (11:25–27), and the disciples in the boat have worshipped Jesus as the Son of God (14:33), so although Peter is congratulated on his insight, the real interest of the passage lies in what Jesus goes on to say: 'You are Peter, and on this rock I will build my church, and the gates of Hades will not overcome it' (16:18). This is one of only two places in the four Gospels that Jesus speaks of the Church (the other being Matthew 18:17, where it refers to a local congregation). To understand it, we need to know that the Greek word *ecclesia* was used to translate the Hebrew *qahal*, which in turn was sometimes used in the Old Testament to refer to Israel as the assembly of the Lord. Jesus has in mind, then, a new Israel, reformed about his person and consisting of those who make this good confession. Among these, Peter will be pre-eminent, as Matthew of course knows that he was. To him, as to all the disciples (18:18), Jesus gives the authority to teach in his name and to admit people of all nations into his Church, as we have seen Jesus himself doing (15:21–28).

As in Mark, Peter's confession is followed by Jesus' announcement of his coming death, Peter's rebuke, and Jesus' call to all who want to follow him to take up the cross. There follow the story of the transfiguration and the lesson on faith and prayer arising from the healing of the epileptic boy, but Matthew adds the odd story of the coin in the fish's mouth (17:24–27), whose point seems to be to balance the pains of discipleship with its privileges. As the king's sons are exempt from taxation, so the disciples are exempt from the obligations of the old Israel (although, for the sake of peace, Matthew implies that they may voluntarily observe them).

This section of the Gospel then ends with a discourse of Jesus on the character of his new community (18:1–35). Taking as his starting point Mark's story of the disciples' dispute over which of them was the greatest (which he softens into a simple request for instruction), Matthew adds the parable of the lost sheep, instructions about dealing with offences between members of the community, and the parable of the unmerciful servant. The community is to be marked by humility and by mutual concern. Children are persons of little importance, and that is how disciples are to view themselves. At the same time, however, children are persons of infinite importance, and that is how disciples are to view one another. Disciples are 'little ones' and the community is to try by all means to see that none is lost.

The chief way in which members are likely to be lost is through unresolved quarrels, so Jesus gives practical advice on how to resolve them. It is noteworthy that there is no suggestion that it is the job of leaders to deal with this matter. Responsibility lies on each member and on the church as a whole. Again, there is no suggestion that people are to be put out of the church for the sin they may have committed. Rather, they are to be put out, if at all, because they will not listen to the church or receive correction. The passage is less about church discipline than about conflict resolution, as Peter's question, 'How many times shall I forgive my brother when he sins against me?' and the lengthy and vivid story that Jesus gives in reply make clear (18:21–35). The Church is a community that lives by the forgiveness of sins—a topic of special interest to Matthew (6:14–15; 26:28).

THE COMING OF THE SON OF MAN (MATTHEW 19:1—28:20)

We now come to the final section of the Gospel, leading up to the climax of the cross and resurrection. In outline, these chapters follow Mark. Jesus travels toward Jerusalem, giving teaching on discipleship as he goes (chs. 19—20). He rides into Jerusalem and confronts the leaders of the nation, whom he proceeds to denounce in seven solemn 'woes' (chs. 21—23). His prediction of the destruction of the city follows Mark closely, but is now expanded with a number of parables that tell the reader to prepare for the last judgment, which the destruction of Jerusalem foreshadows (chs. 24—25). Then follows the arrest, trial and crucifixion of Jesus, leading to his resurrection and appearance in glory to his disciples (chs. 26—28). I have called this 'the coming of the Son of Man'. In Daniel, we recall, the human figure who represents faithful Israel comes in clouds of glory, not from heaven to earth, but to God, to be vindicated and given authority by him after suffering. It is as this Son of Man that Jesus appears to his followers at the close of the Gospel, vindicated in resurrection and with all authority in heaven and earth given to him. In this way Jesus' words are proved true: 'I tell you the truth, some who are standing here will not taste death before they see the Son of Man coming in his kingdom' (16:28).

The road to the cross (19:1—20:34)

The events of these chapters take place on the road to Jerusalem. Although their content and thrust are substantially the same as in Mark, Matthew has underlined the message by inserting the parable of the workers in the vineyard (20:1–16). In this story, a man hires men to work in his vineyard, going out at the start of the day, then at nine o'clock, noon and five o'clock. In the end he pays them all the same, despite the protests of those who were hired first, and the lesson is drawn that 'the last will be first, and the first will be last' (19:30; 20:16). This is the centrepiece of the section and provides a link between its various stories. The Pharisees might be expected to be among the first, but their way of keeping the law shows that they fall short of God's perfect will in the matter of marriage and divorce (19:1–9). Yet sexual asceticism, even for those who are called to it, is equally no guarantee of favour with God (19:10–12). By contrast, the kingdom of heaven belongs to children, the last people you would have expected God to take notice of (19:13–15). The rich young man might have expected to be among the first. He is rich and it has been easy for him to live an upright life, but he too falls short of God's limitless goodness. Yet the subsequent conversation with Peter suggests that it may be equally dangerous to take pride in renouncing these things (19:16–30). The last will be first and the first last, even among the followers of Jesus.

After the parable of the workers, Jesus again speaks of his death and resurrection—the ultimate reversal of human expectations—and, as in Mark, this is followed by the request of James and John for the chief seats in the kingdom (20:20–27). The healing of the two blind men (20:29–34) provides a nice contrast with this story. In the first, two leading disciples come to Jesus and are shown to be blind; in the other, two blind men come to Jesus and are shown to have faith. The last are first and the first last indeed!

The last appeal (21:1—23:39)

The story of Jesus' last days in Jerusalem begins, as in Mark, with three prophetic signs. Jesus rides into Jerusalem as king, stages a demonstration against the temple and uses a fig tree to make clear the true state of the nation and its temple and the imminent prospect of judgment. There follow three parables of judgment, two of them added by Matthew. The first is the parable of the two sons (21:28–32). The first son refuses to obey his father, but later changes his mind. The second agrees to go and work in the vineyard, but in fact does nothing. Jesus says that this typifies the response to God's message of the sinners and the respectable people of Jerusalem respectively. This leads to the parable of the wicked tenants (21:33–46), which we also met in Mark. The tenants withhold the fruit due from them and beat and kill the messengers sent to them. Finally the owner sends his son, and they kill him too, bringing upon themselves well-deserved punishment.

Then Matthew inserts the parable of the wedding banquet (22:1–14). In this version of the story, the banquet is given by a king for his son. When the invited guests refuse to come, the king sends an army and burns their city. Then the king tells his servants to go and invite anyone they find to fill the wedding hall. Like its predecessor, this parable clearly intends to portray the nation as disobedient to God and warns of judgment to come. Matthew's message in all this is summed up in the words of Jesus: 'Therefore I tell you that the kingdom of God will be taken away from you and given to a people who will produce its fruit' (21:43).

Three prophetic dramas and three parables of judgment are followed by three controversy stories in which Jesus silences his critics. The first concerns paying tribute to Caesar. While the story does say something about Jesus' attitude to the Roman state, the main thrust lies in the words, 'Give... to God what is God's' (22:21), as Israel was *not* doing. So who is God and what should we give him? He is God of the living before whom all shall stand (22:32), and we should give him loving obedience (22:34–40).

Who, then, is this who acts and speaks with such authority? He is the son of David, certainly, but he is more. He is the Lord, before whom every critic must fall silent (22:41–46). The public ministry of Jesus in Jerusalem ends with a speech in which Jesus solemnly pronounces God's judgment on the teachers of the law and the Pharisees for their ostentation and hypocrisy. We should not think that Matthew takes delight in having Jesus attack the leaders of the nation. He is relating a great tragedy, as he sees it. The nation God chose as his special possession has rejected him, so Jesus concludes: 'O Jerusalem, Jerusalem, you who kill the prophets and stone those sent to you, how often I have longed to gather your children together, as a hen gathers her chicks under her wings, but you were not willing. Look, your house is left to you desolate' (23:37–38).

Judgment past and to come (24:1—25:46)

For Matthew, writing in the last third of the first century, the disasters predicted by Jesus in the first part of this discourse are already an accomplished fact. The great buildings of the temple have been thrown down (24:2). False Christs have come. There have been wars and rumours of wars, and famines and earthquakes. The sanctuary has been desecrated (24:15), the holy city surrounded by armies, and its population slaughtered or enslaved in great numbers. The day of judgment has come for Jerusalem (24:29–31), and all within a generation, just as Jesus said it would (24:34–35). Jesus has been proved terribly right in the warnings he gave the nation.

It was no doubt important to show the young Church that the terrible times through which they had lived had all been in the purpose of God. Yet Matthew sees that these events had been only a dress rehearsal for the final coming of God to judge the world. To bring this out, he has the disciples ask Jesus a double question: 'When will this happen, and what will be the sign of your coming and of the end of the age?' (24:3; cf. Mark 13:4). The first question, concerning the destruction of Jerusalem, is answered in 24:1–35. It will happen within a generation, and there will be clear signs of its coming. Terrible though that day will be, however, no one is to suppose that it is literally the end of the world.

The second question, concerning the end of the age, is answered from 24:36 onwards. No one knows about that day or hour. It will be sudden and unheralded, like Noah's flood, and Matthew extends the discourse he took over from Mark by adding a series of striking pictures whose purpose is to impress on his Christian readers the need to be prepared for it.[2] In the first place, the day of the Lord will be sudden and unexpected, like a thief in the night (24:42–44), or like the unexpected return of an absent employer (24:45–51). You cannot predict it, but you can prepare for it. You can take precautions against a thief; you can get on with your work so as to be found doing your duty. Second, while it will be sudden, it may not be soon—or not as soon as some think. The parable of the ten bridesmaids (25:1–13) is about the delay of Christ's coming. Like the bridesmaids at a wedding, the followers of Jesus may have to be prepared for a long wait and still be ready, firm in faith and not weary in well-doing, when the bridegroom comes. Nor are they to make excuses about the hardness of the times or the smallness of their resources, like the servant in the parable who received only one talent (25:14–30), but are to take the opportunities of the present time to serve God in them in whatever way they can.

Although it will be hard—although they may find themselves hungry, or thirsty, or friendless, or naked, sick or in prison—they are to know that Jesus suffers in them and with them. He will come again to judge the whole world, and on that day it will not just be the Church that is judged. All the nations will be gathered before the Son of Man, and they will be judged for how they have treated Jesus as he has come to them in the guise of his faithful people (25:31–46).[3]

The arrest, trial and crucifixion of Jesus (26:1—27:56)

Matthew follows Mark extremely closely in his account of the Passion of Jesus, and everything we found in Mark is true here too. Jesus knows full well that he is going to his death. Indeed, Matthew's account opens with Jesus solemnly announcing the fact (26:1–2). When the woman pours perfume on him, he sees it as an anointing for burial. When he eats the Passover with his friends, he sees it as foreshadowing his own death as a sacrifice for the forgiveness of sins. He prays in the garden. He is arrested. He is examined by the high priest while, out in the courtyard, Peter denies him. He is examined by Pilate, who offers to release him, but the crowd prefer Barabbas. He is mocked by the soldiers and crucified. As in Mark, he speaks from the cross just once—the cry of desolation, 'My God, my God, why have you forsaken me?'—and the centurion declares that he really is the Son of God. All this is in Mark, but Matthew adds some interesting details.

The famous words 'All who draw the sword will die by the sword' occur only in this Gospel, as Jesus rebukes Peter for resisting his arrest. Jesus goes on to say that, had he wanted to resist arrest, he could have called on twelve legions of angels, 'but how then would the Scriptures be fulfilled that say it must happen this way?' (26:52–54). Matthew alone gives us the story of the remorse and death of Judas (27:1–10), perhaps because it provides him with another opportunity to show how everything happened in fulfilment of prophecy, and therefore as a witness to God's sovereign control; or perhaps because the story helps to fix the blame for the death of Jesus firmly on the Jewish leaders whose cynical behaviour it underlines. That certainly is the motive behind the next two additions. First, Pilate's wife tells him to have nothing to do with this righteous man because she has had a bad dream about him (27:19). Pilate then, convinced of Jesus' innocence, washes his hands and tries to pin the blame for Jesus' death on the crowd, who become the mouthpiece for Matthew's point of view as they declare, 'Let his blood be on us and on our children!' (27:24–25). Finally, Matthew emphasizes the true significance of Jesus' death by recording not only the tearing of the temple curtain but also that there was a great earthquake, tombs were broken open and many holy people who had died were raised to life, and were seen alive by many (27:52–53). The passage is full of difficulties, but it at least serves to show that, for Matthew, the death of Jesus marks the end of the reign of death, and the inbreaking of the kingdom of God.

The resurrection of Jesus (27:57—28:20)

Matthew's account of the resurrection differs from Mark's in three important respects. In the first place, it is much less mysterious or ambiguous. Instead of a young man sitting next to where the body of Jesus had been, we have a mighty angel who comes down from heaven, rolls away the stone and sits on it, striking terror into the guards. Instead of the women running from the tomb in fear, saying nothing to anyone, we have them running in fear and joy and being met by Jesus in person. They clasp his feet in homage and he repeats the message of the angel for the disciples to go to Galilee, where they will see him. Second, Matthew has sandwiched the story of the resurrection between the story of the posting of the guards at the tomb and the story of their being bribed to say that the disciples stole the body while they (the guards) were asleep. The effect of this is to emphasize that the tomb was indeed empty, and that we are dealing with a physical event. If explanations for this differ, the emptiness of the tomb itself is not in dispute—it is attested by Jesus' enemies as well as his friends. Finally, the disciples travel to Galilee as instructed and there meet with Jesus, who sends them to the nations with the promise of his presence with them 'to the very end of the age' (28:16–20).

THE CLOSE OF THE GOSPEL
AND THE MESSAGE OF MATTHEW

Many of the key themes of Matthew's Gospel come together in this closing scene.[4] First, Jesus is the teacher, the new Moses, who appears on the mountain bringing the new law to the new Israel, just as he did earlier in the Gospel (5:1). Discipleship in this Gospel is a matter of doing 'everything I have commanded you'. Second, Jesus is the Lord, the Son of Man to whom all authority in heaven and on earth is now given, and who can properly be worshipped together with the Father and the Holy Spirit. Third, the gospel is for all nations. This has been hinted at several times in the story, from the visit of the magi to the healing of the centurion's servant and the Syro-Phoenician woman's daughter, and the prophecy of Jesus that 'this gospel of the kingdom will be preached in the whole world as a testimony to all nations' (24:14). Previously, the disciples had been sent only to the lost sheep of the house of Israel (10:5–6), but now the road to the Gentiles lies open and the Church must take it.

Finally, for Matthew, Jesus is the presence of God with his people. The Gospel began with Matthew recalling the words of Isaiah, 'They will call him Immanuel—which means, "God with us"' (1:23). Jesus himself said, 'Where two or three come together in my name, there am I with them' (18:20). Now the Gospel closes with Jesus saying, 'And surely I am with you always, to the very end of the age.'

CHAPTER 4

LUKE'S STORY

Mark wrote, so it is usually thought, for a suffering Church, assuring persecuted Christians of the power of Jesus but also of the necessity of suffering, in the experience of both Jesus and his followers. As a result, he gives us a stern and uncompromising portrait of Jesus, the suffering servant. Matthew wrote for a separated Church, a Church whose members had recently separated from the synagogue. They needed to understand why this had come about, and to see Jesus as the true teacher and themselves as the true Israel. The result is an imposing portrait of Jesus, the Son of Man who will come to judge the world.

Luke by contrast writes for a comfortable Church. There is little hint of persecution, and none of the bitterness of religious conflict that we find in Matthew. The danger is of the Church settling down and losing its spiritual vitality. Luke is still very critical of the Pharisees, but whereas in Matthew the Pharisees represent the Jewish leaders who have led Israel astray, in Luke they represent worldly Christians, who are in danger of forgetting how much they need to be forgiven.[1] They are prone to justify themselves while withholding their compassion from others. They are well-to-do and their wealth corrupts their view of themselves and the world. Accordingly, Luke stresses the joy of following Jesus. It is the joy of the forgiven. It typically expresses itself in meals eaten together 'with glad and generous hearts' (Acts 2:46, NRSV). It calls for repentance, a change of heart and life, and it is offered today!

At the same time, following Jesus is demanding. Faith requires persistence. The cares of life can easily divert Christians, and wealth is seen as a particular danger. So Christians must be alert and pray, as Jesus prayed, to be filled with the Holy Spirit, if they are to persevere.

Luke portrays Jesus as prophet and saviour. He is filled with the Spirit. He is in regular communion with God in prayer, and that is the secret of his acts of power. He is joyful and compassionate, bringing good news to the poor, to sinners, outsiders and women. It is an attractive portrait and one intended for our imitation.

THE COMPOSITION OF THE PORTRAIT

A comparison of the Gospels shows that Mark provided Luke with about 40 per cent of his material. There is about 20 per cent of the Gospel that Luke shares with Matthew, either because they both used the same source or because Luke knew and adapted Matthew to his purpose. The remaining 40 per cent is material unique to Luke. We may suppose that these stories were widely circulated among the early Christians and Luke has made his own selection from the Church 'memory banks'. He probably also shaped what he chose to include, so as to present Jesus in a way suited to the pastoral needs of his church. Alone among the Gospel writers, he tells us something of how and why he worked (1:1–14). The stories of Jesus, he says, were handed down by eyewitnesses and were the subject of Christian preaching by 'the servants of the word'. Others (Luke says 'many') had tried their hand at writing the story down (presumably he means at least Mark and probably also Matthew). Luke then conducted his own investigations and is now writing an 'orderly' account so that Theophilus may know the truth of what he has been taught. This implies that Theophilus is a well-to-do Christian (since he has been taught), possibly one of those comfortable Christians whom Luke intends to stir up to love and good works!

The process Luke describes is very close to what we might have concluded on other grounds: the Gospel stories go back to the eye-witnesses, were passed on by the preachers ('oral tradition') and then gathered and arranged by Gospel writers in the second generation. Luke's purpose was apparently to provide a fuller account than Mark and to paint a portrait with a very different emphasis from that of Matthew.[2]

	Markan framework	Lukan additions
Births of John & Jesus		1 Magnificat, Benedictus 2 Visit of shepherds
Galilean ministry	3 Baptism 4 Healing 5 Controversy 8 Further healings 9 Peter's confession	*(genealogy)* *(temptation)* *(call of disciples)* 6 Sermon on Plain 7 Woman forgiven
Journey to Jerusalem		10 Good Samaritan 11 Friend at midnight 12 Rich fool 13 Woman healed 14 Great banquet 15 Lost son 16 Dishonest steward, Rich man & Lazarus 17 Ten lepers healed 18 Pharisee & tax man 19 Zacchaeus, Parable of the pounds
Jesus in Jerusalem	20 Confrontation 21 Judgment foretold	
Passion & resurrection	22 Last supper & arrest 23 Trial & death 24 Empty tomb	*(Emmaus Road)* *(Ascension)*

In the table, the numbers refer to chapters of Luke's Gospel as we have it in our Bibles. The left-hand column shows that Luke is telling the same story as Mark and Matthew. The middle column shows where he follows Mark (with significant additions shown in the right-hand column in italics). The right-hand column shows the extent of Lukan additions, with particularly famous Lukan passages mentioned by name, including especially many of the parables.

From this table, we can draw the following conclusions. First, Luke kept the Markan framework. Jesus' ministry begins with his baptism. He preaches the kingdom of God in word and deed in Galilee and then travels to Jerusalem, where he confronts the authorities and is arrested, tried and crucified. On the third day he is raised from the dead. Second, Luke has added an account of the birth of Jesus, which on inspection turns out to be quite different from Matthew's. Third, Luke has greatly expanded the space given to Jesus' journey to Jerusalem and made it the setting for much of Jesus' teaching. Many of the most famous parables of Jesus are found here. Fourth, instead of grouping the teaching of Jesus into five long discourses as Matthew has done, Luke integrates the teaching of Jesus into the narrative. The teaching on a particular subject is grouped together in a short lesson, often with a narrative introduction. The teaching on prayer in 11:1–13 is a good example. Finally, even where Luke covers the same ground as Mark, notably in his account of the death and resurrection of Jesus, he does so in a quite distinctive way. Luke has adapted Mark more radically than Matthew has done.

THE STORY IN OUTLINE

THE BIRTH AND CHILDHOOD OF JESUS (LUKE 1:5—2:52)

The story begins in Jerusalem in the heart of the temple, where an old priest is burning incense before the Lord. Before long, Jesus himself will be brought into the temple and presented to the Lord. Then, in the only story we have of Jesus' childhood, we find him in the temple with the teachers, listening and asking questions. Clearly Luke wants to tell us that the good news is not a new religion; nor does it reject the old religion and start again somewhere else. On the contrary, Jesus comes as the fulfilment of all that Israel hoped for. In his second volume, Luke will tell us how the good news spread all over the world, reaching even Rome itself; but it starts here in Jerusalem, in the temple, and the Church must not forget the soil from which it sprang.

The people among whom Jesus is born are faithful Israelites— Zechariah and Elizabeth, not forgetting their famous son John; Simeon, who was 'waiting for the consolation of Israel' (2:25); the prophetess Anna and her friends who were 'looking forward to the redemption of Jerusalem' (2:38); the shepherds, who are addressed as representative Israelites who share the hopes of the nation; Joseph and above all Mary, who is chosen by grace, believing and obedient as Israel is or ought to be.

Songs of praise celebrate the dawn of a new age, but it is an age of fulfilment. Mary rejoices because God 'has helped his servant Israel' and shown mercy to Abraham (1:54–55). Zechariah praises God because 'he has come and has redeemed his people' in fulfilment of 'the oath he swore to our father Abraham' (1:67, 73). Simeon praises God because in Jesus he has seen fulfilled the promise that light would shine from Israel to illuminate the whole world (2:30–32).

An important sign that this is true is the renewed activity of the Holy Spirit. It was widely understood that the Spirit was the Spirit of prophecy and that, as such, it had been withdrawn from Israel, but that the Messiah, when he came, would be endowed with the Spirit to an exceptional degree. Now, first Elizabeth, then Zechariah and finally Simeon are filled with the Spirit and prophesy, and the angel announces that John will be filled with the Spirit from birth, and that the power of the Spirit will overshadow Mary so as to bring about the birth of Jesus. Jesus himself will be filled with the Holy Spirit so as to be son of David and Son of God, a Saviour, who is Christ the Lord. The Holy Spirit is once again on the move, and the proper response to this is joy. Elizabeth rejoices that she is no longer barren (and as such she stands for Israel as a whole). Mary rejoices in 'God my Saviour' (1:47). The angel promises the shepherds 'great joy' and the shepherds return home glorifying and praising God. The birth narrative in Luke forms an overture to the Gospel as a whole, and it is marked by joyful and triumphant music, celebrating not just the births of John and of Jesus but the dawn of a new age.

THE MINISTRY OF JESUS IN GALILEE (LUKE 3:1—9:50)

As the table below shows, for most of this section Luke is following Mark, with occasional episodes taken over from Matthew. It is Mark who has provided the framework and the order. Thus we meet the preaching of John the Baptist, the baptism of Jesus, his temptations (closely resembling Matthew's account), the exorcism of the man in the synagogue, the healing of Peter's mother-in-law and the crowd of sick people in the evening, the cleansing of the leper, the healing of the paralysed man, the call of Levi and controversy over fasting and the Sabbath. All of these occur in the same order as in Mark.

Reverting to Matthew, we have a shortened version of the Sermon on the Mount, beginning with a version of the Beatitudes, continuing with its most distinctive teaching about love for enemies and not judging others, and ending with the parable of the two builders. This is followed by the healing of the centurion's servant, and the question of John the Baptist, 'Are you the one who was to come?'

Back with Mark, we have the parable of the sower, the stilling of the storm, the Gadarene demoniac and the raising of Jairus' daughter (inseparably linked to the healing of the woman with the haemorr-hage). Jesus sends out the Twelve and, on their return, takes them into the desert, where he feeds the crowd. Peter then acknowledges Jesus to be the Christ, and the disciples are warned that the Son of Man must suffer and they with him.

The transfiguration, the healing of the epileptic boy and the argument about who will be greatest bring to a close Luke's account of the Galilean ministry. This section of Luke is thus an abbreviated edition of Mark's account of the Galilean ministry with the addition of four stories from Matthew, which themselves occur in the same order as they do in Matthew.

The composition of Luke 3:1—9:50

Luke 3:1–20	The preaching of John	Mark 1:1–8
Luke 3:21–22	The baptism of Jesus	Mark 1:9–11
Luke 3:23–38	**Genealogy of Jesus**	
Luke 4:1–13	*The temptations of Jesus*	*Matthew 4:1–11*
Luke 4:14–30	**Sermon in Nazareth**	
Luke 4:31–37	Exorcism in the synagogue	Mark 1:21–28
Luke 4:38–44	Peter's mother-in-law, and so on	Mark 1:29–39
Luke 5:1–11	**Call of disciples**	
Luke 5:12–16	Leper cleansed	Mark 1:40–45
Luke 5:17–26	Paralysed man healed	Mark 2:1–12
Luke 5:27–32	Call of Levi	Mark 2:13–17
Luke 5:33—6:11	Questions about fasting and the Sabbath	Mark 2:18—3:6
Luke 6:12–16	Appointment of Twelve	Mark 3:13–19
Luke 6:17–49	*Sermon on the Plain*	*Matthew 5—7*
Luke 7:1–10	*Centurion's servant*	*Matthew 8:5–13*
Luke 7:11–17	**Widow's son raised**	
Luke 7:18–35	*John's question*	*Matthew 11:1–19*
Luke 7:36–50	**Sinful woman forgiven**	
Luke 8:1–18	Parables of the sower and the lamp	Mark 4:1–25
Luke 8:19–21	Jesus' family	Mark 3:31–34
Luke 8:22–25	Stilling the storm	Mark 4:35–41
Luke 8:26–39	Gadarene demoniac	Mark 5:1–20
Luke 8:40–56	Jairus' daughter, etc	Mark 5:21–43
Luke 9:1–9	Mission of the Twelve	Mark 6:7–13
Luke 9:10–17	Feeding the crowd	Mark 6:30–44
Luke 9:18–27	Peter's confession and sequel	Mark 8:27—9:1
Luke 9:28–36	Transfiguration	Mark 9:2–13
Luke 9:37–45	Epileptic boy	Mark 9:14–32
Luke 9:46–50	Dispute about greatness	Mark 9:33–41

What is of special interest is what Luke has added that is not in either Mark or Matthew. There is first John the Baptist's practical teaching (3:10–14). Although all the Gospel writers tell us that John called people to repent, Luke spells out what repentance would mean for different groups—the well-off, tax collectors and soldiers—making John into a preacher of Christian duty. In line with this, Luke broadens the target of John's denunciation from the Pharisees and Sadducees to embrace the crowds. No one is exempt from the need to produce fruit and no one should rely on their birth or ancestry.

The second major addition is the genealogy that Luke inserts after the baptism of Jesus (3:23–38). There are many differences between this genealogy and the one with which Matthew begins his Gospel, and I don't propose to offer an explanation for them or suggest how the differences can be reconciled, but one difference is worth noting. Whereas Matthew's genealogy rooted Jesus in the story of Israel all the way back to Abraham, Luke takes his genealogy back still further to 'Seth, the son of Adam, the son of God' (3:38). Jesus is not just the fulfilment of Israel's hopes; he is the answer to the longings of the whole world, for whose sake God chose Israel in the first place (3:6).

The same note of universality is sounded by the next story we must consider, the sermon of Jesus in the synagogue at Nazareth (4:14–30). Luke has placed this story here at the start of Jesus' ministry because it sums up so much of what follows. Jesus comes as one anointed by the Spirit at his baptism (3:22), full of the Spirit (4:1), empowered by the Spirit (4:14), to announce that the long-awaited kingdom is at hand. Luke doesn't use the word 'kingdom' in this story, but that is what Jesus proclaims when he speaks of good news for the poor, freedom for the captives, sight for the blind, release for the oppressed and the year of the Lord's favour. This is what the Messiah was expected to bring, and, to their delight, Jesus says that the time of waiting is over. This is the day that the Lord has made.

Yet who are 'the poor'? The assumption of Jesus' audience is that they themselves are the poor. God is coming to rescue oppressed Israelites—and so he is, but not only them. In fact, Jesus hints, it is possible that his own people will fail to respond, but others will respond instead. The stories of Elijah and Elisha show that God has never confined his grace to one people, and the kingdom Jesus is announcing will reach out to the poor, including sinners within Israel and foreigners outside. This is too much for the synagogue congregation and Jesus narrowly escapes being lynched.

The power of Jesus is seen in the story of the call of the first disciples (5:1–11). Whereas in Mark they leave everything and follow Jesus at his word alone, here the power of God breaks into their lives at the moment when their own expertise has been shown to be powerless. Peter responds to the unexpected presence of God in a way reminiscent of Isaiah's—'Woe is me…!' (Is. 6:5)—and, like Isaiah, receives a divine commission.

The power and compassion of Jesus are then seen in the raising of the widow's son at Nain (7:11–17). The story immediately follows the healing of the centurion's servant and together they fulfil Jesus' promise to bring good news to the poor, and to do so in the spirit and power of Elijah. The 'poor' turn out to include a hated foreigner (who nevertheless himself shows kindness), as well as, more predictably, a poor widow who has just lost her only son. Together they evoke the response, 'A great prophet has appeared among us' (7:16), and provide an answer to John's question, 'Are you the one…?' (7:19).

Jesus is accused of being the friend of sinners (7:34), which, if true, would call into question his loyalty as an Israelite and his status as a prophet. In the story that follows, Luke is happy to admit the charge! Many key Lukan themes come together in the story of the woman who anointed Jesus' feet. In the first place we find Jesus at table, happy to accept hospitality from Pharisees and tax collectors alike. Then it is demonstrated that Jesus is indeed a prophet. Simon questions this because Jesus is apparently unaware of the woman's past life, but Jesus turns the tables on him by showing that, on the contrary, he not only knows about the woman, he can read Simon's thoughts as well. Then there is a little parable that perfectly illustrates what Luke understands by 'justification by faith'. Like the men in the parable, all are in debt to God by varying amounts, no one is in a position to pay, but God freely forgives all who trust him. Faith expresses itself in love, as the behaviour of the woman shows, and through her example we learn the meaning of repentance and salvation.

In the next section it will become clear that this woman is one of several who have been saved. Luke then places the parable of the sower here to show that the word of God has come and created a division between those who accept and do it and those who don't. Those who do, whatever their background, are Jesus' true family (8:1–21).

ON THE WAY WITH JESUS TO JERUSALEM (LUKE 9:51—19:27)

The central section of Luke begins with a solemn notice of Jesus leaving Galilee and travelling to Jerusalem where he will be taken up to heaven, and it ends when Luke rejoins the Markan story and Jesus rides into Jerusalem. For this reason it is sometimes called Luke's 'travel narrative', since all of it takes place between Galilee and Jerusalem and there are occasional references to Jesus being on the road. It is not, however, anything like a diary, nor is it possible to trace Jesus' progress either in place or time. Luke has taken the opportunity to group together a large amount of material that is not in Mark. Some of it is also found in Matthew, but much of it is unique to Luke, including a number of Jesus' most famous parables.

There is little agreement about how Luke has structured his travel narrative. My proposal is that new sections are usually begun by someone coming to Jesus and asking a question or presenting a problem of some kind, and that we should look for a theme uniting the stories and sayings that follow. This is not always easy because Luke's method has been to place units of discourse side by side while leaving the reader to work out the logical connection between them. Sometimes this may be a matter of one story reinforcing another; sometimes they may provide a contrast.

Discipleship (9:51—10:24)

The opening stories can be grouped around the theme of discipleship. We learn of the true spirit of discipleship as James and John are rebuked for their vengefulness towards the Samaritans who reject Jesus (9:51–55). Then we learn of the cost of discipleship as some would-be disciples are challenged about their commitment (9:57–62). The task of discipleship is outlined as Jesus sends out 72 disciples as heralds of the kingdom (10:1–20). On their return, Jesus assures them of the privilege of disciples in knowing the Father and the Son (10:21–24).

Love for God and neighbour (10:25—11:13)

The next section begins with the lawyer asking, 'What must I do to inherit eternal life?' The answer is, love God with all your heart and soul, and your neighbour as yourself. And who is my neighbour? Anyone in need, of course. But what if the person in need is a hated foreigner? Worse still, what if he were to prove a neighbour to me (10:25–37)?

Closely linked with this story, and balancing it, is the story of Martha and Mary (10:38–42). Loving our neighbour is the second commandment—what about loving God? From this homely tale of a domestic tiff, it emerges that the way to love God is to listen to him and to put this before everything else. Appropriately enough, this is followed by teaching on prayer (11:1–13). First, Jesus teaches his disciples to pray. Luke gives us a shorter version of the Lord's Prayer, shorn of Matthew's explanatory clauses, either because he thought them unnecessary or because he was going behind Matthew to an older tradition, closer to what Jesus originally said. This is followed by the parable of the friend at midnight, one of two parables that urge persistence in prayer (the other is the persistent widow, 18:1–8). Luke then adds the exhortation to ask, seek and knock and concludes by changing Matthew's general assurance that God can be trusted to give good things to the assurance that God will make discipleship possible by giving the Holy Spirit to those who ask him (11:13; cf. Matt. 7:11).

The blindness of the people and their leaders (11:14—12:12)

A dumb man is brought to Jesus and is healed, but some people attribute his success to sorcery. Jesus replies by asking how they can think that Satan would act against his own interests. This is nothing less than the finger of God at work, and proof, for those with eyes to see, that the kingdom of God is breaking in. But eyes to see is precisely what they do not have (11:33–36)! A Pharisee who is amazed at Jesus' failure to perform ritual ablutions before the meal provokes Jesus into a stinging attack on those who concentrate on the finer points of religious etiquette while neglecting justice and the love of God. The disciples are warned against the insidious influence of the Pharisaic mindset and called to live openly and boldly with the help of the Holy Spirit.

Wealth and watchfulness (12:13–59)

The request from a man in the crowd that Jesus might arbitrate in a family dispute provides the occasion for the first of Luke's warnings on the dangers of wealth. It begins with a general warning against greed, and the parable of the rich fool who laid up treasures on earth but not in heaven. To this Luke adds the teaching on anxiety and possessions from the Sermon on the Mount (12:22–34; cf. Matt. 6:19–34) and the teaching on watchfulness from Matthew's eschatological discourse (12:35–48; cf. Matt. 24:43–51). This is the hour of crisis for Jesus and the nation, a fiery baptism that only the single-minded disciple will survive (12:49–53).

The present crisis (13:1–35)

Current events give Jesus the opportunity of speaking about the crisis facing the nation. The governor has acted with brutality towards some Galilean dissidents and, in a separate incident, eighteen people have been killed in the collapse of a tower. Jesus says that this is as nothing compared to the bloodshed there will be if the nationalists continue to try to bring in God's kingdom by violence. Thousands will be slaughtered and the temple itself will come crashing down (13:1–5). The chapter ends with Jesus raising a lament over Jerusalem, whose coming desolation he sees so clearly (13:34–35). It is in this context that Luke has placed the story of Jesus healing the crippled woman in the synagogue, despite the indignation of the orthodox (13:10–17). As the woman has been bound by Satan for eighteen long years, so the nation of Israel has been in chains. The power of God is present to rescue Israel too, but most people do not recognize it—and a day will come when God will not recognize them (13:25). Meanwhile, Jesus goes on his way undeterred by threats and rumours of arrest or assassination, confident that it is his destiny to die in Jerusalem and so, in some way, take God's fiery judgment on himself so that others might be saved.[3]

The dangers of wealth (14:1—17:10)

In this central section of the travel narrative, the Pharisees are continually shown in a negative light. They disapprove of Jesus' healing on the Sabbath (14:1–6). They exalt themselves in God's sight and despise the poor (14:7–14). They grumble when Jesus welcomes sinners (15:1–2). They have the teaching of Moses and the prophets but they do not listen to it (16:29).

What is their basic problem? Luke tells us: they love money (16:14), and that is the root of all their evil. The love of money blinds them to human need and dries up the springs of compassion for the crippled and the poor. Although they would not dream of grabbing the best seats for themselves at a dinner party, they have no hesitation in fancying themselves superior to others in the game of life and exalting themselves before God (14:7–11). Their attachment to possessions means that, like the people invited to the great banquet, they cannot see what is really important and so fail to respond to God's gracious invitation (14:15–24). They are unable to share the heavenly Father's heart for the lost, just as the elder brother in the parable of the prodigal son was unable to share his father's joy (15:11–32). They show less sense than the shrewd manager (16:1–13), for he at least used money to secure his future, but they are heedless of the day of reckoning (16:19–31). The poor lie at their gates, and the Bible lies unopened on the coffee table! Jesus' verdict is, 'You are the ones who justify yourselves in the eyes of men, but God knows your hearts. What is highly valued among men is detestable in God's sight' (16:15). It is the love of money that distorts their values and warps their perception.

The danger is not confined to the Pharisees, however. Anyone can succumb to the attractions of money, and so Luke inserts a passage in which Jesus challenges the crowds with the cost of discipleship (14:25–35), and another in which he warns the disciples against ever thinking that they are more than forgiven sinners, unworthy servants who have only done their duty (17:1–10). Luke knows that the Pharisaic mindset remains a continuing danger for his readers, whom we suppose to include comfortable Christians—and money and possessions are at the root of it.[4]

Entering the kingdom (17:11—19:10)

The final section of the travel narrative begins with a typical Lukan story. Ten lepers ask Jesus for healing and receive it. Only one of them turns back and gives thanks to God, and he is a Samaritan (17:11–19). As such, he stands for all who are excluded from the community of God's people, who cry out to God for salvation, turn back in repentance and give praise to God. The story makes plain the power of the kingdom operating through Jesus, and also the unlikely recipients of it.

The Pharisees then ask when the kingdom is coming, and Jesus says that they cannot see what is under their nose. The kingdom is already at work through the words and deeds of Jesus (17:20–21). Of course it is not here in its fullness, and before it comes there will be terrible days of judgment on the city that has rejected Jesus. The disciples of Jesus need to be prepared for this and not to get prematurely excited or overly attached to the old order, as Lot's wife was (17:22–37). They should still pray for the coming of the kingdom with all the persistence of a widow pleading for justice before the local judge, but they need to be prepared for a long delay, not because God is unjust but because he is merciful and is keeping the door open for still more people to find salvation (18:1–8).

What kind of people will find their way into the kingdom? Not those who are confident of their own righteousness but those who cry out to God for mercy and help—tax collectors rather than Pharisees (18:9–14), and little children who make no great claims for themselves (18:15–17). At this point in the story we meet an old friend, the rich young ruler, familiar to us from Mark and Matthew. He is confident of his own goodness and too attached to his possessions, so he fails to enter the kingdom (18:18–30). His case is followed by that of a blind man who asks only that he may see (18:35–43), and by that of another rich man who welcomes Jesus, gives away half his possessions and is declared by Jesus to be a son of Abraham (19:1–10). Zacchaeus provides a contrast with the rich young ruler, proving the truth of Jesus' words, 'What is impossible with men is possible with God' (18:27), and he makes a pair with the thankful Samaritan with whom the section began, since like him he finds salvation and a place among the people of God.

JESUS IN JERUSALEM (LUKE 19:11—21:37)

Now we are almost ready to rejoin the Markan story and ride with Jesus into Jerusalem, but before we do, Luke inserts another parable, traditionally known as the parable of the pounds but more appropriately entitled the parable of the returning king (19:11–27). There is a similar story in Matthew, the parable of the talents, but its purpose is quite different. The parable of the talents is about being ready for Jesus' second coming. This parable explains the meaning of his first coming, and what is happening as Jesus rides into Jerusalem as king.

The parable concerns a nobleman who goes away and gives a sum of money to each of his servants, with instructions to use it profitably in his absence. On his return, while some of the servants have done well, one of them has done nothing with his money and is punished for his lack of faith and enterprise. So far, the story is very like the parable of the talents, only the amounts being different, but in this case there is something else going on. The nobleman goes away in order that he may return as king. This is not to the liking of his future subjects, who hate him and send a delegation after him contesting the appointment. At the end of the story, as well as the unprofitable servant being punished, those who tried to stop his appointment are summarily executed.

The rightful king of Israel is God. In Jesus, he is now coming to his own, but many of his subjects hate him and others have been unfruitful. Those who have been idle will suffer loss, but for those who hate him, judgment will be swift and terrible. In the stories that follow, Jesus does indeed ride into Jerusalem as king. He encounters hatred and opposition, and he predicts that God's judgment will fall on the rebellious city. The parable is a warning to those who refuse the king, as many in Jerusalem are doing.[5]

The rest of Luke's account of Jesus' ministry in Jerusalem closely follows Mark. Jesus rides into Jerusalem, but now there are tears in his eyes because Jerusalem has not recognized the time of God's coming. Jesus foresees the city's destruction at the hands of foreign armies, something that he proceeds to enact by his demonstration in the temple. The chief priests ask Jesus what is his authority. For the moment, Jesus gives them no direct answer. Instead he tells them the parable of the tenants who refuse the owner his fruit, beat his servants and eventually kill his son—and there is the answer. Jesus is God's Son and, as such, he is far more than the Messiah of popular expectation (20:41–44).

There follows Luke's version of Jesus' discourse on the fall of Jerusalem. It has the same form and the same meaning as in Mark. Jerusalem will be destroyed within a generation, but this will not be the end of the world. In place of Mark's cryptic, 'When you see "the abomination that causes desolation" standing where it does not belong' (Mark 13:14), Luke has, 'When you see Jerusalem being surrounded by armies, you will know that its desolation is near' (21:20). When that happens, it is time for those who live through those days to run for their lives—but what of Luke's readers for whom these things are now history? Luke finishes the discourse with words of Jesus that apply to people at all times and in all places, warning them, 'Be careful, or your hearts will be weighed down with dissipation, drunkenness and the anxieties of life, and that day will close on you unexpectedly like a trap' (21:34).

THE DEATH AND RESURRECTION OF JESUS
(LUKE 22:1—24:53)

The story of the last 24 hours of Jesus' life was almost certainly the first part of the story of Jesus to be written down, probably before any of our Gospels were written. It was so important for the first Christians to understand what had happened to Jesus, and to be able to explain to others why an event that appeared to be abject failure and tragedy was in fact a great victory. As a result, the Gospel writers had less freedom than elsewhere to order their material or to include or leave out details, and so this is the point where their accounts most closely resemble each other. Accordingly we find in Luke the familiar story of the last supper, Gethsemane, Peter's denial, Jesus' trial before the Jewish council and before Pilate (Luke adds an appearance before Herod), the crucifixion, death and burial of Jesus—but Luke has managed to present a very different picture by focusing on two themes.

We may notice once again the attractiveness of Luke's portrait of Jesus. He gives proportionately more space to the last supper at which Jesus gives final instructions to his disciples. As Jesus says, he is among them as one who serves (22:27). His care for them is seen in his praying that Peter's faith not fail, which softens the bleak prediction of his denial (22:31–32). When the disciples try to prevent Jesus' arrest and wound the high priest's servant, Jesus not only restrains them; in this Gospel he actually heals the man's ear (22:51). On his way out to be crucified, he pauses to comfort the women of Jerusalem who are weeping for him (23:27–31). On the cross, he prays for the forgiveness of his executioners: 'Father, forgive them, for they do not know what they are doing' (23:34). When one of the criminals crucified with him turns to him in some sort of faith, he is able to find a word of comfort and hope: 'Today you will be with me in paradise' (23:43). Finally he dies with words of trust on his lips: 'Father, into your hands I commit my Spirit' (23:46).

The contrast with Mark could hardly be greater. There we found Jesus silent except for one terrible cry, 'My God, my God, why have you forsaken me?' Not only has Luke omitted the cry of desolation altogether; in its place we have these three utterances of Jesus that do not occur in any other Gospel. Jesus goes to his death in this Gospel with nobility and serenity, displaying love to others and trust in God.

In line with this, we may also notice Luke's stress on the innocence of Jesus. Five times during his trial and death Jesus is declared to have done nothing wrong. Pilate says it twice (23:4, 14). Herod too declares him innocent, if disappointing as an entertainer (23:15). In contrast to Mark and Matthew, where both criminals join in abusing Jesus, here one of them makes a speech asserting his own guilt and the innocence of Jesus (23:40–41). Finally, the centurion in charge of the execution squad responds to the death of Jesus by praising God and saying, 'Surely this was a righteous man' (23:47). This is all the more striking when we remember that Luke had in front of him Mark's christological confession, 'Surely this man was the Son of

God', and *changed* it! Why did he do this? We can only guess. Possibly it was part of his purpose to present the Christian movement in a favourable light. Despite the fact that Jesus had been put to death by the religious and secular authorities as a criminal, he was in fact an innocent man and his death a miscarriage of justice.

More likely, and more importantly, Luke intends us to see that Jesus dies as a righteous man in place of the unrighteous. He has gone to great pains to emphasize that the last supper was a Passover meal and that accordingly the death of Jesus there portrayed in bread and wine is to be understood as a sacrifice. He will go on, in the resurrection stories, to emphasize the necessity of Christ's death. On this showing, the penitent thief is the first interpreter of the atoning significance of Jesus' death: 'We are punished justly, for we are getting what our deeds deserve. But this man has done nothing wrong.' As a letter attributed to Peter puts it, 'Christ died for sins once for all, the righteous for the unrighteous, to bring you to God' (1 Pet. 3:18).

Luke's account of the resurrection is distinctive too. In place of the mystery of Mark's ending, or Matthew's mighty angel and his interest in explaining the empty tomb, we have three stories. The first is familiar enough. It is the story of the discovery that Jesus is no longer in his grave. The second is the story of two disciples who were walking to Emmaus when Jesus came and walked and talked with them, unrecognized until, at the supper table, he broke the bread. The third story tells how Jesus appeared to the whole group of his disciples in Jerusalem and commissioned them as his witnesses.

The second and third stories are unique to Luke. What is striking, however, is the way in which, in each story, Luke is concerned that we understand the death of Jesus. In the first story, the words of Jesus that the women are instructed to remember are not that he is going ahead of them to Galilee where they will see him, but the Passion prediction that 'the Son of Man must be delivered into the hands of sinful men, be crucified and on the third day be raised again' (24:7). On the road to Emmaus the conversation is once again about the death of Jesus as the stranger says, 'Did not the Christ have to suffer these things and then enter his glory?' (24:26). He then proceeds to conduct an extensive Bible study on the same theme. The same thing happens when the risen Christ appears to his disciples in Jerusalem. He opens their minds to understand the scriptures, but what they are to understand is that it was necessary for the Christ to suffer and rise from the dead.

Matthew ended his Gospel by stressing the authority of Jesus, the command to make disciples and the promise of Jesus' presence with his Church. In bringing his Gospel to a close, Luke has his own way of making the same points. The ascension of Jesus declares his authority. The disciples are commissioned as witnesses to preach repentance and the forgiveness of sins, and in place of the presence of Jesus they are promised the gift of the Holy Spirit. And so the story ends, not as in Matthew on a mountain in Galilee, but in Jerusalem where it began, in the temple itself, and on the characteristically Lukan note of 'great joy'.

CHAPTER 5

JOHN'S STORY

In almost every respect, John stands apart from the other Gospels. Where the other Gospels locate Jesus in Galilee and bring him to Jerusalem only for the last week of his life, much of the action in John takes place in Judea and Jerusalem, to which Jesus makes several visits in the course of the story. Not surprisingly, then, we meet a different selection of stories and characters in John—Nicodemus, the Samaritan woman, the blind man healed at the pool of Siloam, Lazarus and others. There are a number of outstanding miracles, called 'signs' in this Gospel, but no exorcisms. Jesus tells no stories like the good Samaritan or the prodigal son, and he has little to say about the kingdom of God. Instead he delivers long speeches, mainly about himself, speaking of himself as the bread of life, the light of the world and so on.

As a portrait of Jesus, this Gospel is both more divine and more human than the others. On the one hand, Jesus goes about displaying divine attributes (such as knowledge of other people's thoughts) and making divine claims (for example, the claim to have come down from heaven). On the other hand, he displays real human emotion and weakness—he is tired; he weeps—and he engages in real conversations with disciples and opponents. The language and style of this Gospel are distinctive too. Jesus talks a lot about eternal life, light and darkness and God's love for the world. Words are used with double meanings, such as 'lifted up' to refer to Jesus being lifted up on the cross and exalted to glory. Characters in the story regularly misunderstand Jesus by taking his words literally where a deeper meaning is intended, and John often uses irony so that the characters in the story speak more wisely than they know, or fail to see what is obvious to the reader.

Despite these differences, John has still written a Gospel with the same basic 'shape' as Mark. The story still begins at the Jordan and ends in Jerusalem with the trial, death and resurrection of Jesus. The events of the last week of Jesus' life still occupy nearly half the story. It is a matter of dispute whether he assumes that his readers know Mark, and perhaps the other Gospels. Occasional touches suggest that he does.[1] For example, the reference to John's not having yet been put in prison (3:24) makes sense only if the intention is to relate these events to the Markan story that the reader already knows. Yet, clearly, John has not used Mark as a source in the way that Matthew and Luke have done. Instead he has his own sources of historical information, telling us about things we wouldn't otherwise have known, such as the various visits of Jesus to Jerusalem, the early baptizing ministry of Jesus, and the details of the trial before Pilate, of which he gives us a much fuller and more coherent account than do the other Gospels. Then, rather than drawing on the Church's 'memory banks' for sayings of Jesus and putting them together in discourses as Matthew and Luke have done, John has transposed the teaching of Jesus into his own distinctive idiom, putting speeches into the mouth of Jesus which are more likely to express what he believed Jesus meant, and had come to mean, than anything Jesus actually said.

Who, then, was 'John' and can we hope to identify the source of his information? Although traditionally believed to be John bar Zebedee, the author of this Gospel is not, in fact, named (any more than are the others). He is, however, identified as 'the disciple whom Jesus loved'.

Peter turned and saw the disciple whom Jesus loved following them; he was the one who had reclined next to Jesus at the supper and had said, 'Lord, who is it that is going to betray you?' When Peter saw him, he said to Jesus, 'Lord, what about him?' Jesus said to him, 'If it is my will that he remain until I come, what is that to you? Follow me!' So the rumour spread in the community that this disciple would not die. Yet Jesus did not say to him that he would not die, but, 'If it is my will that he remain until I come, what is that to you?' This is the disciple who is testifying to these things and has written them, and we know that his testimony is true.
JOHN 21:20–24 (NRSV)

On the face of it, this is an unambiguous statement that the beloved disciple wrote the fourth Gospel. Yet it is not quite so simple, since whatever else he wrote, he certainly didn't write the closing sentence of this passage and probably not any of it. This has been written by the 'we' who identify the beloved disciple as the author and vouch for the truth of his message. The strong implication of the passage is that the beloved disciple has, in fact, recently died and that someone else is publishing and perhaps editing his work. It has often been noted that the whole of chapter 21 reads like an appendix to a Gospel already complete at the end of chapter 20, and the same person who added this chapter may have made other additions as well. So we need to reckon with at least two people—the author of the fourth Gospel as we now have it (the 'we' of 21:24) and the beloved disciple whose eyewitness testimony and written account he is giving to the world.

So this Gospel claims to rest on and perhaps to incorporate the testimony of someone intimately associated with Jesus and present for at least the closing events of his life. Can we say any more about him? There have been many attempts to give him a name, but the beloved disciple preserves his anonymity still. Assuming, as most scholars do, that he is a real person and not an ideal figure, we can only go on what we are told in this Gospel in the passages that specifically mention him. He is first referred to in the story of the last supper, where he lies next to Jesus (literally 'in the bosom of' Jesus, 13:23). Prompted by Peter, he leans back against Jesus and asks for and receives privileged information. The phrase used for his position relative to Jesus is also used of Jesus' position in relation to the Father (1:18). As Jesus is intimate with the Father and knows his mind, so the beloved disciple is in a position to know the mind of Christ.

Second, the beloved disciple is present at the foot of the cross and sees how Jesus dies (19:26–27, 35). In this he is to be distinguished from the other disciples in general and Peter in particular. Next we meet him on Easter morning, where he is the first to see and believe the significance of the grave clothes in the otherwise empty tomb (20:1–8). In the final appearance of the risen Christ to his disciples by the lakeside, it is the beloved disciple who first recognizes Jesus.

It cannot be accidental that, in all of these stories, Peter plays a subordinate role. He must ask the beloved disciple to ask Jesus for the identity of the betrayer. He comes second to the tomb and late to faith and understanding. He swims to meet the risen Jesus only after the beloved disciple has identified him, and is not made privy to the destiny of the latter. Above all, Peter is not present at the foot of the cross where Jesus says of the beloved disciple to his mother, 'Here is your son' (19:26). While it has usually been seen that Jesus is here thoughtfully providing for his mother, it is much more likely that he is actually nominating the beloved disciple as, in some sense, his heir and accredited representative.[2]

Is this, in fact, the sense in which this disciple is singled out as the one Jesus loved? Jesus presumably loved all his disciples, but if he nominated one disciple as his heir, that would make him 'beloved' in a special sense. We have been too preoccupied with giving the beloved disciple a name, rather than appreciating his importance. 'Here is your son' in the context of Jesus' imminent death means, 'This man takes my place', and if he does so in the first instance in relation to Jesus' mother, it is hard to escape the implication that, at least for the final author(s) of the fourth Gospel, he is the authoritative source of information about Jesus and interpreter of his mind to the Church. Such is the claim to authority that the fourth Gospel makes. We are free to disbelieve it; we are not free to diminish its significance.

John writes for a Jewish community that has been split down the middle by controversy over the person of Jesus. This explains both the Jewishness of the Gospel and its particular concentration on the identity of Jesus. It is likely that the vividness and bitterness of the debates in which Jesus engages with 'the Jews' reflect debates in which John and his readers have themselves recently engaged. Some believers have been put out of the synagogue (16:2) and others are afraid to confess Jesus openly for fear of incurring a similar punishment (12:42). John writes both to strengthen the faith of believers and to bring others to faith, as he says: 'Now Jesus did many other signs in the presence of his disciples, which are not written in this book. But these are written so that you may come to believe that Jesus is the Messiah, the Son of God, and that through believing you may have life in his name' (20:30–31, NRSV).

THE STORY IN OUTLINE

Most readers recognize that the Gospel divides into two main sections, the first section dealing with Jesus' public ministry, often called the 'book of signs', and the second, beginning at chapter 13, dealing with Jesus' death and resurrection, often called the 'book of glory'. Many people also think of the first eighteen verses, or possibly the whole of the first chapter, as a prologue to the Gospel; and the last chapter, which so clearly seems to have been added subsequently, as an epilogue. Recently a number of scholars have suggested that the book of signs ends at the close of chapter 10 and that chapters 11 and 12 form a prelude to the book of glory.[3] This yields the following analysis of the Gospel, which we shall adopt.

Prelude to Jesus' ministry	John 1:1–51
The book of signs	John 2:1—10:42
Prelude to Jesus' hour	John 11:1—12:50
The book of glory	John 13:1—20:31
Postlude to Jesus' ministry	21:1–25

THE PRELUDE TO JESUS' MINISTRY (JOHN 1:1–51)

Where does the story of Jesus begin? At the Jordan when he is empowered by the Spirit? At Bethlehem when he is conceived by the Holy Spirit and born of the virgin Mary? There is truth in both answers, as Mark, Matthew and Luke have shown, but for John the starting point for the story of Jesus lies at the beginning of everything, in the very heart of God himself: 'In the beginning God created the heavens and the earth' (Gen. 1:1). In the Genesis story, God commands things into being—that is, he creates by a word: 'By the word of the Lord the heavens were made' (Ps. 33:6, NRSV). From there, it was a short step in Jewish thought to seeing the word of God as an active partner of God in creation. In a similar vein, Wisdom is represented as declaring:

The Lord brought me forth as the first of his works, before his deeds of old; I
was appointed from eternity, from the beginning, before the world began...
Then I was the craftsman at his side. I was filled with delight day after day,
rejoicing always in his presence, rejoicing in his whole world and delighting
in mankind.
PROVERBS 8:22–23, 30–31

For the devout Jew, Wisdom found her true embodiment in the law
given to Israel through Moses. The law is not a human creation or the
product of human striving after goodness. It comes from the heart of
God himself, and to keep the law is to live life according to the facts,
according to the way things are—and what the Jews said about the
law, John here asserts of Jesus! He is the Word of God and the Wisdom of God, present with God when he created the world and the
clue to its meaning and purpose. Yet what for the Old Testament
writers was only a vivid way of speaking when applied to Wisdom and
law becomes for John a literal statement of the truth: God was not
alone when he created the world.

To put it another way, Jesus is called the Word because through
him God has spoken. God had spoken before, of course. He spoke
through creation and so gave light to humankind, but this light was
only partially successful. It encountered darkness, which did not
understand it (1:3–5). The light was always streaming into the world,
witnessed to by prophets like John, but the story of Israel shows that
while some received him and became his children, many did not
(1:6–13).[4] In those days too he came to his own and his own did not
receive him, but now God has done something better still: *he has come*
in person! 'The Word became flesh and dwelt among us', and there
were those who could say, 'We have seen his glory' (1:14). What the
Jewish thinkers said of the law, John says of a man, known to his
followers as Jesus the Christ, who, as the only-begotten Son of God,
stands closest to the Father's heart and reveals the nature of God as
no other can do (1:18).

Like the other Gospels, John's account of the ministry of Jesus
begins with the witness of John the Baptist. In historical terms, Jesus
had begun as John's disciple, baptized by him and baptizing others in
like manner (3:22). Evidently this idea could cause embarrassment in
some circles, so great emphasis is laid on the fact that John is in no

sense Jesus' master, only a witness to Jesus with no independent significance of his own. The baptism of Jesus is not described, but it is alluded to in terms suggesting that the readers are expected to know about it (1:33), and John declares Jesus to be the Lamb of God who takes away the sin of the world, the one who will baptize with the Holy Spirit, and the Son of God—very much what we learn from the opening of Mark's Gospel also.

The significance of Jesus is further brought out by the story of the gathering of the first disciples. Andrew finds his brother Simon and tells him that they have found the Messiah. Philip finds Nathanael and tells him that Jesus is the one spoken of by Moses and the prophets. Nathanael then is moved to make the first great confession of the Gospel: 'You are the Son of God; you are the King of Israel' (1:49; cf. 6:69; 11:27; 20:28). Jesus declares Nathanael to be a true Israelite and promises that, like Israel of old, he will see the presence and power of God not in a dream but in the person and work of Jesus himself (1:51; cf. Gen. 28:12). This promise is the climax of the prelude and prepares the reader also for what is to come. The 'greater things' that we shall see are signs that heaven is now open and the power of God is streaming into the world through the Son of Man, who is the meeting point of heaven and earth. Like the opening of Mark, these stories serve to put the reader in possession of the truth about Jesus which is hidden from and only gradually revealed to the characters in the story.

THE BOOK OF SIGNS (JOHN 2:1—10:42)

The account of Jesus' public ministry can be further divided into two cycles of stories, each beginning with a miracle of new creation in Galilee and ending with controversy following a miracle of healing in Jerusalem.[5] In the first cycle (2:1—5:47), Jesus' words and works proclaim a new creation that challenges the old order. He changes water into wine, so revealing his glory as the one who transforms lives and brings joy. Then, in Jerusalem, he clears the temple and cryptically proposes himself as the place where human beings can meet with God. John, it should be noted, has moved this story from the end of the Gospel, where it serves as the trigger for the arrest and trial of

Jesus, to the beginning, where it is a sign of the change and challenge Jesus brings. It is followed by Jesus' encounter with Nicodemus, a representative of the old order who is told that he must be born from above if he is to see the kingdom of God. The nature of this new birth is not explained, but clearly it is effected by the Spirit (3:5–6) and issues in eternal life for those who put their faith in the Son of God (3:16). In obvious contrast to Nicodemus, Jesus next encounters a Samaritan woman to whom he offers 'living water', another metaphor for eternal life, and leads her to faith. She becomes a witness to her people, who declare in their turn that 'this man really is the Saviour of the world' (4:42). In Cana once more, Jesus heals the son of a royal official, and then, back in Jerusalem, heals a man who had been waiting by the pool of Bethesda for 38 years.

All of these signs of new life contain a challenge to the old order. The water that is turned into wine is contained in jars for Jewish ceremonial washing. Jesus' action in the temple strikes at the heart of traditional religion. The offer of new birth requires Nicodemus to die to all that he has achieved in a long life and all that he represents. The Samaritan woman is told that a time is coming when people will worship neither on Mount Gerizim nor yet in Jerusalem, but in spirit and in truth—the truth Jesus declares and the Spirit he bestows. The healing of the man by the pool takes place on the Sabbath, provoking an immediate clash with the Jewish leaders. Not surprisingly, they try to suppress Jesus, but Jesus insists that he is acting as the Son of his Father, a claim at once humble and daring. Like a son growing up in his father's workshop, Jesus watches the Father at work and does only what he does (5:19–20). As a son, Jesus is obedient to his Father and dependent on him, but precisely because his Father is the maker and judge of all, a claim to be his Son is a claim to great authority, even over death itself, and his healing miracles are a sign of that. To reject Jesus is to reject the Father who sent him.

When the second cycle begins, we are back in Galilee, where Jesus multiplies the loaves so as to feed a crowd of five thousand (6:1–13). It is presumably not without significance that the first miracle involved wine and this one involves bread. The section is dominated by two great miracles and two corresponding claims. The feeding miracle is followed by a long discourse in which Jesus declares that he is the bread of life (6:35). Then he declares that he is the light of the world

(8:12; 9:5), and this is followed by the giving of sight to a man born blind. In each case it becomes clear that Jesus' words and works provoke division. The bread of life discourse arouses scepticism and offence and we are told that many of his disciples abandoned him. So Jesus asks the Twelve if they too want to leave him and receives from Peter the reply, 'Lord, to whom shall we go? You have the words of eternal life. We believe and know that you are the Holy One of God' (6:68–69). We may note in passing how closely John agrees in substance with Mark, even though he uses different words and stories to make his point, for there too Jesus' words and works meet with a mixed response, and Peter is once again the spokesman for the disciples who believe in him. The miracle in Galilee is followed by two chapters of furious controversy in Jerusalem culminating in the momentous declaration, 'Before Abraham was born, I am!' (8:58).

In the same way, it becomes plain that the light of the world gives sight to some and blindness to others. In the lively story of the healing of the man born blind and his subsequent interrogation by the authorities, two processes are at work. The man himself moves steadily into the light. His physical healing is matched by a growing understanding of who Jesus is until, thrown out of the synagogue, he is asked by Jesus whether he believes in the Son of Man. He then says, 'Lord, I believe', and worships him (9:38). At the same time, with superb storyteller's art, John shows the synagogue elders and the Pharisees moving steadily into a self-imposed darkness, unable to embrace the truth of God that is before their eyes, because in healing the man on the Sabbath Jesus has violated their assumptions of how God ought to work.

The allegory of the good shepherd follows directly on this story. The once-blind man, who has been thrown out of the fold of Israel by the bad shepherds, is gathered in by Jesus and made part of his flock. The allegory is in two parts. In the first part (10:1–10) we have the shepherd and the robbers. The Pharisees show themselves to be robbers because they do not come in by the door—that is, they do not acknowledge Jesus—and the sheep are not fed by them and do not follow them. This relates directly to the events of the previous chapter.

In the second part (10:11–18) we have the wolf, the hireling and the good shepherd. This has its origin in the situation confronting the nation in Jesus' day. The wolf is Rome and the destruction that will be visited by Rome on the nation that follows the path of narrow nationalism, with the violent resistance that such nationalism stirs up. In the face of this threat, the official leaders of the nation will prove to be mere hirelings who will run away when the crisis comes. By contrast, Jesus will face the wolf and overcome it, not by wielding force but by enduring it. He will go to the cross, the Roman instrument of execution, and 'receive in the palms of his hands the nails of rough Roman justice',[6] thus bearing God's judgment on behalf of the nation and the world. In recognition of his faithfulness, God, the owner of the sheep, will give him back his life again, and he will gather his sheep—all who believe in him, not just from Israel but from all nations, the 'other sheep' whom he will bring so that there may be one flock and one shepherd (10:16).

Just as the first cycle ended with the Jews persecuting Jesus because he made himself equal with God (5:18), so this cycle ends in the same way. Jesus declares, 'I and the Father are one' (10:29–30), and the Jews pick up stones to stone him, forcing Jesus to withdraw from them. And so the public ministry of Jesus ends where it began, down by the Jordan, with the witness of John the Baptist proved true by the signs that Jesus has performed (10:40–42).

THE PRELUDE TO JESUS' HOUR (JOHN 11:1—12:50)

There have been several references in the story so far to Jesus' 'hour' (or 'time'). Jesus tells his mother that his hour has not yet come (2:4). The authorities are unable to arrest Jesus because his hour has not yet come (7:30; 8:20). But now the hour is about to strike. It is the hour when the Son of Man will be glorified (12:23). It is the hour to which all of Jesus' life has been leading (12:27). It is the hour for him to leave this world and go the Father (13:1), and Jesus will shortly declare, 'Father, the time has come' (17:1). Clearly, the 'hour' is the hour of his death, but the hour of his death is the hour of his glory, both because in it he reveals the full extent of God's love and completes the work the Father has given him to do, and because his death is followed by resurrection and becomes the way in which he ascends to the Father. This is the climax to which the whole Gospel has been moving, and this section prepares us for it.

The raising of Lazarus can be seen both as the climax of the book of signs, the greatest of the 'greater things' that Nathanael was promised, and also as a preparation for what is to come and as the event that triggers the arrest and death of Jesus. Jesus will shortly die and be placed in a tomb, but not before we learn that he is the master of death and 'the resurrection and the life'. The story itself is notable for its portrayal of the emotions of Jesus. There is grief—everyone knows that Jesus wept—but there is also anger. Twice we are told that Jesus was 'deeply moved' (11:33, 38), but the translation is weak here. The word conveys the idea of anger, an anger that could be seen and heard by those around, and the best guess is that Jesus is angry at the sight of all the grief and devastation that death wreaks in God's world.[7] 'The reason the Son of God appeared,' says John in his letter, 'was to destroy the devil's work' (1 John 3:8). As well as anger, there is also love. We are told three times that Jesus loved Lazarus. This was the basis of the sisters' appeal (11:3), the reason for Jesus' delay in answering it (11:6), and the reason for the greater answer they eventually received (11:36), making the story a potent lesson in prayer.

In John, it is the raising of Lazarus that leads directly to Jesus' death as the Jewish leaders call a meeting of the council and resolve to do away with Jesus. Caiaphas speaks more truly than he knows: 'It is better for you that one man die for the people than that the whole nation perish' (11:50). From this incident we gain a remarkable insight into how John understands the death of Jesus. On the one hand he was put to death as a troublemaker by the authorities. On the other hand he died for the nation, that is to say, he died for his own people, to gather them back into God's fold and so avert the judgment that he saw so clearly was coming in the form of Roman retribution. Ultimately, his death was seen as being for the whole of the world that Israel was called to serve, 'for the scattered children of God, to bring them together and make them one' (11:52). The shepherd of Israel dies for his sheep, but has 'other sheep' also, which he must bring in (10:16).

These themes are continued in the next chapter. The raising of Lazarus is mentioned three more times as the reason for the Pharisees' hostility (12:1–2, 9–10, 17–19). They too speak more truly than they know as they despairingly declare, 'Look how the whole world has gone after him!'(12:19), and, as if to prove them right, Jesus is approached by some worshippers from the diaspora—Greeks asking to see Jesus. Jesus responds by likening himself to a seed sown in the ground. The seed 'dies', but from it comes a great harvest. As he goes on to say, 'But I, when I am lifted up from the earth, will draw all men to myself' (12:32). Jesus dies, the one for the many, to gather together a new people of God out of every nation. The shepherd dies but the flock lives and grows. The seed dies but the harvest is gathered. Jesus is put on trial but it is the prince of this world, and the princes of this world, who are condemned, while Jesus goes on to gather the world to himself.

THE BOOK OF GLORY (JOHN 13:1—20:31)

Like the other Gospels, John tells us how Jesus met for the last time with his disciples before being arrested, tried and executed, but he has devoted much more space to the teaching Jesus gave his disciples before he was taken from them. The result is that the book of glory itself divides into two main sections: the testament of Jesus (chs. 13—17), and the glory of Jesus (chs. 18—20).

The testament of Jesus

The ancient world gave a lot of attention to the last words of famous people. Plato recorded the last words of Socrates. Jewish writers wrote books in which patriarchs and wise men encouraged their successors to walk in their footsteps, warned them of troubles ahead and assured them of ultimate salvation. This literary form is known as a 'testament'. What we have here in the upper room discourse is the testament of Jesus. It begins in a particularly solemn way: 'Now before the festival of the Passover, Jesus knew that his hour had come to depart from this world and go to the Father. Having loved his own who were in the world, he loved them to the end' (13:1, NRSV).

The words 'he loved them to the end' can be translated 'he now showed them the full extent of his love' (so NIV) and refer both to the whole story of the cross that is about to unfold and also to the immediate drama in which Jesus washes his disciples' feet, which is an acted parable of the whole life and death of Jesus. That this is not just an object lesson in humble service is plain from the elaborate way it is introduced. It is not said (as in many sermons!) that Jesus saw that no disciple was willing to perform this menial task. Rather, we are told that Jesus 'knew that the Father had put all things under his power, and that he had come from God and was returning to God' (13:3), and that is why he got up from the meal... took off his outer clothing... wrapped a towel round his waist... poured water into a basin... began to wash his disciples' feet and dry them with the towel. The storyteller has slowed the action right down for us, so that we see in this acted parable the far greater sacrifice of Jesus to which it points. He left the glory of his Father; he emptied himself and took the form of a servant; he died to make us clean and take away our sin.

Peter's protest is a typical Johannine misunderstanding whereby the reader is better able to see the true meaning of Jesus' actions. Peter sees only an act of humble service, which he feels to be inappropriate. Jesus' solemn words, 'Unless I wash you, you have no part with me' (13:8), show that much more is at stake here. To refuse to be washed by Jesus is to refuse the forgiveness of sins he died to make possible. John does not record the institution of the Lord's supper, but this story takes its place and says the same thing. As he said, 'Unless you can eat the flesh of the Son of Man and drink his blood, you have no life in you' (6:53). The washing that Jesus speaks of does not refer to baptism, any more than 'eating the flesh of the Son of Man' is a reference to the eucharist. Rather, the acted dramas of eucharist and baptism convey the same message as Jesus' words: eternal life is by faith in Jesus alone.

Of course, the lesson in humble service is there as well, as Jesus goes on to make plain (13:14). Those who are saved by the self-sacrifice of Jesus need to serve one another and wash one another's feet, but as the deepest meaning of Jesus' action is forgiveness, so the first obligation on disciples is to forgive one another 'as God in Christ has forgiven you' (Eph. 4:32, NRSV).

A good leader tries to ensure that his followers will be able to continue when he is gone. This is the subject of the next chapter and, indeed, of the whole discourse of Jesus. The disciples' hearts are troubled, naturally enough. Jesus has been speaking of going away, and he has just predicted that Peter will disown him. In this context, the famous assurance 'In my Father's house are many rooms' (14:2) refers not to the believer's life after death, but to the believer's life on earth after Jesus' death and resurrection. The Father's house is a metaphor for the relationship with his Father that Jesus enjoyed while on earth.[8] For him, heaven was always open (1:51). Like an apprentice son, he did only what he saw the Father doing (5:19). At every turn he was in the closest communion with his Father (11:41; 12:27). As he says, 'I am in the Father, and the Father is in me', and this was the basis of his fruitful work (14:10–11). Now, he says to his disciples, this relationship with God is open to you too. There is plenty of room in my Father's house. The same Spirit that was given to Jesus at the start of his work is now to be given to the disciples (14:16–17), and he will be their teacher (14:26). As a result, the same relationship with God that Jesus enjoyed is now to be theirs also. Where in 14:10 he says, 'I am in the Father, and the Father is in me', he now says in 14:20 that when the Spirit comes, 'you will realize that I am in my Father, and you are in me'. A little later he says, 'Those who love me will keep my word, and my Father will love them, and we will come to them and make our home with them' (14:23, NRSV).

Interestingly, the Greek word used for 'home' here is the same word that is used in 14:2 for many 'rooms'. Entrance into this relationship is made possible by Jesus' going away and coming back again, a reference in this context to his impending death and resurrection. He is 'the way and the truth and the life', and the way leads to the Father and to the Father's house. At the beginning of the Gospel we were told that the effect of Jesus' coming was that believers received the right to become children of God (1:12), and at the close of the Gospel, in the light of the cross and resurrection, we see Jesus beckoning Mary Magdalene into the same relationship with the Father that he himself enjoys (20:17). The result of this is that the troubled disciples are assured that they too will be able to do what Jesus has been doing, 'and even greater things' (14:12).

You might think that the testament of Jesus had finished with Jesus' words, 'Come now; let us leave' (14:31), but in fact the discourse continues for another two chapters and ends only with the prayer of Jesus. Chapters 15 and 16 address the same underlying question, 'How can we manage when you are gone?' and give the same answer.

The invitation to remain in Jesus, the true vine (15:1–8), corresponds to the invitation to dwell in the Father's house. There is the same assurance of the Spirit's presence and help (16:5–15) and, at the close, the same assurance that Jesus by his death has overcome the world (cf. 14:30; 16:33).

We shall understand Jesus' claim to be the true vine if we remember that in the Old Testament the vine is a symbol for God's people, Israel itself (Ps. 80:8; cf. Is.5:1–7). As such, it spoke of Israel's vocation to bring joy to the world, to be the means of its healing and the channel of its peace. So when Jesus says, 'I am the vine', he is claiming to embody the people of God and fulfil their ancient purpose. When he says, 'You are the branches', he is inviting the disciples to share in this vocation and to recognize that they can fulfil it only by remaining united with him. There is perhaps, too, a hint of sacrifice here, for the vine achieves nothing by its wood, nothing by its leaves. It is valued only for its fruit, and that fruit must be picked and crushed and turned to blood, and only then will it bring joy.

If, for Shakespeare, all the world's a stage, for John all the world's a courtroom in which is being argued out the great lawsuit between God and the world, as can be seen from the wealth of legal terms employed to describe the work of the Holy Spirit in this passage (15:26—16:11). The suit is brought against God by someone whom John calls 'the prince of this world'. It is a battle for the hearts and minds of men and women, a battle for the control of the world, and in his bid to control the world and the people of the world the prince of this world will argue that God is not loving and faithful, and that God's way of love doesn't work. Representing the prince of this world is what the Bible calls 'the Satan', a word which means 'adversary', who is presented in the Bible as the accuser of God's people (Rev. 12:10; cf. Job 1—2). Of course, he works through human accusers, just as the prince of this world works through the princes, governments and opinion formers of this world. On the other side stands Jesus, who in this Gospel appears as the chief witness and advocate for God, proving in his life and death that God is true (3:31–34). Jesus is well qualified to speak for God because he has come from God, but his case is not just a matter of words and ideas. The case against God can be defeated only by lives and deeds, by costly choices made by a human being on earth. So Jesus must not merely argue that God is true; he must demonstrate it by his life and death.

So for John, as for the other Gospels, the supreme test, the clinching argument for the defence, is the cross. At first sight you would suppose that the cross belongs to the prosecution: this is what happens to people who trust God—they end up dead! If the death of Jesus had been the end, the Satan's case would have been proved. But of course it was not the end. God, who did not keep Jesus from dying, raised him from the dead and so proved himself a faithful God and Jesus a faithful witness. The resurrection means that the cross itself is seen in a new light. Jesus will prove in the most extreme way that God is love and that he will keep faith with those who choose his way, and in so doing he has taken the Satan's most powerful argument and turned it against him. That is why, as he approaches his death, Jesus can say, 'Now is the time for judgment on this world; now the prince of this world will be driven out' (12:31).

Yet despite this victory in the highest court in the universe, the prince of this world fights on, bringing his case not against Jesus but the followers of Jesus. Just as Jesus stood trial before Caiaphas and Pontius Pilate, so the followers of Jesus will have to stand trial for their beliefs (15:27—16:2), and Jesus looks to them to be his witnesses, and to plead God's case before the world. And if they cry out, 'How can we possibly manage on our own?' Jesus replies, 'You don't have to manage on your own! I am sending you an advocate, who will plead God's case as I have pleaded God's case, and be with you for ever in every time and place.'

One of the most puzzling and widely disbelieved of Jesus' sayings is, 'I tell you the truth: it is for your good that I am going away' (16:7). The disciples must have struggled to believe that they could be better off without Jesus with them, and we struggle to believe that we could be better off than those who walked and talked with Jesus face to face. But, as we have seen, when Jesus talks of going away he is speaking of going to the Father by way of the cross and resurrection, and who can doubt that it is to our advantage that Jesus has died and been raised and is at the right hand of the Father? For this means that though the battle goes on, it is not the same battle and does not have to be fought again from scratch. The decisive victory has been won, and Jesus risen from the dead has sent his own Spirit to point people's eyes to Easter as the decisive argument for the faithfulness of God. The disciples, then or now, do not have to fight the case on their own. They do not have to be advocates, only witnesses, while the role of advocate is played by the Holy Spirit, of whom it is said: 'And when he comes, he will prove the world wrong about sin and righteousness and judgment: about sin, because they do not believe in me; about righteousness, because I am going to the Father and you will see me no longer; about judgment, because the ruler of this world has been condemned' (16:8–11, NRSV).

As the climax of his testament, Jesus turns to God in prayer. The burden of his prayer is, 'Glorify your Son, that your Son may glorify you' (17:1). Outside religious circles the word 'glorify' is hardly used today, and never in a good sense. It usually suggests that someone is pretending to be better than they are, as if we said of a dictator that he was nothing but a glorified gangster. So what does 'glorify' mean in the Bible? The word comes from 'glory', and glory is God's true nature revealed to human beings, so 'glorify' means 'to reveal the true nature of' someone, especially God. Jesus is praying, 'May all people see me as I truly am, so that I may show you as you truly are', and the point to notice is that Jesus prays this just before he goes to his death on the cross. It is by the cross that Jesus glorifies God: that is, he reveals God's true nature as a God of love and faithfulness.

In the second part of his prayer, Jesus prays for his disciples. He describes them as those who, by God's grace, have seen God in Jesus and who have received his word and obeyed it (17:6). He prays that they will be one and that they will be protected from the evil one. The two requests belong together. He prays that they will not be overcome by the world's ways of thinking, and that in that way they will remain united in the truth he has given them.

In the third part of the prayer, Jesus prays for those who come to believe through the message of those first disciples, among whom John's readers in every age may rightly place themselves. Here too he prays that we may be one. This is not just a hope that we may stick together, but that we may be one in will and purpose, like the Father and the Son, just as a musical conductor does not merely want us to sing in harmony but to sing what the composer actually wrote. With this prayer Jesus offers himself to the Father to do his will as he steps out into the darkness of Gethsemane.

The glory of Jesus

The story of the death and resurrection of Jesus is familiar to us from the other Gospels, but John's account differs in detail and emphasis. It starts with Jesus' arrest in the garden. We do not hear of Jesus' agony or prayer because these things have been dealt with already. John has placed Jesus' agony in his prelude to the book of glory: 'Now my heart is troubled, and what shall I say? "Father, save me from this hour"? No, it was for this very reason I came to this hour. Father, glorify your name!' (12:27–28).

After Jesus' long, 'high-priestly' prayer in the previous chapter, there is no need to say more. Jesus comes across as a commanding figure throughout his arrest and trial, always in control even when he is a prisoner. The trial before the high priest is greatly abbreviated (perhaps because John knows that the decision has already been taken at the earlier meeting of the council, 11:47–53). Instead of a formal indictment before Caiaphas, we have an otherwise unrecorded examination before his father-in-law, Annas, sandwiched in the middle of the story of Peter's repeated denial of Jesus. By contrast, the trial before the Roman governor, Pilate, is much more fully recorded than in the other Gospels—a drama in seven scenes in which we watch Pilate being steadily outmanoeuvred by the Jewish leaders. Finally, Jesus is handed over to be crucified. Even on the cross, Jesus speaks as one fully in control of his own destiny. He finally dies with his mother and the beloved disciple standing by and is buried by Joseph of Arimathea and Nicodemus with lavish care.

Jesus had declared, 'Now is the judgment of this world' (12:31, NRSV), and John's account of the trial of Jesus brings this out. While notionally it is Jesus who is on trial, in reality it is the rulers of this world who are condemned. While Pilate is supposed to be in charge of the proceedings, in reality we see him running backwards and forwards between Jesus, who is inside the palace, and the Jewish leaders outside. Jesus appears as a figure of quiet authority. He knows who he is and why he is there. By contrast, Pilate can only take instruction from him, about the nature of Jesus' kingship and about his own authority. The Jewish leaders also know what they want, and even though it is not what Pilate wants, they get it. Pilate appears weak, easily manipulated and outmanoeuvred. In the end, although

Pilate sits down on the judge's seat, he does not so much pass sentence as capitulate to the mob. The chief priests are much tougher. They emerge from the trial victorious, but their victory is, in reality, a terrible defeat. They get what they want but only at the cost of having to declare before the hated Roman governor that they have no king but Caesar. In this way they judge themselves, not Jesus.

Meanwhile, the true king of Israel comes to his throne. Jesus has spoken several times in this Gospel about being 'lifted up', with the double meaning of being lifted up on the cross and exalted by way of the cross to the Father's right hand. More than any of the other Gospels, John's account of the trial of Jesus emphasizes the kingship of Jesus. 'The king of the Jews' becomes a constant refrain. Pilate opens proceedings by asking, 'Are you the king of the Jews?' Jesus gives qualified assent, and explains the nature of his kingship. The soldiers mock him, saying, 'Hail, king of the Jews.' Finally, Pilate presents Jesus to the Jewish leaders with the words, 'Here is your king', but they reply, 'Take him away! Crucify him!' When Pilate asks, 'Shall I crucify your king?' they reply, 'We have no king but Caesar.' All the Gospels tell us that Jesus died with the charge against him fastened to the cross: 'Jesus of Nazareth, the King of the Jews'. John alone tells us that it was written in Hebrew, Latin and Greek, making plain that Jesus is king not only of Israel, but of the whole world.

Jesus himself speaks three times from the cross in this Gospel. John does not record the cry of desolation that we hear in Mark and Matthew: 'My God, my God, why have you forsaken me?' Such a cry is impossible on the lips of the Johannine Jesus, who enjoys uninterrupted communion with his Father. Equally absent are the gracious words of Luke's Jesus, forgiving his enemies, assuring the dying thief, commending his soul to God. Instead, Jesus commits his mother to the care of the disciple whom he loved. As was suggested at the start of this chapter, this is more than evidence of Jesus' loving care for his mother. It is recorded because it legitimates the beloved disciple as Jesus' heir and the source of authoritative tradition about him to the circle of disciples who have produced this Gospel. Then he says, 'I am thirsty.' Considering the elaborate way this is introduced, with reference to the completion of all things and the fulfilment of scripture, we are surely justified in seeing here, too, more than meets the eye. Remembering that Jesus said on one occasion that his food was to do the will of him who sent him and to finish his work (4:34), and on another occasion that he was determined to drink the cup the Father had given him (18:11), we may infer that Jesus is expressing his thirst to do the will of God.[9]

It is the bystanders who suppose that wine will meet the case, a typical example of Johannine misunderstanding. This is confirmed by the way the third utterance of Jesus is so closely attached to the preceding one. 'When he had received the drink, Jesus said, "It is finished"' (19:30). Jesus has fully completed all that the Father had given him to do, and so, in command to the last, he bows his head and dies, making good his own words, 'No one takes my life from me, but I lay it down of my own accord' (10:18).

There is no believing centurion in John's Gospel to testify that Jesus is the Son of God. Instead, the Roman soldiers go about their normal, brutal tasks, and we have an unnamed witness to the flow of blood and water when a soldier pierces Jesus' side (19:35). A comparison of this verse with 21:24 makes it likely that we are meant to identify this witness with the beloved disciple. Whatever their physiological explanation, the blood and water presumably are meant to point to the cleansing effect of Jesus' death. John appends two scriptures. The first, 'Not one of his bones will be broken', is taken from the instructions for eating the Passover, and marks Jesus out as the Lamb of God. The second, 'They will look on the one they have pierced', continues in the book of Zechariah from which it is taken, '… and they will mourn for him as one mourns for an only child, and grieve bitterly for him as one grieves for a firstborn son' (Zech. 12:10). By their actions the soldiers unconsciously attest that Jesus is the only begotten Son of God and the Lamb of God who takes away the sin of the world.

All the Gospels begin their accounts of the resurrection of Jesus at the same place, but thereafter they diverge quite widely. They all begin with the discovery of the empty tomb by women disciples, but whereas in Luke the women's testimony is not at first believed, in John it leads to Peter and the beloved disciple running to the tomb to see for themselves, so that the beloved disciple becomes the first person to believe that Jesus has been raised from the dead. Jesus then appears to Mary Magdalene and she becomes the first person to declare, 'I have seen the Lord!' (20:18). Next, Jesus appears to all the disciples as they are gathered in Jerusalem and sends them out in the power of the Holy Spirit to represent him to the world, as he has represented the Father, and so to bring people the forgiveness of sins that he has died to make possible. Finally Jesus appears to Thomas and elicits from him the crowning confession of the Gospel: 'My Lord and my God!' (20:28). So the book of glory ends, with a succinct summary of the purpose of the Gospel: 'These things are written that you may believe that Jesus is the Christ, the Son of God, and that by believing you may have life in his name' (20:31).

These four stories bring out John's gift as a storyteller. He is recording extraordinary happenings, but he does it so simply that we feel it is the most natural thing in the world. Whether or not he was an eyewitness of these events, he makes us feel that we are eye-witnesses. We hear the pounding footsteps and laboured breathing as Peter and the other disciple run to the tomb. We have no difficulty imaging the collapsed grave-clothes or the cloth that had been round Jesus head, lying folded by itself. We share in Mary's grief and confusion as she searches for the body of Jesus in the garden, and her incredulous delight as the 'gardener' turns out to be Jesus himself. We huddle with the disciples behind closed doors 'for fear of the Jews' (20:19), and share their joy as Jesus shows them his hands and his side. Who has not felt the force of Thomas' doubts or his capitulation before unanswerable evidence? We notice the way too that the four stories progress from darkness to light, beginning in the grey dawn with an empty grave and wondering, hesitant faith, and ending with joyful reunion and confident confession. Between them they present the reasons the Church has always believed in the resurrection: the grave was empty, a necessary but not sufficient condition of Easter faith; Jesus was seen alive by his friends; and the Holy Spirit has been given, the presence of Jesus to all subsequent generations.

John has placed together things which, under Luke's influence, we are accustomed to think of separately. The resurrection and ascension are all part of the same event as Jesus returns to his Father. Mary is told to tell the disciples, 'I am ascending to my Father and your Father, to my God and your God' (20:17). Similarly, Jesus gives the Holy Spirit to the disciples on the occasion of his first appearance to them and not after an interval of fifty days. It is possible to reconcile John's and Luke's accounts by saying that what happens in John is an acted promise of something that was in fact to happen later, but it is probably better simply to give our attention to the portrait John has painted and ask what he wants to tell us. When we do that, we learn that the death, resurrection and ascension of Jesus, together with the gift of the Spirit, are all to be seen as one great event. Jesus returns to his Father by way of the cross and resurrection in which his true glory is seen, and in that event he is 'lifted up', exalted to the right hand of God, to the glory that he had with God before the world was made (17:5). Because of this, believers can now enter into the same filial relationship with God that Jesus has enjoyed on earth; his Father is now their Father, and his God their God. This is so because the same Spirit that came on Jesus at his baptism is now given to believers, and the Spirit is given because Jesus has been glorified, just as John had earlier promised (7:39). So the cross and the Spirit—Easter and Pentecost in Lukan terms—belong inseparably together.

All this is made plain to the first disciples by the resurrection of Jesus, but what about subsequent generations? Will Jesus appear to them too? This is the importance of the Thomas story. For here is *a man who wasn't there*—just as we were not there. He demands and receives the proof that we too would like to be given, and he makes the great confession that we too should make, but Jesus pronounces a blessing, not on Thomas, but on those who have not seen and yet have believed—in other words, on us, the readers of the book. Jesus has returned to the Father. He will not show himself repeatedly in every generation to provide proofs for the sceptical. Thomas should have believed the word of the apostles, who said to him, 'We have seen the Lord!' So should we.

POSTLUDE TO JESUS' MINISTRY (JOHN 21:1–25)

After the resounding conclusion with which the book of glory ends, we are surprised to find the Gospel continuing as it does in chapter 21. It is a reasonable guess that the Gospel was originally intended to end at chapter 20, and perhaps in an earlier edition it did so, but that makes it all the more important to ask why this extra material was added and what we are supposed to learn from it. If John thought it was worth adding, even at the cost of some violence to the shape of his Gospel, we may be sure he thought it was important. But why?

The story of the fishing expedition with the extraordinary catch of fish recalls the story in Luke when something similar happened and Jesus called his first disciples with the promise that henceforth they would be catching people rather than fish (Luke 5:1–11). Presumably John's readers are familiar with the story. Here it leads directly into the story of the meal that Jesus shares with the disciples. Jesus takes bread and fish and gives it to them, and it is hard not to think that the meal is meant to symbolize the eucharist. Both these stories answer the question, how do we encounter the risen Lord today? Life goes on, and Jesus is alive, but we shall encounter him at his table and as we go about his business in the world.

The third story, the restoration of Peter, serves a double function. Within the agenda of those who edited and published this Gospel, it serves to affirm Peter as a true Christian leader, but at the same time to subordinate him to the beloved disciple, on whose testimony their church and their faith is founded. To the general reader it issues a message of assurance. As Jesus forgave and reinstated Peter, he can do the same for you. The question that all must answer is, 'Do you love me?' and if, despite all our sins and failures, we answer, 'Yes', he will say to us, 'Show your love to me by feeding my sheep.' This latest Gospel ends by recalling the summons with which, in Mark, Jesus' ministry begins: 'Follow me!' (21:19).

PART TWO

THE CHURCH'S STORY

CHAPTER 6

LUKE'S STORY:
THE ACTS OF THE APOSTLES

Dear Friends of God,

I'm delighted that, after all these years, people are still wanting to read my little book on the early Christian movement. As I explained to my first reader (whose name, Theophilus, also means 'friend of God'—there's a coincidence!), the story you are going to read is really the continuation of the story of Jesus, which in turn is the climax of the story of Israel. God always intended Israel to be the light of the whole world, and through the death and resurrection of Jesus, their king, he has got that plan back on course. My little book tells how that light was carried like an Olympic torch from its beginnings in Jerusalem to the ends of the earth and the capital of the empire.

It may help if I tell you what you won't find here. You won't find a complete 'chronicle of the early Church'. That would need far too many volumes and be very tedious. So I tell you nothing about how the gospel spread east to Asia or south to Africa, and I make no attempt to tell you everything that happened even in Jerusalem. Instead I provide you with short summary accounts of early Christian life (2:42–47; 4:32–36) illustrated by one or two exciting stories. You may notice that most of chapters 1—5 is taken up with the events of just two periods of 24 hours. You'll find nothing like the 'Lives of the Twelve Apostles' here. Instead I've chosen to tell my story, broadly speaking, as the 'Acts of Peter' followed by the 'Acts of Paul', with a few other characters thrown in. I knew Paul, of course, and played some part in the story myself, but even here I've given you a few representative incidents, not an exhaustive biography, because my real hero is not Paul so much as the gospel itself and its triumph over all obstacles. Then you won't find a manual of church organization. Jesus left no blueprint for the Church. Things happened differently in different places and the Holy Spirit blessed all of it. So please don't enlist me to settle your disputes about elders and deacons, or baptism and the Holy Spirit because that's not where my interest lies.

So what are these chapters about? First and foremost they are about Jesus, who is now reigning in heaven and continues his ministry through the apostles. It is he who pours out the Spirit (2:33). It is his name that has power to save (3:16), and he is the subject of each of Peter's three speeches. Second, they are about the Holy Spirit, who is Jesus' agent on earth and the secret of the apostles' courage (4:8) and the Church's growth (9:31). It is the Holy Spirit who makes it possible for the good news to be taken to the ends of the earth (1:8), and I show how each stage of the Church's expansion is prompted and validated by the Spirit, whether by prophecy or by acts of power. Third, they are about the Church itself, which Jesus is gathering out of all nations (2:47), but as I've said, I'm less interested in the details of its organization than in its unity. God's plan, as Paul saw more clearly than anyone else, was for a Church that embraced people from 'every nation under heaven' without distinction, living together in harmony. Of course it didn't always work out like that. There were quarrels and disagreements, but if I have chosen to emphasize the unity of the early Church rather than its disagreements, I hope you will understand.

I hope you enjoy my little book. It contains some good stories and several humorous touches. There's serious theology too, of course, but I've tried to make this as digestible as possible by putting it in the form of short summary speeches. If these stories give you a new confidence in the name of Jesus, a deep hunger for the power of the Holy Spirit, and a commitment to the unity of God's Church across every barrier of race or culture, then I will have achieved my purpose.

Your friend,
Luke

The Acts of the Apostles is unique. It is the only record we have of thirty years that changed the course of history—the only witness to the rise of the Christian movement after the death and resurrection of Jesus. No other book of the New Testament gives us anything like a connected account of those momentous years, and no book outside the New Testament has anything to tell us at all. If we want to hear the Church's story, we have no choice but to listen to Luke and then try to fit the rest of the New Testament into the framework he provides. So who was Luke and what kind of story has he written?

Like the Gospels, the Acts of the Apostles is, strictly speaking, anonymous. The author does not identify himself. What we do know is that Acts was written by the same person who wrote the third Gospel, and that this person was a companion of Paul for part of the time, as is shown by his use of the pronoun 'we' in some of the stories (16:10–17; 20:5–15; 21:1–18; 27:1—28:16). Traditionally, as we have seen, he has been identified with the Luke mentioned by Paul in two of his letters (Col. 4:14; Philemon 23), and this is probably reliable, if only because anyone wanting to attribute Acts to a friend of Paul to increase its authority would surely have found a more prominent person than Luke for the purpose.

We do not know for certain when he wrote. All we can say is that if, in writing his Gospel, Luke used Mark, and if Mark wrote around AD70, as most scholars think, then Acts—which is volume two of Luke's work—cannot have been written before AD70. If we allow ten years to elapse between Mark and Luke, and a further ten years between Luke and Acts, we arrive at a date around AD90. But ten years is a suspiciously round number, and there is no reason why the intervals should not have been very much smaller.

Assuming that Luke wrote some ten or twenty years after the death of Paul, and fifty or sixty years after the birth of the early Church, how did he know what to write? Partly he could draw on his own recollections, as an eyewitness of some of the events he records. Partly, he tells us, he drew on his own researches (Luke 1:1–4), and partly he used his creative imagination, like the best historians of his day—especially in the speeches, which play such a key role in holding the reader's attention in Acts. These cannot be verbatim accounts, since they are too short, but neither do they read like mere summaries. They are little gems, artfully composed so that they appear to be complete speeches, presenting the Christian message in a way appropriate to the audience on each occasion. Like the great Thucydides 400 years earlier, Luke has 'put into the mouth of each speaker sentiments proper to the occasion', while at the same time endeavouring 'to give the general import of what was actually said'.[1]

Each of Luke's volumes is addressed to Theophilus, who is called 'most excellent', suggesting that he was a person of high rank— possibly Luke's patron—but nothing else is known of him. He might simply be a convenient symbol for Luke's intended readership (his name means 'friend of God'), who were presumably Greek-speaking, Jewish Christians. Luke writes in an elegant Greek style, but his concern to show from Scripture that the Christian movement is the fulfilment of God's promises to Israel would probably appeal only to people who knew their Old Testament.

What sort of story has Luke written? The best way to find out is to read it. If that seems a rather daunting task, let me give you a guided tour.

THE STORY IN OUTLINE

The story falls into four main sections, each ending with a key speech in which the issues of the preceding section are summarized. The first section, from 1:1 to 8:3, recounts the beginnings of the Church in Jerusalem, seen as the promised restoration of God's people, and concludes with Stephen's speech (7:2–53). The second section, from 8:4 to 15:35, describes the expansion of God's people to embrace Samaritans and Gentiles, and concludes with James' speech at the Council at Jerusalem (15:13–21). The third section, from 15:36 to 20:38, might be called the Acts of Paul. It tells how Paul took the gospel to Europe, founding churches at Philippi, Thessalonica and Corinth and spending three years working in Ephesus, and concludes with his speech to the Ephesian elders (20:17–35). The final section, from 21:1 to 28:31, relates the sufferings of Paul, his arrest and trials and his perilous journey to Rome as a prisoner, and it ends with his speech to the Jewish leaders in Rome (28:23–28).

THE RESTORATION OF GOD'S PEOPLE (ACTS 1:1—8:3)

Acts begins with the departure of Jesus in glory, making plain that everything that happens in the book will be the acts of the ascended Lord ('Exalted to the right hand of God, he has... poured out what you now see and hear', 2:33). The disciples ask, 'Lord, are you at this time going to restore the kingdom to Israel?' (1:6). This has been seen as a silly question and as a sign that the disciples are still lacking in understanding, but this is unfair to them and to Luke, who has no interest in presenting the disciples as obtuse. Israel had been for centuries under pagan rule and the promise of the kingdom had always included the restoration of Israel. Now, with Jesus' resurrection, the kingdom has actually begun to arrive, so will Israel be restored to its former glory? The answer Jesus gives is both 'no' and 'yes'. This is not the time for the Roman rulers to be driven out of the land of Israel, and the Davidic monarchy is not about to be restored, 'But you will receive power when the Holy Spirit comes on you; and you will be my witnesses... to the ends of the earth' (1:8). In this way the kingdom will be restored to Israel, now to be seen as a worldwide international family bringing blessing to 'all peoples on earth' (Gen. 12:3).

Jesus departs in clouds of glory, but the promise is made that he will return 'in the same way you have seen him go into heaven' (1:11). In context, this must refer in the first place to the descent of the Spirit. This is what has just been promised, and sure enough, 'in a few days' (1:5), the Spirit comes 'from heaven' (2:2) with supernatural signs, wind, fire and foreign languages. To be sure, the Pentecost event is not an exact replica of the ascension, but then neither is it precisely what was foretold by Joel, but this does not stop Peter equating the two events (2:16–21). The signs accompanying the coming of the Spirit show the character of the Church's mission and ministry. It will live by the power of God (the wind); it will experience persecution and suffering (the fire); it will preach to people 'from every nation under heaven' (the languages). Peter loses no time in calling Israel back to God and to his Messiah, Jesus, and in the overwhelming and immediate response we see the beginning of the restoration of God's people. Luke gives the first of his summary descriptions of the life of the early Church designed to show the extent of that restoration (2:42–47; see also 4:32–35).

That it is Jesus who has returned in the Spirit is made plain by the next incident Luke relates—the healing of the crippled beggar at the temple gate. It is an event full of echoes of the ministry of the earthly Jesus, and Peter makes plain that it is the name of Jesus and through faith in him that the healing has occurred (3:16). Yet this is not just an act of compassion to an individual. The healed beggar is a sign of God's purpose to restore his people so that they too can walk and leap and praise God. Jesus is seen to be a new Moses, calling Israel to repentance and faith so that they can fulfil their historic mission to the rest of the world, as promised to Abraham (3:15–26). Now it becomes plain that not all Israel will accept the call. The ordinary Israelites respond in increasing numbers, but their rulers reject Jesus in this second visitation just as they did at his first. This leads to the final act of the section.

It begins with the choice of seven leaders to oversee the distribution of food to the poor. Although Luke has presented this as the origin of the order of deacons that was emerging in the Church by the time he wrote, and of the principle according to which some need to be set apart for the ministry of God's word and freed from other responsibilities, he allows us to see that behind the account lies the spread of the gospel to Greek-speaking Christians and the need to provide them with their own leaders. The seven are more than deacons: they are powerful preachers to whom will fall responsibility for the next stage of Christian expansion. One of them is Stephen.

Stephen brings to a head the opposition of Israel's rulers to the new movement. He is accused, like Jesus before him, of wanting to destroy the temple and abolish the law of Moses, and he replies with a long speech in which he presents a new reading of Israel's story, showing the marginal place of the temple in that story and the way in which it is his opponents who show themselves to be against Moses. Just as their fathers twice rejected Moses (7:27, 39), so they have twice rejected Jesus, both during his earthly life and now as he comes to them through the Spirit.[2] The immediate outcome is Stephen's death, but the outcome in terms of Luke's story is the rejection of the Jerusalem rulers, who play no further part in the story.

THE EXPANSION OF GOD'S PEOPLE (ACTS 8:4—15:35)

In the second part of Luke's story we see the prophecy of Jesus (1:8) beginning to be fulfilled as the Church moves outward, first to Samaria and then to include the first Gentiles in its membership. Philip preaches to the Samaritans and, as a sign of their inclusion in the new people of God, we are told in some detail how the Holy Spirit was given to them. Significantly, this required the involvement of the leading apostles from Jerusalem as a sign of reconciliation and of the Samaritans' full acceptance. Then, as a sign that the gospel will eventually be carried to the ends of the earth, the ends of the earth come to Philip in the form of a man from Ethiopia, who had come up to Jerusalem to worship and finds through the message of Jesus a joy that he presumably had not found in the temple.

The 'acts of Philip' (8:4–40) are followed by the 'acts of Peter' (9:32—12:19), but before that, Luke tells us of the conversion of Saul from persecutor to confessor, and his call by the risen Christ 'to carry my name before the Gentiles and their kings and before the people of Israel' (9:16). This event is related three times in Luke's short history, each time with a slightly different emphasis, but always with the aim of showing that Paul's life was changed by God and that it was God who called him to the controversial ministry he went on to exercise.

Meanwhile, Luke shows us that the inclusion of Gentiles within the Church did not originate with Paul, but that, in fact, Peter was instrumental in welcoming the first Gentile convert. The story of the conversion of Cornelius, which might with equal justice be called the conversion of Peter, is narrated by Luke at great length (10:1—11:18). First we learn how God prompted Cornelius to seek out Peter, then how God prepared Peter to receive him and broke down his Jewish scruples about associating with Gentiles. Each character then tells the other of their experience. Peter preaches a sermon beginning, 'I now realize how true it is that God does not show favouritism' and going on to tell the story of Jesus. Before he can even finish what he has to say, God pours out his Spirit on his Gentile hearers as a mark of their acceptance. Finally Peter is made to recount the whole incident all over again to the disapproving church leaders in Jerusalem, who declare, like the chorus in a Greek play, the moral of the tale: 'So then, God has granted even the Gentiles repentance unto life' (11:18).

From the 'acts of Peter' we move to the 'acts of Barnabas and Saul'. First we are told how Barnabas was instrumental in bringing Saul to the notice of the church at Antioch (11:26). From Paul's account in Galatians, we know that some fourteen years have elapsed between Paul's conversion and our next sight of him in Antioch, years that he presumably spent in and around his native Tarsus, being prepared for the ministry he was soon to exercise. Antioch was the first church to combine Jewish and Gentile believers in large numbers, and Barnabas and Saul were among their teachers. Before long, however, the Holy Spirit calls them out of this ministry into itinerant preaching, and the Gentile mission is born. Once again we can see the importance Luke attached to this move, from the fact that he devotes two long chapters to it (chs. 13—14). Yet the largest part of the story is taken up not with the conversion of Gentiles but with Paul's preaching in the synagogue at Pisidian Antioch and its sequel (13:14–52).

Like Peter and Stephen before him, Paul addresses a largely Jewish audience to show that Jesus is the fulfilment of Israel's story. Only when the Jews reject this message do the missionaries turn to the Gentiles (and we catch a glimpse of how Paul went about preaching to a non-Jewish audience in 14:15–17). Luke does not, in fact, give much space to describing how Paul evangelized the Gentiles; he spends more time defending the Gentile mission against its critics.

All of this leads to the meeting at Jerusalem which forms the watershed of Luke's book. The council is precipitated by the arrival in Antioch of messengers demanding that the Gentiles must be circumcised to belong to the people of God. Apparently they also visited the newly planted churches of Galatia with the same demand and met with some success. It was probably at the height of this controversy that Paul wrote his letter to the Galatians, using the arguments he would also use at the Jerusalem meeting. At Jerusalem, Luke tells us, the issue was laid before the leaders there. Peter once again relates his experience of mission among Gentiles (presumably the Cornelius incident), and James sums up in favour of Paul's position: the Gentiles need not be circumcised. They are only to respect Jewish scruples by abstaining from 'food polluted by idols, from sexual immorality, from the meat of strangled animals and from blood' (15:20), and the church makes a formal resolution to that effect.

Interestingly, the conversion of the Gentiles is seen by James as the rebuilding of David's fallen tent (15:16), as prophesied by Amos 9:11. The Gentiles can belong to the people of God without submitting to circumcision, and this is the way in which Israel itself will be restored. Gentiles do not have to become Jews in order to become Christians, and this is not to be seen as the rejection of the Church's Jewish heritage but as its fulfilment and enlargement.

THE ACTS OF PAUL (ACTS 15:36—20:38)

Paul now moves centre stage in Luke's account, which from now on focuses exclusively on Paul's evangelistic exploits and then on his trials. The exploits occur during what are usually referred to as the second and third missionary journeys, although it is not clear how far Paul was, strictly speaking, a *missionary* at this time (that is, one sent out by a church as he and Barnabas had been from Antioch), and how far he was quite independent.

The second journey begins with Paul, now accompanied by Silas, revisiting the churches planted at Derbe and Lystra, where Timothy joins the team. Rather to our surprise, Paul has Timothy circumcised —something we would not have expected from reading Galatians. This is one of several incidents where Luke presents Paul as a faithful Jew despite his insistence on Gentile freedom (16:3; 18:18; 21:26). Further evangelistic opportunities do not open for Paul in Asia Minor, and the team, now apparently including Luke himself (16:10ff.), crosses over to Europe to spread the message in the cities of Greece.

This is the part of Paul's career that Luke describes in most detail and the part that links most closely with the evidence of Paul's own letters. We learn of his visit to the Roman colony of Philippi, where a church forms in the house of Lydia, a businesswoman from Thyatira. The unforgettable story of the conversion of the Philippian jailer follows the arrest and overnight detention of Paul and Silas (16:11–40). Despite being released in the morning, the missionaries are forced to move on to Thessalonica, where the message about Jesus once again divides the Jewish community, as it does in Berea (17:1–15).

Paul moves on to Athens, where there seems to be no Jewish community for him to preach to, so he preaches instead to the philosophers, and this enables Luke to present a sample of the way Paul used to present the gospel to audiences with no knowledge of the Jewish scriptures (17:16–34). Some hearers believe the message, but apparently no church is formed in Athens. Paul moves on to Corinth, and the familiar pattern unfolds. First he preaches in the synagogue, but when he runs into opposition he moves into the house next door, taking Crispus the synagogue ruler, and his family, with him (a detail that is confirmed by 1 Cor. 1:14). We might have expected to see Paul once again on the road, forced out of Corinth as he had been at Philippi and Thessalonica, but here at last the Roman government comes to his aid in the person of the proconsul Gallio, who dismisses the Jewish case against Paul. This intervention makes it possible for Paul to stay over eighteen months in the city and to plant one of the churches that was to give him most heartache, and about which we are best informed. A brief account of this time appears in Acts 18:1–18.

Paul then leaves Corinth and crosses the Aegean sea to Ephesus, which was to be the focus of his activity for much of the third journey. Before embarking on this journey, Paul for some reason visits Jerusalem and Antioch, but Luke provides us with no details of these visits. Instead he introduces us to Apollos, a learned Jew from Alexandria, who is converted to the Pauline understanding of the gospel and sent off to Corinth, where we shall meet him again. Paul meanwhile returns to Ephesus, where he was to stay for nearly three years. When the synagogue was closed to him, he 'had discussions daily in the lecture hall of Tyrannus' and to such good effect that 'all the Jews and Greeks who lived in the province of Asia heard the word of the Lord' (19:9–10).

True to his selective method, Luke illustrates these years with only three vivid stories. There is the puzzling encounter with the disciples who knew only John's baptism (19:1–7). There is the amusing story of the Jewish exorcists and the impact of their experience in a city noted as a centre for magic and the occult (19:11–20), and there is the long and graphic account of the riot in the theatre in Ephesus (19:23–41). Once again, a period of years is illustrated by three afternoons' work and otherwise covered in brief summary statements. During this time we know that Paul engaged in correspondence with the church in Corinth (and also, I shall argue, with Colossae and Philippi), but of this Luke says nothing.

Paul then leaves Ephesus (perhaps not voluntarily) and travels back through Macedonia to the troubled church at Corinth again. He stays three months at Corinth, presumably writing his letter to the church at Rome to prepare the way for his projected visit, although again Luke says nothing about this. From Corinth, Paul sets out for Jerusalem with a considerable party of delegates from the churches, in what we know to have been a 'make or break' attempt to win the approval of the Jerusalem church for his mission and churches. On the way he stops at Miletus, where he addresses the elders of the church at Ephesus (20:17–35). This is the only speech in Acts addressed to a Christian audience and it nicely expresses the values and style of the Pauline mission. Paul looks back on the work he has accomplished and forward to the dangers facing the churches after he has gone.

THE SUFFERINGS OF PAUL (ACTS 21:1—28:31)

If Acts had ended with Paul's speech to the Ephesian elders, we should not have been surprised. It reads like a farewell and would have brought Luke's account of Paul's ministry to a perfectly satisfying conclusion. In fact, of course, the story continues for another eight chapters—more than a third of its total length—describing Paul's arrest in Jerusalem and his trials before a variety of 'governors and kings' (Matt. 10:18). It is likely that Luke intends us to see a parallel between Jesus' journey to Jerusalem, where he was arrested, and Paul's similar fate at the hands of the Jewish leaders.

These chapters are probably the least interesting part of Acts for the modern Christian reader, but we may be sure that Luke thought them of the utmost importance to his purpose of vindicating Paul and the Christian movement against charges from Jewish critics that Paul had died as an apostate and that the Christian movement lacked all legitimacy. Paul twice tells the story of his conversion as evidence that he was responding to a call from God, and he twice declares that his belief in the resurrection puts him firmly in line with mainstream Judaism (24:21). Paul is happy to acknowledge himself a Pharisee (not an ex-Pharisee! 23:6), and claims to be on trial 'because of the hope of Israel' (28:20).

The book ends with Paul's voyage to Rome, his shipwreck, his eventual arrival in the capital and concluding dialogue with Jewish leaders there. Again we are surprised at the amount of space given to the voyage and shipwreck and the curiously low-key, even anti-climactic, ending to the book as a whole. The story of the voyage is lively and enjoyable, but seems short of theological significance, while the much-heralded arrival in Rome leaves us asking what happened to Paul in the end. It is as if we are watching a film in which the picture and sound fade out while the main character keeps on talking, his voice growing fainter and fainter. This is the point at which to remember that Luke's real hero is not Paul but the word of God. The story of the voyage tells us that God's word will reach to the ends of the earth despite all obstacles, while God is able to keep his messenger safe through all perils. In line with this, the climax of the book is not, as we might wish, Paul's trial before Caesar, leading perhaps to a triumphant acquittal or a noble martyrdom, but the presence of God's word in the capital of the world and the triumphant, even defiant, declaration in the face of continued rejection by the Jewish leaders, 'Therefore I want you to know that God's salvation has been sent to the Gentiles, and they will listen!' (28:28). If Luke knew what happened to Paul, as presumably he did, he has not chosen to tell us, perhaps because there was nothing very inspiring about it anyway.

CONCLUSION

So what sort of story has Luke written? As our imaginary letter from Luke tried to make clear, it is first of all a *continuing* story. Acts continues the story of what 'Jesus began to do and to teach' (1:1), as recorded in the Gospel. It also sets out to show that the story of the Church continues the story of Israel in fulfilment of the promise to Abraham (3:24–25).

Second, it is a *selective* story. It tells us of the spread of the Christian message from Jerusalem to Antioch, and from Antioch through Asia Minor and Greece, but when Paul arrives in Rome there is already a church in existence and Luke tells us nothing about how it got there, any more than he tells us of the founding of the church of Alexandria in Egypt. Even in what he does tell us, there are huge gaps. Luke gives us some vivid stories that describe the events of a few days, and strings them together with summaries that cover an unknown number of years (e.g. 6:7; 9:31). Paul spent three years in Ephesus, but, as we have already seen, Luke gives us just three stories (19:1–41) that would hardly fill a couple of afternoons.

Third, it is an *apologetic* story. Luke writes to convince and defend —but defend what exactly, and against what charge? In the first place, Luke defends the whole Christian movement and shows it to be the true Israel. It is not an upstart, breakaway movement, but the proper fulfilment of 'all that the prophets have spoken' (Luke 24:25), to which Israel's long history has been pointing all along.

He also defends Paul as the teacher of Israel.[3] While, in our eyes, Paul may appear as the foremost missionary statesman of his age, to his contemporaries he was a much more controversial character, and after his death his disciples had to fight to preserve his memory, free from slander and misrepresentation. Almost half of Acts is devoted to Paul's career, and his conversion is told three times, making plain that Paul was what he was by God's call, and that his teaching and life were fully in accord with the Old Testament scriptures.

Especially, Luke defends the Gentile mission and the decision to allow Gentiles to join the Church as full and equal members without the need for circumcision. The Jerusalem meeting of Acts 15 is a pivotal chapter in Luke's story, and the story of Paul is told in such a way as to show the importance of the decision reached there.

Finally, Luke defends the faithfulness of God himself—faithful to his promises to Israel, and faithful to Jesus and to his followers: 'The God of Abraham, Isaac and Jacob, the God of our fathers, has glorified his servant Jesus' (3:13). Throughout the book, it is made plain that God keeps the promises he makes to his servants (e.g. 1:8; 23:11) and that even the arrest and imprisonment of Paul demonstrate the faithfulness of God.

Fourth, it is an *exemplary* story. Generations of Christians have looked to Acts for examples to follow or to see the early Church as an ideal to return to. Luke intended us to do so, and his account of the life of the Church is intentionally idealistic, smoothing over the difficulties and tensions we know to have existed. But it is the unity of the Church and the love and courage of the first Christians that he intends us to imitate and not the details of their organization. If Acts tells us anything about the organization of the early churches, it tells us that there was no single pattern valid for all times and all places— but the faith, the prayers, and the dependence on the Holy Spirit of these early Christians are always to be coveted and imitated.

Finally, though, is it a *reliable* account? Where it can be checked, the answer seems to be 'yes'. In particular, Luke is correct in geographical details, and he knows the correct titles for the different magistrates and officials in different places. This gives us confidence to believe him when he tells us things that cannot be checked. Similarly, things that Luke tells us that can be dated, like the proconsulship of Gallio in Corinth, or Festus' procuratorship in Judea, enable us to construct a reasonable outline of the history of the first thirty years of the Christian movement.

As we have seen, however, there are big gaps in Luke's account. The most contentious issue concerns Luke's portrait of Paul. There are some surprising omissions (like the lack of any mention of Paul as a letter writer), and some surprising inclusions (like Paul's apparent willingness to conform to Jewish legal and ritual requirements). Some scholars claim to find irreconcilable theological differences between Acts and the Pauline letters, but these can usually be explained as simply a difference of emphasis and audience. Paul wrote for his own Christians, often to correct a particular error or misunderstanding; Luke wrote for a wider audience and with the aim of showing that Paul was not a dangerous maverick. If Luke's portrait of Paul is smoother and more flattering than one that we might construct for ourselves from reading his letters, it is not for that reason a distortion. Many of us will appear better in the memory of our friends than we allow ourselves to appear in the heat of argument—and what are friends for?

CHAPTER 7

PAUL'S STORY: GALATIA

THE STORY BEHIND GALATIANS

Behind every letter there is a story—something that prompts the writer to write at all, often an ongoing relationship between sender and recipients. The recipients know the story, of course, so while the writer may refer to it, he or she will not usually need to tell it. A third party reading the letter, however, perhaps long after it was written, may miss the point unless they understand what was going on. Behind Galatians there are two stories—the Galatians' story, which we pick up from hints and allusions, and Paul's own story, which he tells at some length.

THE GALATIANS' STORY

The Galatians lived in the towns of Pisidian Antioch, Iconium, Lystra and Derbe in central Asia Minor (modern Turkey). They are called Galatians because these towns lay within the Roman province of Galatia, although before the coming of Roman administration, Galatia proper had been an area rather to the north. They had become Christians during the missionary journey of Paul and Barnabas described by Luke in Acts 13 and 14. From Paul's letter to them, we learn that Paul had preached to them only 'because of an illness' (4:13)—perhaps because he was recuperating from sickness of some kind and was forced to spend more time with them than he had planned. Whatever the details, the Galatians had given him a warm welcome. Formerly, many of them had been pagans (4:8), but now they accepted the message of Christ crucified and had received a powerful and confirming experience of the Holy Spirit (3:1–5).

After Paul had left them, there came other preachers with 'a different gospel' (1:6). Paul does not at first tell us what this message was, because of course the Galatians knew what he was talking about. In fact, it is clearly spelled out only near the end of the letter: 'Mark my words! I, Paul, tell you that if you let yourselves be circumcised, Christ will be of no value to you at all' (5:2). Taken with the reference to 'observing special days' (4:10), it is clear that the new message was a demand for the converts to undergo circumcision and to conform to the distinctive requirements of the Jewish law in order to belong to the people of God. Paul does not tell us who had brought this message, but evidently they were Christians, since they claimed to preach the gospel. Presumably they were Jewish—like Paul himself, of course—but, unlike Paul, they believed that Gentile converts should be obliged to keep the law. We might properly call them 'conservatives', who viewed Paul as a dangerous 'liberal'! In their own eyes they were simply being faithful to Scripture: circumcision was demanded by Genesis 17. In Paul's opinion, their motivation was to avoid persecution (6:12). For many Jews, circumcision was seen as a matter of national loyalty, and those who stepped out of line were likely to incur hostility, if not from the authorities then certainly from their neighbours. Some Jewish Christians, at least, saw no reason why the Christian movement should bring trouble on itself by relaxing the entry requirements for Gentiles wishing to embrace the faith.

PAUL'S STORY

Paul begins his letter by telling parts of his own story. He does this partly because the 'conservatives' had cast doubt on his credentials and partly to show that this issue of requiring Gentiles to keep the law was not a new one, but had been faced and dealt with before. In answer to those who said that Paul was only an apostle at one remove, with a second-hand and incomplete knowledge of the Christian message, Paul stresses that he was commissioned directly by Jesus Christ (1:1) and received his understanding of the gospel directly from Jesus (1:12). He tells us what he was before his conversion—a Jew, and a Jew of a particular type, 'extremely zealous for the traditions of my fathers' (1:13–14). He has stood where these conservatives stand

and knows the arguments from the inside. Next he tells us of his conversion, describing it as a prophetic call from God, like that of Jeremiah or one of the other prophets, in which there was no human intermediary. The conversion was followed by a three-year period in Arabia, presumably to think through the implications of his Damascus road encounter, and during this time he had no contact with other Christian leaders.

Next, Paul tells us of two visits he made to Jerusalem. The first, three years after his conversion, was very short and unofficial (1:18–24). Paul only met Peter and James, and only for a few days. The second visit, fourteen years after his conversion, was more important. He went up to Jerusalem, presumably from Antioch and as part of an official delegation, to discuss the very issue that was now troubling the Galatians—the circumcision of Gentile converts. The Jerusalem leaders had endorsed Paul's stand on this matter and his mission to the Gentiles, and had not required the circumcision of Titus, whom Paul had taken along as a test case (2:1–10).

It is an intriguing puzzle to reconcile what Paul says here with the account given by Luke in Acts. Luke mentions an initial visit to Jerusalem by Paul following his conversion (Acts 9:26–30). Then he tells us of a visit made by Barnabas and Saul, bearing a gift from the church at Antioch for the relief of famine (Acts 11:27–30). The next visit is for the apostolic meeting at Jerusalem (Acts 15:1–35). Which of these three visits mentioned by Luke is Paul referring to in Galatians? Most scholars equate the first visit described by Luke (Acts 9:26–30) with the brief visit described by Paul (Gal. 1:18–19), although the two accounts are quite different. They then see the meeting described in Galatians 2:1–10 as Paul's version of the apostolic meeting of Acts 15, on the grounds that the same topic, the circumcision of the Gentiles, was discussed on both occasions. On this view, Paul has simply omitted all mention of the 'famine' visit of Acts 11:27–30. The alternative view is that Galatians 2:1–10 describes the 'famine' visit, and that the apostolic meeting of Acts 15 is not mentioned in Galatians because it has not yet taken place.

There are good reasons for preferring this second view. To make his case to the Galatians, Paul needs to record every visit he made to Jerusalem. He ought not to have omitted a visit, and moreover he is writing on oath. He says that his second visit was made in response to revelation (2:2), which fits well with Acts 11, where the church sends a gift to Jerusalem in response to Agabus' prophecy of famine. This also explains why Paul does not mention the decree issued by the apostolic meeting of Acts 15, as he surely would have done had he known of it. Paul does not mention it because it was still in the future when he wrote Galatians. On this view, Galatians is Paul's earliest surviving letter, written before the Jerusalem meeting, as part of the 'sharp dispute' (Acts 15:2) that preceded it.

The final piece of his story that Paul tells is the Antioch incident just referred to (2:11–14). The church at Antioch was a mixed church, with Jewish and Gentile Christians worshipping together and breaking bread together around one table. According to Acts, this was the first church of its kind. When Peter came to Antioch, presumably after his escape from Herod's prison, he found nothing objectionable in this and joined in the fellowship meals, until 'certain men came from James' (2:12). We do not know who these men were or why James sent them, but the effect of their arrival was to make Peter discontinue table fellowship with the Gentile Christians. According to Paul, Peter acted out of fear—fear of what more conservative Jews might say—the same fear that, according to Paul, lay behind the attempt to impose circumcision on the Galatian converts (2:12; 6:12). Paul therefore opposed him openly and denounced what he saw as Peter's hypocrisy. Either Peter had not been sincere in his earlier acceptance of the Gentile Christians or he was not now acting from conviction in separating from them and demanding that they submit to the demands of the law.

Although the Antioch incident concerned table fellowship and the problem in Galatia was about circumcision, Paul evidently sees them as closely related. Both concern the application of the law, and both had the effect of discriminating against Gentile Christians. The demand for circumcision would exclude large numbers of Gentiles from joining the Church at all, and the refusal of table fellowship would divide the Church along racial lines into first- and second-class members. Both were contrary to the agreement that Paul had made with the other apostles on his visit to Jerusalem, and, as the debate intensifies in Antioch (Acts 15:1), he writes this passionate letter to the Galatians to dissuade them from surrendering to the conservatives' demands.

THE MESSAGE OF GALATIANS

CRUCIFIED WITH CHRIST

We shall best grasp the message of Galatians by focusing on three key passages. The first, 2:15–21, follows so closely on the report of the Antioch incident that some people see it as part of what Paul said on that occasion, while others see it as the explanation Paul is now giving of the stand he took then. He appeals first to a belief that had apparently come to be well understood by all of them in the earliest days of the Christian movement: 'a man is not justified by observing the law, but by faith in Jesus Christ' (2:16). 'Justified' is a legal metaphor used to describe someone's acceptance by God as belonging to his people, as God had long ago accepted Abraham (Gen. 15:6). No doubt Peter and Paul had both believed that such acceptance depended on 'observing the law', especially in those things that had come to define faithful Israelites, but Jesus had changed all that. In his life he had accepted sinners and eaten with them (Luke 15:2); in his death he had died for them and exposed the hollowness of the legal system that had excluded them so, from the start, his followers knew themselves to be accepted only by their faith in him. No doubt, in the eyes of the upholders of the law, that meant that Jesus was actually encouraging people to sin, but Paul knows better! (2:17). The real sinners are those who, like Peter, are inconsistent, setting aside the demands of the legal system one minute and reimposing them the next (2:18). Either acceptance from God is through the legal system or it isn't. If it is, then Peter was wrong to abandon it; if it isn't, then he is wrong to require it of others.

The truth is, Paul says, that those who belong to Christ Jesus have died to the law and passed beyond its jurisdiction (2:19). They should no longer seek its approval or fear its penalties. How so? They have been 'crucified with Christ' (2:20). When a man is crucified, he dies as an outlaw, condemned by the legal system as no longer fit to belong to that society. Jesus was not assassinated by a mad man or knocked down by a bus. He was executed by the due process of law, condemned by the authorities, both secular and religious. Raised from the dead, he showed what God thinks of these authorities and their sentence, and has passed for ever beyond their jurisdiction. *And now Paul has publicly identified himself with Jesus.* If you identify yourself with an outlaw, an outlaw is what you become. Paul, the former guardian of the law, has become an outlaw. He is no longer concerned with the law's rewards or penalties, or with the good opinion of his former associates.

To be crucified with Christ is a matter of public identification. It refers to the social cost of conversion. The moment of truth is the moment of baptism, as any convert from Islam or Hinduism today will tell you. That is when you are publicly identified with Christ, and that is when you can expect to start sharing his fate. Paul knew the truth of this in his experience. Almost the last thing he says in the letter to the Galatians is, 'I bear on my body the marks of Jesus' (6:17).

What follows? Those who have shared Christ's crucifixion share his risen life as Christ lives in them by his Spirit. They are no longer living to please those whose opinion formerly mattered to them. Instead they 'live by faith in the Son of God… [or possibly, 'by the faithfulness of the Son of God']¹ … who loved me and gave himself for me' (2:20). This means, among other things, that they should no longer be slaves to other people's opinions. Peter had caved in because he feared the circumcision group (2:12). The 'conservatives' in Galatia wanted to avoid persecution for the cross of Christ (6:12). Paul says, by contrast, that the world has been crucified to him and he to the world (6:14). 'The world' is the world of public opinion and applause and, for a Jew like Paul or Peter, that world was the world governed by the Jewish legal system. What matters now is God's opinion. Righteousness no longer comes from the law; it comes entirely by the grace of God (2:21).

ALL ONE IN CHRIST JESUS

Galatians is not about how to get to heaven, but about who can belong to the people of God on earth. That was the issue in Antioch: Can Jews and Gentiles eat together? It is now the issue in Galatia: Must Gentile men be circumcised in order to be the 'children of Abraham'? In pressing the case for circumcision, the 'conservatives' had naturally appealed to the example of Abraham and to the command of God that all his male descendants should be circumcised (Gen. 17). But Paul claims Abraham in support of his own position. First, Abraham was accepted by God simply on the ground of his faith, before there was any mention of his being circumcised (3:6; cf. Gen. 15:6). Second, Abraham was called by God to be the means of blessing to all the nations on earth. Therefore, the family of God was never meant to be confined to Jews alone but was, through the Jewish people, intended to embrace everyone. And what is that 'blessing'? No doubt, under the influence of Old Testament texts such as Isaiah 44:3, Paul sees it as the gift of the Holy Spirit (3:14), which the Galatians had so manifestly received (3:2–5).

By contrast, the law pronounces a curse on those who fail to fulfil its commands, and the Jewish people are well aware of that curse since they have lived for centuries in exile and under foreign rule, just as Deuteronomy had said they would. Happily, the Messiah has come and lifted the curse by taking it on himself (which was why he had to die by being 'hung on a tree': see Deut. 21:23), so that Israel can be restored to its proper place in God's plan, and all of us can receive the Spirit promised to Abraham.

The legal system, whose most prominent symbol was male circumcision, has effectively been left behind by the coming of Christ and his act of faithfulness in dying on the cross. (The same Greek word can mean 'faith' or 'faithfulness' and refers either to our believing or Christ's faithfulness to God on our behalf: when Paul says that 'faith came' (3:23) he means that Christ came and was faithful.) Not that the whole apparatus of law was a colossal mistake! Not at all. It was given to Israel for the purpose of keeping them safe precisely so that they could function as a channel of blessing to the nations (although it took the coming of Christ to get this plan of God back on course). Now that Christ has come, however, the days of Israel's legal system are over. Paul likens the law to a child's guardian (3:24). The function of this guardian was to see the children safely to school, like a crossing attendant or 'lollipop lady' in our society. When the children are small, they need help in crossing the road, but adults do not need this help, and continued dependence on a crossing attendant would not be a sign of maturity.

The conclusion of the somewhat involved arguments of 3:6–25 is that 'you are all sons of God through faith in Christ Jesus' (or 'through the faithfulness of Christ Jesus') (3:26). That is the meaning of your baptism, as it was the meaning of Jesus' baptism (Mark 1:11), and the social consequence of this is that 'you are all one in Christ Jesus' (3:28). Old distinctions of race, status or gender are obsolete, as those of colour or caste must be in our world. This cannot simply be true in the sight of God; it must be true also here on earth and in practice, wherever the children of God meet around his table. That, we remember, was the issue in Antioch, and it would have been no use for Peter to protest that, while God might make no distinctions, his Church regrettably needed to do so.

Apart from Christ, all peoples, Jew and Gentile alike, are like children, subject to the discipline of their own national deities and religions. (NIV speaks of 'basic principles' in 4:3, but the word embraces gods as well as rules, as 4:8–9 shows.) The Jews would have agreed with that assessment of the function of pagan religion, but Paul daringly includes the Jewish legal system and sees it as functioning in the same way. This was no better than slavery, but now God has sent his Son to die for us and his Spirit to live in us, and the Spirit enables us to pray to God as our Father and to live as his free children, with all that that implies for the future (4:4–7).

THE FRUIT OF THE SPIRIT

The final two chapters deal with the moral consequences of what Paul has been saying. We must remember that the 'conservatives' were not concerned with religious rites for their own sake. They no doubt believed that the law was the way to make people holy, and that the law was indivisible. Once you let people in without circumcision, they would have said, you don't know where it will lead. All sorts of wickedness will flourish unchecked in the Church!

Paul has identified the gospel with freedom (5:1), but freedom can be abused. The law as a religious system peculiar to Israel may have been superseded, but the law as God's revealed will for human behaviour certainly hasn't. It can be summed up in one sentence: 'Love your neighbour as yourself.' Not even the present crisis, it is implied, dispenses us from that obligation (5:13–15). However, there is a better way than law to make people holy. The Spirit they have received is a Spirit of holiness, and he is able to counter the natural, selfish desires that so easily dominate people's lives. With his help they can choose the good and reject the evil that they might otherwise like to do (5:16–18). A list of these evil things is given (5:19–21), followed by a list of the qualities that mark behaviour inspired by the Holy Spirit (5:22–23).

But how does it work? It is striking that Paul nowhere suggests that the Holy Spirit relieves the Christian of the need for moral effort. To follow through his agricultural metaphor, we must both clear the ground and plant good seed. Clearing the ground takes place when we 'crucify the sinful nature with its passions and desires' (5:24). This is a matter of decision and it is something that each person must do for themselves.

'Crucifixion' is here being used in a sense quite different from that in 2:20 and 6:14. There it was being used to spell out the inevitable result of being publicly identified with Christ. It is something to be recognized and endured. Here it is something that the believer must do as a result of that recognition. In practical terms, it means turning decisively from all that we know to be wrong and putting our sinful desires to death. Then we must walk in step with the Spirit, planting the seeds of Christian character according to his directions. Some examples follow, and then Paul returns to the agricultural metaphor with a warning: we reap what we sow, for better or worse. In all this, Paul is not guilty of starting with the Spirit and ending with mere human effort (3:3). He is not paying lip service to the Spirit, while falling back on exhortations and threats. The Spirit is the Spirit of the new creation, beside which neither circumcision nor uncircumcision mean anything at all (6:15).

THE OUTCOME OF GALATIANS

FOR PAUL

If we are right in our reconstruction of events, and Galatians was written before the Jerusalem meeting, then the letter must be reckoned a success. The meeting decided in Paul's favour, and that surely will have put a stop to the circumcision of Gentile believers in Galatia. The dispute rumbled on, however, as we learn from Paul's letters to the Philippians and Colossians (Phil. 3:2–11; Col. 2:11–12), and Paul still needed to defend his churches against Jewish-Christian counter-missions. The demand for circumcision needs to be fought even in the letter to the Romans (2:17–29).

FOR US

Circumcision is not, for most Christians, a pressing issue today, but that does not mean that Galatians is of merely historical interest. The presenting issue has changed, but the underlying issue has not: How can all be one in Christ Jesus? The Church struggled for centuries to come to terms with Paul's insight that in Christ 'there is no longer slave or free' (3:28). In many parts of the world, Christians still have difficulty accepting as brothers and sisters those of another ethnic group, tribe or caste. To our shame, we have been forced into accepting the equality of women and men in the Church not by the logic of the gospel but by the pressure of secular feminism. Yet the gospel Paul preached still has the same power to break down barriers. It still offers a new relationship with God (4:6–7) and equal membership of his people on the ground of faith alone. It still has power to subdue our fallen human natures (5:16) and produce the fruit of love, joy and peace in those who respond. Galatians stands as a charter of freedom and acceptance for the Church in any age. But be warned! It will never be easy. Freedom still attracts the hostility of the guardians of cultural and national boundaries. For that reason we shall find ourselves having to die to the world's good opinion (2:20; 6:14), as we seek to break down every barrier of ethnicity, class or gender (3:28) within the Church, which is 'the Israel of God' (6:16).

CHAPTER 8

PAUL'S STORY: THESSALONICA

THE STORY BEHIND THE THESSALONIAN LETTERS

The church at Thessalonica was born to trouble. The circumstances that led to the founding of the church are narrated by Luke as follows:

After Paul and Silas had passed through Amphipolis and Apollonia, they came to Thessalonica, where there was a synagogue of the Jews. And Paul went in, as was his custom, and on three sabbath days argued with them from the scriptures, explaining and proving that it was necessary for the Messiah to suffer and to rise from the dead, and saying, 'This is the Messiah, Jesus whom I am proclaiming to you.' Some of them were persuaded and joined Paul and Silas, as did a great many of the devout Greeks and not a few of the leading women. But the Jews became jealous, and with the help of some ruffians in the marketplaces they formed a mob and set the city in an uproar. While they were searching for Paul and Silas to bring them out to the assembly, they attacked Jason's house. When they could not find them, they dragged Jason and some believers before the city authorities, shouting, 'These people who have been turning the world upside down have come here also, and Jason has entertained them as guests. They are all acting contrary to the decrees of the emperor, saying that there is another king named Jesus.' The people and the city officials were disturbed when they heard this, and after they had taken bail from Jason and the others, they let them go.
ACTS 17:1–9 (NRSV)

Paul is on his way from Philippi, where he has been flogged, locked up for the night and asked by the authorities to leave town. Luke is keen to stress that Paul began his mission to Thessalonica in the synagogue, expounding the scriptures to a Jewish audience because,

146

as we have seen, he wants to portray the preaching of the gospel as bringing about the restoration of Israel—but he does not disguise the fact that the positive response came mainly from Gentiles (even if God-fearing ones, 17:4). This agrees with what we learn from Paul's letters. On the one hand, Paul's extensive use of Jewish apocalyptic imagery in relation to the coming of Jesus (1 Thess. 4:13–18; 2 Thess. 2:1–12) suggests the presence of Jewish listeners, but otherwise the impression we get is that the Thessalonian Christians had been mainly pagans, who had 'turned to God from idols' (1 Thess. 1:9).

Paul's message to the Jews, 'Jesus is the Christ', is understood by the Greeks as saying, 'There is another king named Jesus', and this too agrees with the emphasis in these letters. Paul speaks repeatedly of the coming of the Lord, using the Greek word *parousia*, a term often used for the official visit of a person of high rank. It was a message likely to produce a hostile reaction, not only from Jews, who could not accept the idea of a crucified Messiah, but also from native Thessalonians, who were proud of their city's status as a free city within the Roman empire. Accordingly, these letters contain several references to suffering, persecution and the need for steadfastness under trial.

We do not know how long Paul spent establishing the church at Thessalonica. The reference to three Sabbaths tells us how long he was able to preach in the synagogue, but the letters suggest a longer period during which we may suppose that a house church was established and that it gathered to be taught in the house of Jason, a well-to-do convert. Before long, however, Paul was forced to leave Thessalonica also. Acts 17:10—18:4 tells us that he went to Beroea and then to Athens, before finally being able to settle for a reasonable period of time in Corinth. It was apparently while he was still in Athens that word reached him of a disturbing development in Thessalonica. Some people have got the idea that the kingdom of God has already arrived, and others in their enthusiasm have given up work, perhaps expecting the church to support them while they spread the word. There is no reason to think that this was the result of 'false teachers' or visitors to the church. Paul does not attack anyone, as he does in Galatians and 2 Corinthians, though he thinks it possible that they have received a bogus apostolic letter. In fact, it is much more likely to have been a misunderstanding of his own teaching on the part of very young Christians. However it may be, nothing could be more calculated to give the new movement a bad name, and Paul hastily wrote them the letter we know as 2 Thessalonians and sent it back to Thessalonica with Timothy.

THE ORDER OF THE THESSALONIAN LETTERS

There is nothing inherently improbable in the view that the two letters have been placed in the wrong order in our Bibles, although most scholars have rejected it.[1] The titles of New Testament books are not part of the original text (as we saw with the Gospels), being added by church librarians when the books began to be collected together. The traditional order is as likely to be due to the relative length and popularity of the two letters as to any certain knowledge of the date of writing.

Some of the best reasons for reading them in reverse order are as follows. First, of the two, 1 Thessalonians appears the more finished letter both in structure and style. By contrast, 2 Thessalonians looks as if it has been hastily put together and fired off to deal with a sudden crisis. Second, both letters refer to the need for people to work. It is easier to believe that this was the presenting problem, dealt with effectively in 2 Thessalonians and then merely alluded to in 1 Thessalonians ('Now about brotherly love *we do not need to write to you…* Make it your ambition to… work with your hands, *just as we told you*', 1 Thess. 4:9–11), than that Paul wrote briefly about it, only to find the problem getting worse. The reason Paul doesn't need to write about it is that he has done so at length already (2 Thess. 3:6–15).

The same is true, third, of the teaching in the two letters about the day of the Lord. The main problem has been the belief that the day of the Lord is imminent or, indeed, has already come, and Paul deals with this at length in 2 Thessalonians 2:1–12. What he says in 1 Thessalonians is by way of clarification. If the day of the Lord is not so imminent, what will happen to people who die first? They will be safe and we will share their joy. (We do not need to suppose that any Thessalonians had actually died. Paul writes in answer to a question raised by his own teaching that the end is not yet.) Also, just because the day of the Lord is not yet, it doesn't mean that we can relax. On the contrary, Christians should always be ready and watchful, just as Jesus had taught.

Fourth, 1 Thessalonians appears to presuppose that some time has elapsed since the church was founded. There has been time for their story to inspire the new churches of Corinth and Achaia (1 Thess. 1:7–8), which would not even exist if 1 Thessalonians had been written, as is usually thought, a few weeks after Paul left Thessalonica. The church members can be asked to derive encouragement from remembering both their own conversion (1:9–10) and the character of the original mission to them (2:9)—again, not something that would be natural if the events concerned had only recently occurred. Of course, it is impossible to be certain which letter was written first, but I invite you to read them in the order I propose and see what sense it makes.

AN OUTLINE OF 2 THESSALONIANS

You have just planted a church in a city without previous Christian witness. It is a small group of people, meeting in the home of one of the few well-to-do converts. You yourself have been forced to leave sooner than you would have wished, before you have had a chance to finish teaching them or to appoint leaders to carry on the work. The young church is at risk, both from persecution and from error. The authorities are suspicious; neighbours are hostile and quick to inform against it. A stone-throwing mob may at any moment surround the house or harass members on their way to worship. From bitter experience you know that other teachers may gain a hearing from the church or send plausible letters that contradict what you have so painstakingly taught, and now you hear that, in their enthusiasm, some of your little group believe that the day of the Lord is already here, and others are trying to live at the church's expense. You cannot go back to see them, so you write a letter and hope that a nice, inconspicuous fellow like Timothy will be able to deliver it without attracting too much attention. How will such a letter begin?

It will begin with lots of encouragement! Paul begins by saying how he thanks God for them all. It is often said that Paul's letters begin with a prayer of thanksgiving, but this is not quite accurate. They begin with Paul *reporting* his prayers of thanksgiving, and the reason he does this is to tell the church how pleased he is with them, in this case with their faith, love and perseverance under trial (1:3–4). Then he reminds them of the contrasting fate of believers and unbelievers when Jesus comes again (1:5–10). Then he tells them how he prays for them, which is a further encouragement, both in the fact that people are praying for them and in the implied assurance that God will answer prayer, and that those whom he has so obviously chosen, he will not abandon (1:11–12).

Now it is time to tackle the problem of those who think that the day of the Lord has already come. Paul says that that is impossible. Things will have to get much worse before they get better. The Lord will not come until the Antichrist comes and instigates a great rebellion against God. Only then will the Lord come, and only then will evil be finally overthrown. Despite the troubles the church is facing, in reality God is holding back the forces of evil at the present time, presumably so that the gospel can be preached and people have the opportunity to repent and be saved. This is a time for endurance and witness, not premature celebration (2:1–12). (The really difficult verses here are 6 and 7. Nobody is quite sure either what the words refer to or even if they are correctly translated, but I think I have given the overall sense of the passage.)

More encouragement is needed. Paul gives it by reminding the Thessalonians of God's choice and call of them (for which he gives thanks). He calls for them to stand firm and prays for them to do so. He also asks for their prayers, showing that he shares their difficulties and that they can have a significant part to play in his mission, and he models that prayer by praying once more for them to know the love of God and the perseverance of Christ.

Only now is Paul ready to deal with the people who want to live at the church's expense. It clearly concerns only a few of the members, so it cannot be a case of mass hysteria prompted by a belief that the day of the Lord is at hand. They cannot be elderly widows or people who cannot work, because these the church gladly supports. They cannot simply be lazy or work-shy, because these the church would have no inclination to support, and the instruction would be unnecessary.

Most probably, they are self-appointed 'evangelists', possibly itinerant 'prophets' who have left off working to go round spreading the word, and who are imposing on the goodwill of the church's more impressionable members and demanding meals. Hence the relevance of Paul's example: their own missionaries had not claimed the right to live off the church, and neither should these people. To do so places an unfair burden on those who have to feed them and gives the church a bad name. The word Paul uses for 'idle' means literally 'disorderly', and the word he uses for 'busybody' means someone who goes round meddling. They were standard terms of social disapproval in the ancient world. The young church is in enough trouble already without some of its members acquiring the reputation of being idle busybodies.

With a final word of blessing Paul, quite literally, signs off, drawing attention to his signature in a way that suggests that this is the first such letter he has written to them. It is well known that Peter found some things in Paul's letters hard to understand (2 Peter 3:16), and this letter contains its share of those, but the basic message of this letter is clear to the point of bluntness: 'If a man will not work, he shall not eat' (2 Thess. 3:10)!

So Timothy was sent back to Thessalonica, taking with him, we believe, the letter we have just been reading. We do not know how long he was away, but it must have been some time, during which Paul left Athens and moved to Corinth and established a new church there. Eventually Timothy joined him there (1 Thess. 3:6; Acts 18:5), bringing good news. The church had taken Paul's warning to heart. The idlers had returned to work and there was no need to press the point, but the idea that the day of the Lord might not be coming for some time was raising other questions, and the church was still under a lot of pressure from hostile neighbours. So Paul wrote to them, again, a letter full of encouragement and pastoral guidance—the letter we know as 1 Thessalonians.

AN OUTLINE OF 1 THESSALONIANS

The letter falls naturally into two halves, chapters 1—3 forming a sustained encouragement to the church and chapters 4—5 providing instruction on a variety of matters. In the first place, Paul wants them to know that he is pleased with them and confident of their ability to survive and grow despite the difficulties of their situation. He begins by drawing attention to 'your work produced by faith, your labour prompted by love, and your endurance inspired by hope in our Lord Jesus Christ' (1:3). Paul thanks God for these things, but he mentions them as a way of assuring the church of his confidence in them. He then recalls the profound change the gospel made in their lives. They turned to God from idols. They modelled their lives on the example of Paul and of Jesus, and Paul has been able to hold them up as an example to the new churches in Philippi and Corinth (that is, Macedonia and Achaia, 1:8). In all of this, the power of God has been very evident (1:2–10).

That power has been no less evident in the lives of their apostles (2:1–16). The ministry that gave birth to the church was marked by courage (2:2), integrity (2:3–6), hard work and sacrifice (2:7–9), love and gentleness (2:7, 11). Paul is not here defending himself against charges brought by the Thessalonians. If anything, it is the accusations he has faced in Corinth that have given shape to what he says here. In all their difficulties it will help the Thessalonians to recall the character of the apostolic mission and assure themselves that they have not been duped, that they were not wrong to give their trust to these travelling preachers with their strange and subversive message. It really was the word of God (2:13), and if accepting it has got them into severe trouble, they are to know that such trouble has been the lot of all God's messengers, including supremely Jesus himself, and that Paul knows only too well what it is to be rejected by his own countrymen, just as they have been. Paul feels the pain of this acutely and allows his feelings to show (2:15–16). The last sentence of verse 16 is difficult, but probably asserts the imminence of God's judgment on those who consistently reject him.

Finally, the power of God has been confirmed in the report Timothy has brought. Paul explains how his failure to come himself was no reflection of his love for them. On the contrary, he was very worried about them, and since he could not come himself he sent Timothy to them. Now Timothy has brought a most positive report, which Paul is glad to share with them. The first section of the letter ends fittingly with a prayer for their continued growth in love and holiness, which in turn prepares the way for the exhortations to follow (2:17—3:13).

The ethical instructions that follow are quite general, being the sort of thing Paul regularly had to tell his churches by way of reminder, but not reflecting any particular problems in the life of the church (contrast 2 Thess. 3:6–15). They are to live to please God (4:1), avoid sexual immorality (4:3–8), practise brotherly love (4:9–10), and get on with their daily work as previously instructed (4:11–12).

Some further clarification is needed, however, regarding the day of the Lord. If it is not necessarily going to happen immediately, what about those who die first? There is no reason to suppose anyone has actually died, but the Thessalonians have raised the question since, if the day of the Lord is delayed, believers may obviously die first. Paul assures them that the Christian dead will be quite safe. They will rise first, but those who are still alive when the Lord returns will join them (4:13–18). Still, the fact that the day of the Lord is not imminent is no reason for slackness or immoral living. It will come 'like a thief in the night' (5:2), just as Jesus had warned (Matt. 24:43–44). Christians are to live as those who eagerly expect the kingdom of God and practise faith, hope and love as if it were already here (5:1–11), just as the Thessalonians have been doing (1:2).

In his closing remarks, Paul tells the church to respect their leaders (5:12–13), whose presence in comparison with 2 Thessalonians is another sign that we are dealing with a later letter. He then addresses the leaders about their pastoral responsibilities (5:14–15). Finally, he sketches the character of the Christian life as one of joyful thanksgiving and openness to God's Spirit, and commends the church confidently to God's sure keeping.

THE MESSAGE OF THE THESSALONIAN LETTERS, THEN AND NOW

The particular interest of the Thessalonian letters lies in the window they open on Paul's missionary preaching. We tend to think that Paul went around the cities of the Mediterranean world preaching that people are justified by faith and not by observing the law, but this was only a corrective message made necessary where Jewish Christians interfered with his work by demanding that Gentile converts submit to the yoke of the law, as they did in Galatia. It would have made no sense to preach such a message in a city like Thessalonica apart from such interference. Instead, Paul preached that Jesus was Lord, that God had raised him from the dead and inaugurated the last act of human history. 'Jesus has become King!' was the good news that the apostles delivered. 'Submit to him before it is too late!' From these letters it is clear that Paul presented the coming of Jesus in the language of Jewish apocalyptic expectation, with trumpet call, blazing fire, everlasting destruction and clouds of glory, with a full supporting cast of archangels and the 'man of lawlessness'. Although such language and imagery remains precious to many Christians today, not many evangelists employ it in speaking to our secular world. Its absence from Paul's later letters suggests that he too may have found that, in Gentile circles, it raised more problems than it solved. But 'Jesus is Lord and King' remained as the central message, and it is a message that still has power to 'turn the world upside down' (Acts 17:6, NRSV).

CHAPTER 9

PAUL'S STORY: CORINTH (1)

THE STORY BEHIND 1 CORINTHIANS

After the apostolic council at Jerusalem, Acts tells us that Paul set out on what was to become a lengthy expedition lasting as much as two years, which we know as the second missionary journey. He revisited the Galatian churches, no doubt taking with him news of the council's decision, and then headed further west. Finding no opportunity for church planting in Asia Minor, Paul and his team were persuaded to cross over into Europe. Churches were planted in Philippi and Thessalonica, but the missionaries were unable to settle anywhere for long, being forced to move on by the opposition they encountered, until finally they reached Corinth. Here, although there was the usual opposition from elements of the Jewish community, which was split in two by Paul's strange message about a crucified Messiah, the civil power came to his aid in the person of the proconsul, Gallio, who dismissed the charges against Paul. As a result, Paul was able to stay for more than eighteen months, establishing the new church. So much we learn from Luke's account in Acts 15:36 to 18:17.

Corinth was a famous seaport. It was also, in Paul's day, a new town, having been refounded as a Roman colony by Julius Caesar less than a hundred years before. It was prosperous, go-ahead and cosmopolitan, 'a pluralistic melting pot of cultures, philosophies, life-styles and religions... an economic boom town'.[1] Corinth was a lively place and the new Christian congregation seems to have reflected this. The believers were a mixed bunch. There were Jews—including at least two former synagogue rulers, Crispus and Sosthenes—but Greeks too. There were slaves, but also free men and women. Paul says that 'not many of you were wise... powerful... of noble birth' (1:26, NRSV), but clearly some were quite well-to-do. Paul mentions by name Crispus (1:14); the former synagogue ruler, Stephanas, who is mentioned with his household (1:16; 16:15–16), suggesting a person of some means; and Gaius, who, according to Romans 16:23, was able to host the whole church in his house. Romans, which was written from Corinth, also furnishes us with the name of Erastus, a local government official, so there were people of wealth and influence in the church and they brought with them the competitiveness, appreciation of rhetoric, and comfortable lifestyle typical of their class.

Paul wrote 1 Corinthians some two or three years after leaving Corinth to return to Antioch (Acts 18:18–22), but he did not lose contact with the church during this time. He wrote them at least one letter, now lost (1 Cor. 5:9), and the church wrote to him, raising a number of questions that Paul is now answering (7:1; 8:1; 12:1). Other friends brought reports of trouble in the church (1:11), much of which seems to have centred around a man who arrived in Corinth after Paul's departure, namely Apollos. Apollos is described in Acts as an Alexandrian Jew, learned and eloquent. Intentionally or not, he seems to have become the focus for anti-Paul sentiment in Corinth, which split the church. Some favoured Paul, others Apollos (1:12), apparently impressed by his superior learning and eloquence. In the first part of the letter, Paul has to defend his own ministry without directly attacking that of Apollos (3:4–5, 21; 4:6). So, with a letter to answer, worrying signs of immaturity, and a growing faction that rejected his leadership of the church, Paul begins to dictate the letter we know as 1 Corinthians.

THE MESSAGE OF 1 CORINTHIANS

THE THREAT OF DIVISION (1 CORINTHIANS 1—4)

Paul has heard from members of Chloe's household that there are 'quarrels' in the church, with different factions boasting of their allegiance to different leaders and teachers: 'One of you says, "I follow Paul"; another, "I follow Apollos"; another, "I follow Cephas"; still another, "I follow Christ"' (1:12). There is no suggestion in the letter that these divisions were doctrinal. The issue seems rather to have been a matter of style and personality, to judge from the arguments Paul marshals against them, and to have centred around Paul and Apollos. There is no reason to think that Cephas (that is, Peter) was or ever had been in Corinth. Those who said, 'I follow Cephas' were probably Jewish Christians trying to make trouble for Paul by claiming that he had not 'seen Jesus our Lord' in the flesh as Peter and the Jerusalem leaders had done (9:1). It is not known who was saying, 'I belong to Christ', or why, and some have even suggested that this should be read as Paul's rejoinder to those who boasted their human allegiances. Alternatively, Paul may just be adding 'Cephas' and 'Christ' for rhetorical effect so as to deflect attention from himself and Apollos.

Greek culture set a high value on philosophical speculation and on rhetoric, the art of public speaking. There was a ready audience for itinerant teachers of philosophy, provided they delivered their message with elegance and wit. Some at least of the Corinthians prided themselves on being able to identify a good speaker, and in Apollos they thought they had found one. By implication, they accused Paul of lacking depth and style in his preaching. He admits the charge! Indeed, he glories in it! If his preaching lacked 'eloquence or superior wisdom' (2:1) or 'wise and persuasive words' (2:4), this was deliberate. He is the messenger of a God who has displayed his power and glory through something that is ordinarily associated with utter weakness and shame, and confounded human ideas of power and wisdom. Nobody who wanted to save the world would go about it by sending his Son to die on a cross (1:18–25). Come to that, nobody who wanted to save the world would choose people like the Corinthians as his fellow workers (1:26–31). But that is what God has done.

It is impossible to do justice to the Christian message while at the same time trying to acquire a reputation for wisdom and eloquence. It is impossible at one and the same time to glory in the grace 'that saved a wretch like me', as John Newton's hymn puts it, and also in one's own taste and refinement. Of course, properly understood, the Christian message is the profoundest wisdom, but it is not the wisdom of this world and can be understood only with the help of the Spirit of God (2:6–16). Yet this is precisely what the Corinthians, by their quarrelling, show that they lack! (3:1–4).

What, after all, are apostles, and Paul and Apollos in particular? They are only servants, each with a particular responsibility. Like workers on a farm, one plants the seeds and another waters them: neither is more important than the other, and in any case it is God who makes the seeds grow. Similarly, one workman lays the foundation and another builds on it: neither is more important than the other and both are accountable to God for what they do. It is God who gives any success his servants enjoy, and it is God who will test the worth of their work, so the Corinthians should not set themselves up as judges (3:5—4:7).

There is no doubt that the Corinthian church had a rich experience of the power of the Holy Spirit. Paul says that they did not lack any spiritual gift (1:7), and goes on to speak of miracles and healings as well as prophecies and speaking in tongues (12:28). Unfortunately, they lacked the spiritual maturity to handle this experience or to understand what it meant (3:1). Spiritual power easily breeds arrogance in those who are still judging success by the standards of this world, and so it did with the Corinthians. They thought they had arrived (4:8). Rather, they thought that the kingdom had arrived and that they were already reigning with Christ—but this was a misunderstanding. The kingdom has certainly arrived in the sense that, in Jesus, the resurrection has begun, but it is not here yet in its fullness, which is why Paul and his fellow apostles suffer as they do (4:9–13). The powers of the age to come are at work, but the old age is still very much with us. So long as it lives in this 'already and not yet' situation, the church will experience pain as well as power, death as well as life. Failure to realize this gives people an inflated idea of their own power and holiness, and leads them to pass dismissive judgments on those who are suffering persecution for the cross of Christ. This may be seen as the fundamental error lying behind many of the problems Paul encountered in this young church.

Paul ends this section with a personal appeal for the Corinthians' loyalty. He is their father, someone to whom they owe their very existence as a church, and they should respect him and imitate him. They should also remember that a father's love may need to show itself in discipline (4:14–21).

IMMORALITY AND LITIGATION (1 CORINTHIANS 5—6)

The Corinthians are confident of their spirituality, but in fact they have little to be proud of. They have tolerated an irregular union between a man and his stepmother (5:1). We cannot be sure, but it is likely that the man in question was a member of the church's social elite (which is why he was not disciplined). Paul is outraged, and directs that the church should meet as the body of Christ, empowered by his Spirit, and put the man out of the fellowship until such time as he repents. He reinforces this demand by reference to the Old Testament practice of ridding the house of leaven before celebrating the Passover (5:7). Christ is our Passover lamb, and the church as his household is to be pure. Paul had written to the Corinthians about this before, telling them not to associate with immoral people, but they had misunderstood him. He was not telling them to cut themselves off from the world, but to refuse to countenance immorality within the church.

Paul believes that the church should live by different standards from those of the world around. This becomes clear from the way he handles the next problem. The Corinthians (again, presumably the wealthier members) have been resorting to litigation in the city courts instead of letting the church decide between them (6:1). Paul has nothing against the city courts as such. He had every reason to be grateful for Gallio's help when the Jews took him to court, but he will not have missed the note of contempt for religious quarrels in the proconsul's verdict (Acts 18:12–17). Yet such behaviour shames the church, both because such disputes exist among Christians and because the church cannot sort them out. Paul sees the church as fully competent to arbitrate, and those who confess Jesus as Lord should not be going to law in the first place (6:7; Matt. 5:40). The gospel enables and demands a clean break with the old way of life (6:9–11).

As a final example, Paul returns to the problem of sexual immorality. Apparently some of the Corinthians are continuing to resort to prostitutes and justifying this with the slogan, 'Everything is permissible for me' (6:12). It is likely that this is another example of the Corinthians' misunderstanding of Paul's teaching. No doubt Paul had come to them fresh from telling the Galatians that 'it is for freedom that Christ has set us free' (Gal. 5:1). Such a message might spell liberation for those under the yoke of the law, but in a place like

Corinth it was asking for trouble! *Not* everything is permissible. Perhaps, too, they had a typically Greek contempt for the body as compared to the soul. If so, Paul needs to remind them that they belong, in body as well as soul, to the Lord who bought them. God lives in their bodies by his Spirit, making them members of Christ himself and temples of the Holy Spirit, and in the coming kingdom they will be raised to life in bodies transformed by God's power. The conclusion is plain: 'Honour God with your body' (6:20).

SEX, MARRIAGE AND SINGLENESS (1 CORINTHIANS 7)

Paul now turns to problems raised by the Corinthians in their letter to him. Their basic concern seems to have been whether marriage is compatible with life in the Spirit. It was widely believed in the ancient world, and not just among Jews and Christians, that in order to have communion with God a person needed to abstain from sex—to fast, in fact, and not just from food. It is easy to see why, in the heady spiritual atmosphere of the Corinthian church, some people might interpret Paul's call to 'honour God with your body' to mean abstinence even within marriage—that married people might do well to dissolve their marriages in order to concentrate on the things of the Spirit (especially if their partner were not a believer) and that single people should not get married at all. Surely Paul, with his celibate lifestyle, would agree?

Paul is sympathetic to their concerns, but also realistic. It is not realistic for married people to give up sex. In their letter the Corinthians had written, 'It is good for a man not to have sexual relations with a woman' (7:1). The verse does not refer to marriage but to sex, and it does not give Paul's opinion but the Corinthians' view as expressed in their letter. (As we have seen, Paul quotes the Corinthians' opinion in 6:12, and he will do so again in 8:1.) Paul's reply is clear. Married people should give to one another their conjugal rights. Abstinence for the sake of prayer is permitted, but only for a short time (7:2–6). Paul may be called to celibacy, but most people are not (7:7–9). Those who are married should stay married, according to the Lord's instructions, and that applies even when the other partner is an unbeliever, unless the unbeliever refuses to remain in the marriage (7:10–16).

The underlying principle here is that people should stay where they are. No doubt there were Corinthians who said, 'If only my circumstances were different, I could serve God better. If only I were not married! If only I were not a slave!' Paul says that circumstances that cannot be changed must be accepted as a calling from God. Marriages contracted before conversion may not be abandoned in search of a deeper spiritual life. Getting circumcised will not bring you nearer to God. Even slavery makes no fundamental difference to a person's spiritual state or capacity, and emancipation, though desirable, will not change that. God is with you where you are; stay where you are *with God* (7:17–24).

In the rest of the chapter Paul addresses single people. They are free to marry, but should they do so? Paul makes it clear that he is only giving his own opinion, but he thinks that they too should be in no hurry to change their situation. There are two reasons for this. First, he expects that the Lord is coming back soon, and the days before his return are likely to be times of trouble. This is no time to be taking on family responsibilities. Second, unmarried people do have more time for serving the Lord, and this is not to be disregarded. (That marriage might double a person's effectiveness in Christian service is not something Paul considers!) So even engaged people might consider putting off their marriage, but once again Paul is realistic: 'If his passions are strong, and so it has to be, let him marry as he wishes; it is no sin' (7:36, NRSV). Widows similarly are free to marry, but Paul would discourage this (but compare 1 Tim. 5:14).

Paul's advice is not fashionable today, but then the situation he is addressing is not common either. Not many Christians today contemplate giving up sex and marriage for the sake of drawing near to God. Viewed against the background of such extreme ideas, the advice Paul gives in this chapter might seem a model of wisdom and moderation.

IDOLATRY AND FREEDOM (1 CORINTHIANS 8—10)

This section of the letter too is prompted by a question asked by the Corinthians. What about food that has been sacrificed to idols? May we eat it? And if we are free to do so, should we make use of this freedom? It becomes plain on examination that there are two different situations in view. There is food served in the restaurants attached to temples, and there is food sold in the marketplace, and Paul gives different answers in each case.[2]

Temples provided the Greek city with many of its restaurants. Meat sacrificed in the temple would subsequently appear on the menu downstairs. The problem for Christians was that those who ate in the temple restaurant were deemed to be the guests of the god whose temple it was. For this reason, Paul warns them off eating in such places. Idolatry caused Israel to fall, and it could cause them to fall too. If eating Christ's bread at the Lord's Supper makes us participants in Christ, eating in a temple will make us participants with demons (10:1–22).

On the other hand, food sold in the marketplace presents no problems, even if it has most probably been killed with prayers to a pagan god. The Christian is not bound to enquire whether this is so or not, but may eat it with thanksgiving to God (10:23–26).

Yet there is another issue here. Once again, it was probably the well-to-do who cherished the freedom to eat meat, whether from the temple or the market, because they could afford it. They were probably better educated and, as such, saw only too well that the logic of Paul's message was that an idol is nothing, the supposed gods did not exist, and so there was no reason why a Christian should go in fear of them or pay them any respect. As they said, 'We all possess knowledge' (8:1). But Paul knows that not all the Corinthians had this knowledge. Many were simple folk, imperfectly emancipated from the fear of idols and the gods that stood behind them. Such people would need to make a complete break with idolatry, and could easily be led back into it if they saw more liberated Corinthians eating in the temples, or even if they were told that the food on the table had earlier been offered in sacrifice. So Paul insists that love is more important than the knowledge of which they are so proud, and love will lead them to limit their freedom voluntarily for the sake of the 'weak' brother or sister (8:1–13). He then digresses from the topic of meat offered to idols to show that he himself, though an apostle, voluntarily limits his own freedom for the sake of others' salvation, and this is what being a Christian is all about (9:1–27; 10:31—11:1).

PROBLEMS IN THE MEETING (1 CORINTHIANS 11—14)

It is convenient to lump these chapters together because the problems they deal with all relate to things that went on when the church met for worship. From another point of view, though, the problems of chapter 11 are closely connected with what precedes, since they too are all about the voluntary limitation of freedom.

Women in Paul's churches are free to pray and prophesy. That is not in dispute. Some of them, however, are doing so with their heads uncovered and perhaps with their hair loosed. That is not culturally acceptable. Some of what Paul says here is difficult to understand, but the main point is clear enough: women who pray or prophesy in the meetings should be decently dressed according to the notions of that time and place. The new freedom that the gospel has brought is not to be abused (11:2–16).

The second matter concerns the abuse of the Lord's Supper (11:17–34). Once again Paul speaks of divisions, but these are not divisions over personalities, still less over doctrine. It is rather that the Corinthians are maintaining social distinctions between the richer and poorer members.[3] Some are starting to eat before others arrive. Some are overindulging to the point of drunkenness, while others are going hungry. The poorer members are being treated with utter contempt. If we ask how such things could be happening at a celebration of the Lord's Supper, we need to bear in mind three things. One, the Supper was part of a real meal and not just a liturgical event. Two, the church met in a private home. Three, it was quite normal in Roman society (and Corinth was a Roman colony) for the rich to entertain large numbers of people while preserving social distinctions, entertaining their social equals more lavishly than mere 'hangers on'. When the church met in the house of Gaius, it would have been all too easy for people to sit with their friends and fall back into observing social customs and distinctions.

Paul will have none of it, however, and rebukes them sharply. He reminds them of the sacred nature of the occasion and the true purpose of their coming together (11:23–26). In holding the poorer members in contempt, they are despising the Lord who has saved them by his blood, and failing to recognize that the Church is nothing less than his body (11:27–29). God will not overlook such sacrilege and, in fact, the church has already begun to experience his judgment (11:30–32). To avoid this, they need to examine themselves with a view to repenting of their worldly attitudes. They should welcome one another as equals when they meet together as a church. Those who wish to eat more or better than others should do so in the privacy of their own homes (11:33–34). It is likely that the kind of problem Paul deals with here, and the advice he gives, were one of the reasons that, before long, the Lord's Supper came to be separated from the fellowship meal.

Paul now turns to deal at some length with a matter that had apparently been raised by the Corinthians themselves in their letter— 'spiritual gifts' (12:1). As often in Paul's letters, the nature of the problem emerges only gradually. This is partly because the church knew what he was talking about without being told, and partly because Paul tends to begin by stating the spiritual principle at stake before giving practical directives.[4] In this case, it becomes plain that the problem concerns the misuse of glossolalia, or 'speaking in tongues', in the church meeting. Apparently this practice was highly prized by some of the Corinthians as the mark of true spirituality, but its unrestrained use in the meeting led to disorder (14:23, 40).

Paul proposes three tests that all speech in church must pass, to be acceptable. The first is the test of Christian orthodoxy (12:1–3). In a world full of cults and occult practices, it is not enough for somebody to claim inspiration, however impressive or apparently supernatural their delivery. What is the content of their message? Does it proclaim Jesus as Lord?

Before going on to the other tests, Paul explains the nature and purpose of the Spirit's work in the Church. He begins with a redefinition of terms, which is not always picked up in our English translations. The Corinthians had asked about *pneumatika* (12:1), meaning manifestations of spiritual power. When Paul answers, he talks about *charismata* (12:4), meaning manifestations of the grace of God. If everything we possess or are enabled to do is a gift of grace, we have nothing to boast about. God's grace is infinitely varied, being seen in all sorts of Christian activity, spectacular and humdrum, so one is not more spiritual or important than another. Every spiritual gift is given to benefit the Church as a whole, and anything that benefits the Church as a whole is a spiritual gift. The Church is the body of

Christ and, like a body, it consists of many different parts. All are needed, and none is to be despised. If, in practice, some parts of the body are more vital than others, then in the body of Christ it is those who bring the word of God in intelligible speech who come first— apostles, prophets and teachers (12:28). Speaking in tongues is listed last (12:10, 30)!

The second test is the test of love. Love is more important than anything else in the Church, and without love, no ability or activity is of any worth (13:1–3). And what is love? Paul describes it: 'Love is patient, love is kind. It does not envy, it does not boast, it is not proud…' (13:4–7). If some ability in the Church leads to boasting and division, it is not being correctly exercised. In the justly famous thirteenth chapter of 1 Corinthians, Paul compares love to the things the Corinthians prided themselves on possessing—prophecy, tongues, knowledge—and tells them that (unlike these) love is the only thing they will take with them into the coming age of the kingdom.

When dealing with the debate over food offered to idols, Paul had said, 'Knowledge puffs up, but love builds up' (8:1). Accordingly, the third test Paul proposes is that of edification, or upbuilding. Does an activity build up other church members in faith, hope and love? If not, it has no place in the church meeting. If the test of spirituality is love, and the test of love is upbuilding, then the test of upbuilding is intelligibility. What I do not understand (a sermon in a foreign language, for example), cannot benefit me. So prophecy is greatly to be preferred to glossolalia precisely because it can be understood. Glossolalia needs interpretation and without this should be exercised in private (14:1–19). Nor is it just a matter of the needs of insiders. The church needs to consider the effect of its meetings on visiting unbelievers. If everybody speaks in tongues, the outsider will think them mad, but if someone brings a message from God in plain speech there is every chance that the visitor will be converted (14:23–25). It is not just a question of intelligibility; it is also a question of orderliness. People should speak one at a time, and politely give way to one another, 'for God is not a God of disorder but of peace' (14:33).[5]

WAITING FOR GOD'S FUTURE (I CORINTHIANS 15)

At first sight, this long discussion of the resurrection of the dead might seem to have nothing to do with what has gone before, and we are surprised to find it here. But in fact it has everything to do with what has gone before and, by addressing the underlying error in the Corinthians' thinking, serves to tie the various topics of this long letter together. The Corinthians denied the resurrection of the dead, not just because, as Greeks, they found the idea ridiculous (though they did, 15:35), but because they believed that, in the only sense worth talking about, it had happened already. They believed that the kingdom of God had already come in its fullness and that they were already in it (4:8). Through the indwelling of the Spirit, they were already immortal and spoke the language of the angels (13:1). It is this that lies at the root of their arrogance, their contempt for their struggling apostle, and their loveless disregard of people less well-endowed than themselves.

It is important to remember that, for Paul, with his Jewish heritage, the resurrection of the dead is not simply a way of speaking about life after death or the immortality of the soul. It is not something that happens to individuals when they die. It is a future event, something that God is going to do for the whole world, to restore the world to what it ought to be and to vindicate his honour and the honour of those who have waited for him and believed in him. What distinguishes the faith of Paul and the other early Christians is that they believed that this great event had actually begun with Jesus. The kingdom of God, which is another way of speaking of the age to come, has broken into present time. Jesus is the firstfruits of a mighty harvest, and the rest of the harvest cannot be long delayed. *But it hasn't happened yet!* Paul knows that while the resurrection has begun with Jesus, it has not yet happened to anyone else. This means that, as Christians, we are still waiting for God to complete his work of renewal in us and in the world. This should make us humble and realistic about what we are and what we can expect.

Paul begins by establishing common ground with the Corinthians. They believe, do they not, that Christ has been raised from the dead? This was the centre of the gospel they have received and is well-attested as a fact of history (15:1–11). If this were not so, there would be no Christian faith and no hope for anyone (15:12–19). However, since it is so, the rest is sure to follow. Christ will come, the dead will be raised, death itself will be destroyed, and the whole world will be restored to reflect the loving intention of its maker (15:20–28). Of course, in speaking of resurrection we do not mean that everyone will be dug up, so to speak, to resume the life they had before! Resurrection will mean transformation. Just as the seed is transformed into the fully grown plant, so we shall be changed to participate in God's new world order. We shall not be disembodied spirits, but our bodies will be spiritual bodies (15:35–50). But this is for the future; we are not there yet; and as Paul was to say to the Romans, 'If we hope for what we do not yet have, we wait for it patiently' (Rom. 8:25). This is what the Corinthians must learn to do too (15:58).

PRACTICAL MATTERS (1 CORINTHIANS 16)

Like the announcements in church following a great sermon, the rest of the letter comes as something of an anti-climax. Paul gives some sensible advice about the administration of the great collection he is organizing for the church in Jerusalem. He tells them of his travel plans, commends Timothy to them, and refers warmly to Apollos, making clear that there is no personal animosity between the two men. He affirms Stephanas and his family as leaders of the church in Corinth, and passes on the greetings of the churches in Asia, especially those of Aquila and Priscilla, who played such an important part, with Paul, in establishing the church in Corinth. He ends with the watchword of the Aramaic-speaking churches: 'Maranatha! Come, O Lord!'

THE OUTCOME OF 1 CORINTHIANS

FOR PAUL

The situation got worse before it got better! As we shall see, a Jewish Christian counter-mission arrived in Corinth and gained a hearing among some of the people who were giving Paul such trouble. Paul made an unsuccessful visit to Corinth in an attempt to deal with the matter and had to retreat. He wrote to them at least twice more before matters were resolved.

FOR US

Although different from us in many ways, the Corinthians' problems were very much like ours. They lived in a materialistic, competitive society that knew nothing of the God of Israel or the Jewish Scriptures. They wrestled with how to maintain their own boundaries while still being relevant to the society round about them. They struggled to hold together in one church people of different social backgrounds. They were confused about sex, and about charismatic powers. Who isn't?

CHAPTER 10

PAUL'S STORY: EPHESUS

THE LETTERS FROM PRISON

At least three of Paul's letters were written when he was in prison—the letters to Philemon, the Colossians and the Philippians—and with these we shall also look at the letter to the Ephesians, although it is not certain either for whom this letter was originally intended or even who wrote it.

Paul was in prison when he wrote these letters.[1] So much is clear. But where and when was he in prison? The traditional answer, still given by a majority of scholars, is that these letters were written from Rome in the closing years of his life and that the imprisonment is that described by Luke at the end of Acts. The view that I wish to put forward, however, is that Paul is in prison in Ephesus and that the letters should be dated to the three-year period Paul spent in Ephesus during the so-called third missionary journey described in Acts 19.

It is true that Luke says nothing about Paul being in prison during this time, but as we noted, Luke covers this significant period of Paul's life with three short stories—the story of the Ephesian disciples who received the Holy Spirit, the story of the Jewish exorcists, and the riot in the theatre. Not much for three years' ministry! There is plenty of room here for an imprisonment, and reason to think that Luke may have told us less than he knew, perhaps for the same reason he tells us nothing of Paul's final trial and execution. He does not want to portray Paul as a troublemaker. Certainly Paul had troubles while he was in Ephesus, for he alludes to them in very strong language in a letter written shortly after he left Ephesus:

We do not want you to be unaware, brothers and sisters, of the affliction we experienced in Asia; for we were so utterly, unbearably crushed that we despaired of life itself. Indeed, we felt that we had received the sentence of death so that we would rely not on ourselves but on God who raises the dead.
2 CORINTHIANS 1:8–9 (NRSV)

We do not know what happened, but it is not unlikely that Paul's afflictions included imprisonment and that the sentence of death he escaped is the same as the one he is contemplating in Philippians 1:21. We do not need to think of a long period of imprisonment. People were not generally sentenced to prison as a punishment in the Roman world. They were remanded in custody prior to a trial, but given the arbitrary nature of Roman justice, this would be a time of uncertain length and great danger.[2]

What makes the idea of an Ephesian imprisonment attractive is the sense it makes of the travels described in two of the prison letters, Philemon and Philippians. In Philemon, the slave Onesimus has made his way to Paul and is now being sent back. Paul himself hopes to follow soon and asks that a guest room be prepared for him. It is easier to think of Onesimus making the hundred-mile journey from Colossae to Ephesus than to suppose that he travelled over 800 miles (which would take him probably two months); and why would Paul, if released from prison in Rome, be planning to go to Colossae? Similarly, in Philippians, the church hears that Paul is in prison, Epaphroditus is sent by the Philippians to Paul, news of his illness travels back to Philippi, Paul hears that the Philippians are anxious about him and so on. It is much easier to think of all this coming and going taking place between Philippi and Ephesus than between Philippi and Rome. Paul, then, has run into serious trouble in Ephesus and is in prison awaiting a trial and possible execution. While there, he has a visitor by the name of Onesimus.

ONESIMUS' STORY

Onesimus was the slave of a man called Philemon, one of the leaders of the church in Colossae, and in whose house the young church met for worship (Philemon 2). We do not know for sure how and why Onesimus came to visit Paul. Traditionally, it has been thought that he was a runaway slave, and that it was this that had landed him in prison himself, but there are difficulties with this view. If that were the case, how would he have come into contact with Paul, and how would Paul have had authority to send Onesimus back to Philemon, or anywhere else, for that matter? It is more likely that Onesimus has travelled to Ephesus to seek out Paul, as a friend of his master, to enlist his help in interceding with Philemon. What we do know is that he was in some kind of trouble, since Paul writes, 'If he has done you any wrong or owes you anything, charge it to me' (v. 18). If Onesimus is a runaway slave, these words hardly do justice to the seriousness of the situation, but it is established that a slave in trouble with his master might seek the help of someone to intercede for him.

The other thing we know is that, while he was with Paul, Onesimus became a Christian through Paul's witness (as Philemon had done before him, v. 19), since Paul speaks of him as 'my son Onesimus, who has become my son while I was in chains' (v. 10). Paul would have liked to keep Onesimus with him as an assistant of some kind, but in fact he sends him back to Philemon for two reasons. One is that Onesimus and Philemon should be reconciled as Christian brothers. The other is that Philemon will be able to release Onesimus into Paul's service (which will probably entail his emancipation from slavery) of his own free will, and not under compulsion.

THE MESSAGE OF PHILEMON

Philemon, as we have seen, is the letter Paul wrote and gave to Onesimus to smooth the way for him. It begins with the usual greeting, addressed both to Philemon and the church, which makes it plain that although the letter is a personal letter, it is not a private letter, and that reconciliation between two Christians is of concern to the whole church (vv. 1–3). Paul goes on to commend Philemon for his faith and love and expresses the hope that this faith and love will once again bear fruit in practical Christian service (vv. 4–7). Then follows the body of the letter (vv. 8–22), which is an appeal on behalf of Onesimus and a delicately expressed request that he be received 'no longer as a slave, but... as a dear brother' (v. 16), and allowed to return to Paul as a free man That is probably what Paul means by suggesting that Philemon will do 'even more than I ask' (v. 21). The word Paul uses for such a fine expression of Christian generosity is 'refreshment'. Philemon has refreshed the hearts of his fellow Christians in the past (v. 7), and Paul is confident that he will do so again (v. 20). It is worth pondering the idea that generosity and reconciliation affect the whole Church like a cool drink on a hot day.

The immediate outcome of this letter was presumably the reconciliation of Philemon and Onesimus, and perhaps the emancipation of the latter. The letter would hardly have survived had Philemon hardened his heart and refused Paul's request. Its significance for us two thousand years later is the practical demonstration it gives of the power of the gospel to change lives and to break down the sinful structures of society. Some people are disappointed that Paul's condemnation of slavery is not more radical and explicit, but it can be more costly to confront sin in one's own immediate circle than to issue sweeping denunciations. The story of Onesimus shows that Paul's slogan, 'There is neither slave nor free, for you are all one in Christ Jesus' (Gal. 3:28), was not empty rhetoric.

At the same time as he wrote to Philemon, Paul wrote also a general letter of exhortation and encouragement to the young church in Colossae, of which he has heard from Epaphras, the man who first preached the gospel there.

THE COLOSSIANS' STORY

The close connection between the letters to the Colossians and Philemon is shown by the number of names common to both letters. Both letters mention the return of Onesimus, both send a message to Archippus, and the same five people join Paul in sending greetings—Epaphras, Mark, Aristarchus, Demas and Luke. The Colossian Christians lived in a small town in the Lycus valley in south-west Asia Minor, about a hundred miles from Ephesus. They had become Christians through the work of Epaphras, one of Paul's co-workers, during Paul's stay in Ephesus. Similar congregations came into being in the neighbouring towns of Hierapolis and Laodicea (Col. 4:13). Evidently Paul's strategy was to make Ephesus the centre from which the surrounding area could be evangelized, and Luke tells us that in this way 'all the Jews and Greeks who lived in the province of Asia heard the word of the Lord' (Acts 19:10). The church of Colossae was thus a new congregation, probably not very large, and well able to fit into Philemon's house.

It is commonly held that, at some point after the formation of the Colossian church, 'false teachers' infiltrated the fellowship, bringing with them another gospel whose effect was to deny the centrality and sufficiency of Christ. The only evidence for this is, of course, the letter itself, and scholars have tried to define the 'Colossian heresy' by reference to the warnings Paul gives. Unfortunately this has yielded no agreement as to its nature. Some note the reference to the worship of angels (2:18) and conclude that it must be some form of Gnosticism; others point to the reference to circumcision (2:11) and think it must be essentially Jewish. Still others wonder whether there was any Colossian heresy or any infiltration of the church at all.[3]

This last view seems the most likely. The tone of the letter is peaceful and positive. Paul gives thanks for the church's firm faith (1:3; 2:5). You have only to compare the tone of Galatians to see the difference. There, 'another gospel' has gained a hearing and Paul is so angry that he has no time to include any thanksgiving at all before launching his attack. He says he is 'at my wits' end about you' (Gal. 4:20, REB). How different is Colossians, with its emphasis on thankfulness (seven mentions in all) and its steady encouragement to perseverance and faith (2:6–7).

So if there has been no infiltration of the church, what is Paul doing in this letter and why is he doing it? He is writing a letter of pastoral encouragement to a young church he has not visited and warning them against a danger that is ever present but which has not, as yet, become pressing. The Colossians did not live in a vacuum. There were sects and cults all around them, but above all there were synagogues in every town and neighbours who professed the ancient Jewish faith and might be keen to steer the new Christians into their own community. It is Judaism that is the danger. That is why Paul includes an extended meditation that portrays Christ in the terms that Jewish people used for the wisdom embodied in the law (1:15–20). That is why the Colossians must be told that they do not need to be circumcised or keep the Sabbath or submit to the Jewish rules about food and drink. And the worship of angels? Well, Judaism had a lot to say about angels, as we shall see.

So the Colossians' story is an uneventful one. There were no visitors and no crisis of faith. A recently founded church is being warned of possible danger and encouraged to continue in the course laid out for them by the excellent Epaphras. Like 'the dog in the night' in the Sherlock Holmes' story, Paul is not barking, and that is how we know there is no intruder!

THE MESSAGE OF COLOSSIANS

The letter to the Colossians falls into four main sections. First there is a long introduction, including thanksgiving and prayer, aimed at establishing goodwill on the part of the readers, helping them to know who they are in Christ, and introducing the author and his work (1:1—2:5). Then the basic theme of the letter is stated in two short verses: 'Just as you received Christ Jesus as Lord, continue to live in him…' (2:6–7). The third section consists of an exhortation warning of dangers to avoid and goals to pursue (2:8—4:6), and the letter is rounded off with an extensive section of greetings, which again helps to establish trust between the readers and the author (4:7–18).

THE INTRODUCTION (COLOSSIANS 1:1—2:5)

After an initial greeting, this section falls into three sub-sections: Paul's thanks (1:3–8), Paul's prayer (1:9–23) and Paul's work (1:24—2:5). Paul thanks God for the church, specifically for their faith and love. Faith and love spring from hope, hope is conveyed by the worldwide gospel, and the gospel is the message preached to them by Epaphras. In telling them how he thanks God for them, Paul is paying them a compliment. By saying how the gospel is bearing fruit in all the world, he assures this new, small congregation that they are part of something

well-established and significant. The commendation of Epaphras
further assures them that the faith they have received is the real thing.

By reporting his prayer for them, Paul accomplishes a similar
pastoral purpose. What he prays for them to know, he also teaches
them so that they will know it. Paul prays for knowledge and understanding as the best prophylactic against error, but it is not a merely
theoretical knowledge. It is a knowledge that leads to good work, great
endurance and ceaseless thanks. They are to know that they have
been redeemed and so they are fully qualified as members of God's
worldwide family through Christ (cf. 2:18 'Let no one disqualify
you...'). For who, after all, is Christ? 'He is the image of the invisible
God, the firstborn over all creation...' (1:15), and with these words
Paul launches into a magnificent statement of the supremacy and
sufficiency of Christ. It falls into two carefully balanced parts. The first
describes Christ as 'the firstborn over all creation' and says that all
things were created by him and hold together in him (1:15–17). The
second describes him 'the firstborn from among the dead' and says
that all things were reconciled—that is, restored to their proper
relationship to God, through his life, death and resurrection
(1:18–20). And they are included: 'Once you were alienated from
God... But now he has reconciled you' (1:21–22). The purpose of his
prayer is that they will continue in this faith, firmly holding on to the
gospel he has preached to them.

The words of this great passage (1:15–20) make perfect sense as
they stand, but we shall get a better understanding of what Paul is
doing here if we remember that, in the Old Testament, it is humanity
that is the image of the invisible God (Gen. 1:26). Wisdom is the
firstborn of creation (Prov. 8:22), and Jewish sages had taught that
Wisdom had taken up residence in Israel and was embodied in the
law. Paul, by contrast, is saying that Jesus is the image of God and in
him humanity is being restored, and that the wisdom of God is
embodied in Christ, so there is no need to look to the law to complete
what they began when they put their faith in him.

Having reminded his readers who they are in Christ, Paul goes on
to introduce himself and his work as an apostle of Christ. He is a
servant both of the gospel (1:23) and of the Church (1:25), and that
is why he suffers as he does. Why is he in prison? He is sharing in
Christ's sufferings (1:24), taking his share, and more than his share,

of the hardships the Church must bear as it continues the work of Christ in the world and discharges the ministry of reconciliation. He has a special commission to bring to all nations God's open secret, which he sums up in the words, 'Christ in you, the hope of glory' (1:27). That is to say, God is in Christ, Christ is in you, and this means eternal life, not just for the people of one nation but for all the peoples of the world. Such a commission requires and receives Paul's total commitment and energy as he seeks to build up believers in their faith and ensure that the Church grasps the whole truth of the gospel of God (1:28—2:5).

THE THEME OF THE LETTER (COLOSSIANS 2:6–7)

Before he delivers the warnings and instructions that make up most of the rest of the letter, Paul states the purpose of his writing. 'So then, just as you received Christ Jesus as Lord, continue to live in him, rooted and built up in him, strengthened in the faith as you were taught, and overflowing with thankfulness' (2:6–7). The Christian message had been carried like the baton in a relay race, passed from one runner to another until Epaphras had passed it to them. They had confessed Jesus as Lord when they were baptized and now they must live in him as he lives in them. Piling up metaphors, Paul wants them to be 'well rooted like a tree, solidly built like a house, confirmed and settled like a legal document, and overflowing like a jug full of wine'![4]

THE EXHORTATION (COLOSSIANS 2:8—4:6)

Dangers to avoid (2:8–23)

Young Christians want to learn and to grow in their faith, and this makes them vulnerable. Paul knew from bitter experience that his spiritual children could be kidnapped by persuasive people who would take advantage of their immaturity and openness to new ideas to lead them into something that might look like progress but which Paul sees as a backward step. The danger in this case comes from

Judaism, which may present itself as deep and divine, but which Paul sees as hollow and human, just another religion among the many religions of the world that find their completion in Christ (2:8–10).

People will urge the males among them to be circumcised, but this is unnecessary. They have already been 'circumcised' in a far more profound way when they were baptized. In that rite they said goodbye to their old life with all its sinful associations, and entered on a new life, strengthened by the same power that raised Christ from the dead. They had been under sentence of death, but now they have received a royal pardon. The law brought only the knowledge of sin and indebtedness, but Christ has paid the bill and wiped the slate clean. All nations and religions enslave their peoples with demands for obedience and the fear of punishment, Jewish religion no less than others, but Christ has disarmed the spiritual powers that stand behind culture and religion by his death on the cross, and no one who believes in him needs to submit to any other control or direction (2:11–15). The thought is the same as in Galatians 4:8–10.

Similarly, there is no need for the Colossians to observe the Jewish food laws or the regulations for keeping the Sabbath (2:16–17). Why not? In the first place, these things have been superseded by the coming of Christ. To the Galatians, Paul had said that the law was a child-minder designed for our immaturity (Gal. 3:24), but now that Christ has come its provisions are unnecessary. Here he says that those provisions are a shadow of the things that were to come. They are like an illustrated holiday brochure: when you arrive at your destination, you do not spend your time looking at the pictures in the brochure. You enjoy the view. Now that you have Christ in you (1:27), you do not need the things that prepared people for his coming.

First-century Jews made much of the tradition that the law had been given by angels (see Acts 7:53; Gal. 3:19), and they used this as an additional reason why people should submit to its demands. Paul sarcastically calls such people angel worshippers (2:18). Christians should worship Christ alone. Some strands of Judaism claimed to be able to transport their adherents to heaven and give them visions of the glory of God. This is probably what lies behind the very obscure reference to going into great detail 'about what he has seen' (2:18). Paul is wary of such claims. They foster pride, and they distract people from Christ who, as the head of his body, the Church, is the true source of its growth to maturity. Asceticism, much prized by visionaries of all religious traditions, is much more likely to produce arrogance than holiness. True holiness comes from being united with Christ in his death and resurrection (2:20–23).

Goals to pursue (3:1—4:6)

Having warned the Colossians off things that he sees as false friends and blind alleys, Paul now explains what it means to live in the Christ whom they have received as Lord (2:6). The first step is to be clear about what they want. 'Set your hearts on things above' (3:1): holiness is a matter of ambition. 'Set your minds on things above' (3:2): holiness is a matter of thinking straight, being clear about the reality of God and Christ, his present indwelling and future coming.

Then there are habits to get rid of like worn-out clothes—sexual sins and inordinate desires (3:5–7), and social sins that destroy community, aggressive behaviour, deceitful behaviour and discrimination based on racial or social differences (3:8–11).

Next, there are habits to put on like new clothes, qualities that build and preserve community—compassion, kindness, humility, gentleness and patience and, when these are not perfectly present, a willingness to forgive and, above all, love. The Christian community is to be marked by peace, wisdom, joyful praise and thankfulness.

These attractive qualities are not just for Sundays, when the church is meeting and we put on our best face, so to speak. They are qualities for everyday use. We are to take them home and put them on there too—wives and husbands, children and parents, slaves and masters, living Christ's way not only in ideal homes but in the homes they actually have. Some people are disappointed that Paul's instructions are not more radical, but if Christ is introduced into every relationship, as he is here, those relationships will change. The letter to Philemon shows just how this might happen.

Finally, there is a call to prayer, especially prayer for Paul as he makes his witness in prison, and a call for the readers to make their testimony too by wise and gracious conversation.

FINAL GREETINGS (COLOSSIANS 4:7–18)

The final greetings are surprisingly long, when you remember that Paul and the Colossians had never met—but that is the point! Naming these mutual friends and passing on their greetings strengthens the links between the author and his readers and emphasizes that they are all part of one big family. So ends this encouraging letter. If we want to sum up its message in one sentence, we could take words from chapter 3, verse 11: 'Christ is all, and is in all.'

ANOTHER LETTER FROM PRISON

About the same time as he wrote Colossians, Paul also wrote his letter to the Philippians. There are strong similarities. If Colossians sounds a persistent note of thanksgiving, Philippians rings with joy. Both letters base their exhortations on the figure of Christ, described in stanzas of great power and beauty (compare Col. 1:15–20 with Phil. 2:6–11), and both warn against the insidious threat from Judaism (compare Col. 2:8–23 with Phil. 3:2–11). But there are differences. Philippians is a much more intimate letter—naturally enough, given the long and warm friendship between Paul and that church—and besides, he has a gift to thank them for (4:10–19).

THE MESSAGE OF PHILIPPIANS

The letter begins, like many of Paul's letters, with an expression of Paul's confidence in the church, expressed as a list of their attributes for which Paul gives thanks, and his concern for them, expressed as a report of his prayer for their growth in grace (1:1–11). Then he reassures them that his own situation as a prisoner facing an uncertain outcome is no cause for despondency. In the first place, his unsought notoriety 'has really served to advance the gospel' (1:12–14). Like many a victim of a smear campaign in our own times, his attitude is that 'all publicity is good publicity, so long as the name is right'! And if the worst comes to the worst (which it won't), then Paul will be with Christ (1:19–26).

There follows the first extended exhortation in the letter, beginning, 'Conduct yourselves in a manner worthy of the gospel of Christ', and extending from 1:27 to 2:18. This 'worthy' life is characterized by courage and love—courage, because the new movement faces opposition everywhere of the sort that has just landed Paul himself in jail; and love, because it is important that the church stands together in the face of opposition. This will require unselfishness modelled on the supreme example of Christ himself, who did not stand on his rights or exploit his status as Son of God, but laid aside his glory and embraced the depths of shame and suffering for the sake of others, thereby winning eternal renown (2:5–11). This is the pattern of life God intends his people to display as they co-operate with his working in them.

Paul returns to the theme of reassurance, this time with reference to Epaphroditus, whom the Philippians had sent to Paul bearing their gift. Epaphroditus fell ill, but has recovered, and now Paul is sending him back and asking that he receive a hero's welcome for his dangerous mission (2:19–30). We easily forget how precarious life could be for these early missionaries.

A second exhortation follows, which features a warning against an ever-present danger, as well as various other ethical instructions (3:1—4:9). The danger comes from the same sort of Jewish Christian counter-mission that often interfered with Paul's converts. As we shall see, these people had much in common with the group that caused so much trouble in Corinth. They prided themselves on their Jewish credentials. They advocated the circumcision of male Gentile believers. They encouraged their adherents to see themselves as 'perfect' or 'mature', and they rejected the values and lifestyle exemplified by the cross of Christ. Paul's antidote for this disease is that Christians should rejoice in the Lord (3:1; 4:4), and not in any qualifications or accomplishments of their own. Rejoicing in the Lord means rejoicing in his cross, and also in his future, recognizing that we have not arrived and shall not be perfect until we are transformed at the resurrection (3:20–21). Where previously he had referred to the example of Christ, now Paul puts forward his own example. He too had given up privilege and status, and was now looking to God for his vindication (3:2–10).

Finally, Paul returns to the theme of assurance, turning his thanks for their financial support into a general lesson in confidence (4:10–20). God who had supplied all his needs, either through their gifts or by enabling him to put up with privation cheerfully, would also supply all their needs. This most intimate of Paul's letters, then, has the function of encouragement. It was not prompted by the need to correct any massive problems in the church. Despite a quarrel of some kind between two prominent women in the church (4:2–3), the church was plagued neither with false teaching nor disunity. Paul warns them against matters that create division and against the attractions of a false spirituality, but he is not seriously worried about them. On the contrary, they are his joy and crown (4:1).

In the event, just as he told the Philippians (1:25), Paul was released from prison and travelled by way of Macedonia to Corinth. On the way, he wrote to the church in Corinth the letter we know as 2 Corinthians.

AFTER COLOSSIANS

The letter that most closely resembles Colossians, however, is not Philippians but Ephesians. The similarities are of two kinds. There are topics common to both, which are not found (or not found in this form) in the other Pauline letters—for example, the call to 'put off' and 'put on' lists of vices and virtues (compare Col. 3:5–17 with Eph. 4:25—5:2); and the household codes, instructions directed to each member of the Christian household (compare Col. 3:18—4:1 with Eph. 5:22—6:9). There are also distinctive phrases common to both letters—for example, 'In him we have redemption through his blood, the forgiveness of sins' (Eph. 1:7, cf. Col. 1:14); 'From him the whole body, joined and held together by every supporting ligament, grows and builds itself up in love, as each part does its work' (Eph. 4:16, cf. Col. 2:19); 'psalms, hymns and spiritual songs' (Eph. 5:19, cf. Col. 3:16). Many more such verbal echoes could be cited.

At the same time, there are big differences between the two letters. Ephesians is no longer concerned to warn its readers of the insidious threat from Judaism, so out go the great hymn-like passage that attributes to Christ everything that the synagogue teachers claimed for the law (Col. 1:15–20), and the warnings against succumbing to demands for circumcision and observance of the Sabbath and food laws (Col. 2:8–23). Instead, the readers of Ephesians are reminded that they have been included in the true people of God, which is no longer defined by such observances (2:11–22). In addition, Ephesians begins with solemn praise to God for his great plan of salvation (1:3–14), and includes an exhortation to maintain the Church's unity (4:1–16), and a summons to spiritual warfare (6:10–17). It is as if someone has rebuilt an old country house, keeping some bits, pulling down others, retaining some of the old stonework but using it in a new setting, while adding to the building whole new wings.

Ephesians is Colossians rebuilt for a new day, but rebuilt by whom and for whom? Once again, the similarities and differences are a matter of fact, the explanation a matter of opinion. Many scholars now think that Ephesians cannot have been written by Paul himself, or to the church at Ephesus, but was written as a statement of Paul's theology for the Church as a whole by a learned disciple after his death. Briefly stated, the reasons are as follows. First, the style is very different from that of the other Pauline letters, using long sentences and piling up synonyms. Second, it is suggested that there are shifts in theology. Ephesians is more interested in the universal Church than the local congregation, more focused on the exaltation of Christ than on his cross, more concerned with what believers enjoy now than on the future coming of Christ. Third, the perspective has changed. Ephesians now looks back to the 'holy apostles and prophets', including Paul, as the foundation of the Church, in a way that suggests that they are now dead and we are in a new generation (2:20; 3:5). Gentile Christians are no longer threatened by 'Judaizers' but need to be taught to see themselves in continuity with the Israel of old. As for the intended audience, it is not likely that it was the church at Ephesus. The word 'Ephesus' is missing from the best ancient manuscripts and was probably not original. Moreover, Ephesus was a church that Paul knew well, whereas the readers have to be told about Paul as if they had never met him (3:2) and the letter is almost devoid of personal greetings. This suggests that it is more of an essay in Christian theology presented in the form of a letter than a genuine letter addressed to a particular situation. None of this lessens its value.

On the contrary, Ephesians is one of the finest statements of what it means to be a Christian that has ever been penned, and we shall look briefly at its message.

THE MESSAGE OF EPHESIANS

Unlike the other Pauline letters, which were written in the heat of the moment and often jump from topic to topic as the needs of the church demand, Ephesians is a carefully balanced document. Chapters 1—3 set out believers' privileges in Christ, and chapters 4—6 set out how believers should live in the light of them. It has been helpfully shown that the two parts are linked together by the idea of 'calling', the first part being governed by the prayer 'that you may know the hope to which he has called you' (1:18), and the second by the exhortation to 'live a life worthy of the calling you have received' (4:1).[5] It is also helpful to think of Ephesians as a kind of baptismal sermon in which 'we' who have been Christians for some time welcome 'you' who have recently been saved into the privileges and responsibilities of the Christian family, and the best way for us to 'hear' this letter is to return in imagination to the day of our baptism (or confirmation) and to imagine we are being addressed by a saintly old pastor (or bishop).

The writer begins with a solemn prayer of praise to God for all the benefits he has bestowed on us in Christ, from our election, through the forgiveness of our sins, to our final salvation of which the Holy Spirit and our baptism are the pledges, and how this fits into God's great plan to bring healing and harmony to the whole universe in Christ (1:3–14). Then he tells us how he prays for us to know the hope to which we have been called and how it has been guaranteed to us by the resurrection and ascension of Christ (1:15–23), and by the way we have ourselves been brought from death to life (2:1–10) and incorporated into the worldwide family of God (2:11–22). He reminds us that the gospel is something that has been handed down to us by those who were Christians before us, notably Paul of course, often at the cost of imprisonment and even death (3:1–13); and he prays that we ourselves will take our place in that great company, fully confirmed in all the love of God (3:14–21). As this part of the address reaches its climax, we feel ourselves lifted up above the vicissitudes of everyday life and actually seated with Christ in heaven, able to see the world from his point of view—in the words of the hymn, 'ransomed, healed, restored, forgiven'.[6]

The second part of the address brings us firmly down to earth again. If that is our hope, how then shall we live? The old saint reminds us that, as a church, we are here to be a showcase of God's plan to reconcile the whole universe to himself and put an end to every proud division, and that through our ministers God has given us the grace we need to fulfil it (4:1–16). Getting very practical, he tells us that new life means new lifestyle (4:17–32), and calls us away from society's obsession with sex to live together as children of the light (5:1–20). The Christian life is not just for living at church but at home, and not in ideal homes but the homes we actually have (5:21–33). This is where many of our sinful divisions are nurtured, and this is where they are to be overcome in family relationships that demonstrate the character of Christ (6:1–9). Finally, like those newly baptized, we are sent out into the world 'to fight valiantly under his banner against sin, the world, and the devil', together with all Christ's faithful soldiers and servants (6:10–20).

The message of Ephesians might be summed up in the words: 'One Lord, one faith, one baptism; one God and Father of all, who is over all and through all and in all' (4:5–6). In this, Ephesians is completely true to Paul's own life and teaching. It is also a message that speaks to the deepest needs of the Church and the world today, so that one recent commentator can say, 'Of all the New Testament letters Ephesians is perhaps the most relevant for the church as she moves rapidly into the twenty-first century.'[7]

CHAPTER 11

PAUL'S STORY: CORINTH (2)

THE STORY BEHIND 2 CORINTHIANS

The story behind this letter is rather complicated. It begins with the sending of 1 Corinthians. Paul, then in Ephesus, wrote to the Corinthians the letter we have already studied and sent it via Timothy, who would have the job of reading it to the church and reinforcing its message (1 Cor. 4:17). Timothy returned with bad news. Paul's letter had not been well-received. In particular, nothing had been done about disciplining the incestuous man in the way Paul had demanded (1 Cor. 5:1–5) Meanwhile, a Jewish Christian delegation had arrived in Corinth with letters of recommendation, claiming to be genuine apostles and pointing to their impressive oratory and successful ministry as evidence, and the church was listening to them.

Paul immediately set off for Corinth to sort things out, but was rebuffed. He describes it as a 'painful visit' (2 Cor. 2:1). Back in Ephesus, Paul wrote them an angry letter, and sent Titus to deliver it and, if possible, to bring the church back into line. Meanwhile, the situation in Ephesus had become very difficult and Paul was forced to leave. He went first to Troas, but then, as he tells us (2:12–13), went on to Macedonia in the hope of meeting up with Titus and hearing news of the situation in Corinth and how his angry letter had been received. Titus duly arrived and brought a much more hopeful report. The church had accepted Paul's letter and had done everything Paul had asked them to do (7:5–16). Paul then wrote to them a letter of reconciliation, which forms part of what we know as 2 Corinthians.

THE COMPOSITION OF 2 CORINTHIANS

But what is 2 Corinthians? Is it one letter or a patchwork of fragments from different letters written at different times? There are some surprising breaks in the argument, making it hard to believe that the letter we have was all written on one occasion. In particular, chapters 10—13 are quite different in tone from chapters 1—9. While chapters 1—9 express confidence in the Corinthians, chapters 10—13 angrily reproach them for their fickleness and threaten disciplinary action. It is very hard to believe that the later chapters were ever part of the same letter as the earlier. Second, the long passage 2:14—7:4 clearly interrupts Paul's story of how he left Ephesus and met up with Titus. Third, the short passage 6:14—7:1 has no obvious connection with the context in which it now appears. Finally, chapters 8 and 9 both deal with the collection for the church in Jerusalem, but they look like different letters covering the same ground. Chapter 9 starts as if mentioning the matter for the first time, which reads oddly after chapter 8 has been giving instructions about this very thing.

My own view of the explanation for these breaks is as follows. First, chapters 10—13 were indeed originally part of another letter. Many scholars think they were written after chapter 1—9 and show that the improvement in relations reported by Titus was only temporary and that things went from bad to worse. I prefer the view that these chapters are the angry letter sent to Corinth after his painful and unsuccessful visit, and that, as such, they are the letter that brought the Corinthians back to their allegiance to Paul. Paul then wrote chapters 1—9 to cement the reconciliation. Second, 2:14—7:1 were inserted into the account of Paul's journey to Macedonia, but my guess is that Paul inserted them himself, perhaps using material he had written earlier about the character of authentic Christian ministry. It is hard to see any later editor breaking up Paul's narrative in this way. The same is perhaps true of 6:14—7:1, which are an insertion within an insertion. Finally, I think that chapters 8 and 9 were originally separate letters. Chapter 9 originally followed chapter 7, but chapter 8 is part of an earlier letter that has been put in here because it dealt with the same subject.

On this view, we have parts of two major letters combined as one.

Letter A (chs. 10—13) was written first, and letter B (chs. 1—9) was written subsequently. My reason for thinking that the later chapters were written earlier is that we know Paul went on from Macedonia and spent three months in Corinth. During this time he had the leisure to write Romans, in which he mentions that the church in Corinth has contributed to the collection. All this suggests a happy ending to the story and is difficult to reconcile with the idea that things at that time were as bad as chapters 10—13 would suggest. The only way to test this theory is to read the two letters in the order proposed, chapters 10—13 before chapters 1—9, and see what sense it makes.

THE MESSAGE OF 2 CORINTHIANS 10—13

Paul is writing to a church that has been visited by a group of teachers opposed to him and has been deeply impressed by them. Paul even believes that the church is taking their side against him. Who were these visitors? They were Jewish Christians who boasted of their Jewish credentials (11:22) and presumably called for some kind of adherence to the law of Moses (3:7–18). It is certain that they claimed to be true apostles (11:5, 13), marked out as such by their superior oratory, the miracles they performed, the visions and revelations they experienced, and the prosperous lifestyle they enjoyed. Paul, by contrast, was rated a poor speaker (10:10; 11:6), deficient in miracles and visions, seemingly always in trouble, who demeaned himself by working for a living rather than accepting the support from the church due to an apostle (11:7–12). It is not certain what the relationship of these visitors was to the mother church in Jerusalem and to the original apostles among its leadership, but it is likely that the visitors at least claimed their support. There was much in their sales pitch that would have appealed to the Corinthians, given their liking for eloquence and power.

Paul appeals for loyalty and threatens disciplinary action (10:1–11). The visitors are trespassing on another person's God-given territory, something that Paul himself was careful not to do (10:12–18). They have preached another Jesus, a different Spirit, a different gospel. So far from being 'super-apostles', they are not true apostles at all (11:1–15). It is foolish to boast but, if he must, Paul will boast of how much he has suffered for Christ rather than how much he has achieved, and he goes on to list imprisonments, floggings, shipwrecks, dangers, toil, privation and 'the pressure of my concern for all the churches' (11:16–33). The catalogue of troubles is similar to the description of the apostolic calling that Paul had already given the Corinthians in his first letter (1 Cor. 4:9–13). So far from showing him to be inferior, these sufferings show him to be a genuine servant of the crucified Lord.

Paul turns to visions and revelations (12:1–10). Presumably the visitors claimed to have received many such experiences. Paul has had such an experience. He was caught up to 'the third heaven' and heard 'inexpressible things' (12:2, 4). It was an overwhelming spiritual experience, but it was a long time ago, and in any case Paul is reluctant to talk about it. Such experiences, he believes, are essentially private and should not be used to impress other people. It is better by far to talk about his troubles, because through them Paul has learned an important lesson. Nobody knows for certain what he meant by his 'thorn in the flesh' (12:7), whether it was an illness or persistent opposition from some quarter. He prayed for its removal and received instead the assurance that God would give him the grace to bear it. God, who 'chose the weak things of the world to shame the strong' (1 Cor. 1:27), has chosen to allow Paul to be weak, so that Christ's power might be all the more clearly seen in him. That power has been seen in signs, wonders and miracles done by Paul—it has not all been pain and defeat—but he characteristically adds 'with great perseverance' (12:12). Summing up, he says, 'I delight in weaknesses, in insults, in hardships, in persecutions, in difficulties. For when I am weak, then I am strong' (12:10). This is the heart of letter A, and the heart of his answer to his critics in Corinth. It is the great lesson of permanent and universal importance to come out of this angry letter in which so much is hard either to understand or to apply to ourselves.

Paul warns the church that he is coming to them again, and this time he will take effective action to sort them out (12:14—13:10). He is not coming to take their money. He greatly fears that they have done nothing to correct the abuses he wrote about in 1 Corinthians. He calls for self-examination, so that his visit will not be another painful experience. The letter ends with the most beautiful, as well as the most familiar benediction Paul ever wrote (13:14).

THE MESSAGE OF 2 CORINTHIANS 1—9

According to our reconstruction of events, Paul was still in Ephesus when he wrote letter A. He has now left Ephesus and is in Macedonia, most likely in either Philippi or Thessalonica, and Titus has arrived with good news of the church's change of heart brought about by that letter.

Paul's letters normally begin by telling his readers how he thanks God for them. This is a good way of gaining a hearing for his message, since we are all more ready to listen to people who think well of us. In the present case, such thanksgiving might have sounded forced and insincere, so instead Paul begins by praising God for the comfort and help he has himself received in his recent troubles. This both awakens sympathy and enables him to introduce a theme of great importance in this letter, the positive purpose of Christian suffering. Suffering teaches us to rely on God and makes us able to comfort others when they are going through trouble. So if God's servants do not always look very victorious, this is not because they lack faith but because God is teaching them and making them more useful (1:1–11).

After this little homily, Paul turns to the pressing problems in his relationship with the Corinthians. There are two of them. He said he would come and visit them and he changed his mind and didn't come (1:12—2:2). Also, rather than paying them a visit, he had written them an angry letter, and although the letter has been so successful that Paul now feels that, if anything, the Corinthians have gone too far in doing as he had said, the whole episode has left both parties feeling bruised, and Paul is writing to re-establish a good relationship. This is dealt with in 2:3–13 and 7:5–16.

The problem in the first passage is simple: he said he would come, and broke his word. In such a situation you can either say, 'I didn't do it,' or, 'I did do it, but I was justified.' Paul opts for the second: 'I changed my mind, but I had good reason.' Quite simply, it would have been too painful for all concerned (1:23—2:2). A simple matter, you might think, but Paul feels that his honour is at stake and with it the credibility of his ministry, and so he launches into a convoluted explanation. He begins by stating his commitment to straight dealing (1:12–14). He changed his mind, but not in a worldly manner, or out of self-interest. This leads him on to think about the reliability and faithfulness of God, which is demonstrated in two ways—first by the coming of Christ in fulfilment of God's promise, and second by the giving of the Spirit, who confirms that we belong to Christ. The point is clear: God's faithfulness should be reflected in the faithfulness of his servants.

Paul's next concern is to heal the hurt caused by his angry letter. Among other things, the Corinthians had at last got round to disciplining the man whose incestuous relationship had so incensed Paul before (1 Cor. 5). Paul wants to say that his harsh words were prompted by love (2 Cor. 2:4) and that he bears the church no ill will for anything they may have said in the heat of the moment. As a sign of this, he now urges the church to forgive and restore the offender (who is now presumably repentant, though that is not stated) (2:5–11). Having handed the man over to Satan temporarily (1 Cor. 5:5), he is now anxious that Satan gain no lasting advantage, as he would if the man were lost to the church for ever. In what follows, Paul tells the Corinthians how anxious he had felt about their disagreement (2:12–13; 7:5), how happy he now feels at their response and how proud of them he is (7:6–16).[1]

AUTHENTIC CHRISTIAN MINISTRY
(2 CORINTHIANS 2:14—7:4)

For whatever reason, Paul decided to interrupt this simple letter of reconciliation with a profound essay on the characteristics of authentic Christian ministry, which forms his more reasoned response to the challenge of the 'super-apostles'. He begins by thanking God. Despite changing plans and personal difficulties, we are part of Christ's triumphal procession. Christ triumphed through his cross, and we shall do the same. Despite our setbacks, we are assured that Christ is winning a great victory through us, and just as such earthly triumphs are accompanied by the burning of incense to the gods, which impresses the spectators, so our lives offered to God create a profound impression on the watching world—though not always to its liking (2:14–16).

Next, Paul contrasts his ministry with that of 'so many', especially the 'super-apostles' he attacked directly in letter A. They 'peddle the word of God for profit' (2:17); Paul speaks only to please God. They boast of their 'letters of recommendation' (3:1); Paul prefers to rely on the testimony of those whose lives have been changed by his preaching. He is a minister of the new covenant under which God will put his law in people's minds and write it on their hearts, as Jeremiah foretold (Jer. 31:33), in place of the law written on tablets of stone. This leads him to a fresh reading of the story of Moses. No doubt the false apostles appealed to Moses as their authority. Moses' face certainly shone with glory, reflecting the divine splendour, but it didn't last. The glory faded, and the law too was a temporary dispensation, now superseded by the coming of the Spirit under the new covenant. Then again, Moses had to put a veil over his face and, for the Jewish people who have not accepted Jesus as Christ, that veil remains, preventing them from seeing the truth; but where the gospel is preached, the Spirit is given, and the Spirit enables us to see the glory of God in the face of Jesus Christ and to be changed by it.

As a result, Paul is confident and does not lose heart, even though there is plenty that might discourage him. This is the persistent theme of the next two chapters (4:1, 16; 5:6, 8), and Paul uses four pictures to explain his confidence. True messengers of God are like clay pots containing precious treasure (4:7). Outwardly they are very ordinary, and worse than ordinary—beaten and broken down, in fact—but the message they bring and the ministry they exercise is priceless. In the service of Jesus, they experience hardship, pain and danger of death, but this earthly body is just a tent, temporary accommodation until something more solid is provided (5:1). The lasting accommodation is the resurrection 'body', the life of the age to come. So far from being stripped of our present body, at death we shall put on the other like an overcoat—clothing infinitely more substantial (5:4).

Finally, Paul compares himself to an expatriate. Expatriates live in a foreign country, but only for a fixed time determined by their employer. They have a country of their own and they are going home some day. Meanwhile, they are not tourists, but people with a job to do and a responsibility to discharge. However tough things get, Christians know that they have a home elsewhere and they are going there one day. Meanwhile there is work to do and a master to please (5:6–10).

Paul's purpose in all this is to cement his reconciliation with the Corinthians by getting them to see that the life he leads and the ministry he exercises, with all their trouble and strife, are a genuine expression of God's grace and not something that his churches need to feel ashamed of. So he goes on to write about authentic ministry, its motivation, style, goal and cost (5:11—6:10). Authentic ministry is motivated by the fear of God on the one hand, and the love of Christ on the other. True ministers know that they must appear before the judgment seat of Christ (5:10–11), and they are spurred on by the thought of the Son of God who loved and died for us all (5:14–15).

Authentic ministry does not boast of its ecstatic experiences, as the 'super-apostles' evidently did. This is why Paul says, 'If we are out of our mind, it is for the sake of God' (5:13). If Paul has had visionary experiences, that is a private matter between him and God. An account of them would be of no help to others, who need rather a clear and open statement of the truth. Authentic ministry has as its goal the reconciliation of people to God. That is why Christ came, and that is why his servants preach. They are ambassadors for Christ, who embody in their persons the saving power of God, his righteousness, released into the world through the cross (5:18–21).[2] Finally, authentic ministry is costly, and Paul gives a powerful portrait of the servants of God, their sufferings and the paradoxical contrast between what they are and achieve on the one hand, and how they appear on the other (6:3–10).

Before Paul returns to the story of his anxiety over the Corinthians and how Titus brought the good news of their change of heart, he ends his account of authentic ministry with an appeal to the Corinthians to open their hearts to him, and a warning that they must choose one way or the other (6:11—7:4).

THE COLLECTION FOR THE JERUSALEM CHURCH
(2 CORINTHIANS 8 AND 9)

Now that relations between Paul and the Corinthians have returned to normal, Paul can take up with them once more the matter of the collection for Jerusalem. This is a delicate matter, because it is difficult to ask people for money if they have no confidence in you, and easy to lose people's confidence if you do ask. There is also the problem that Paul has consistently refused to accept money from the Corinthians for himself, which they wanted to give, and now wants them to contribute to a project dear to his heart. The material on this subject, which Paul here assembles, falls into four sections. First there is an appeal for generosity based on the example of the Macedonians and the supreme example of Jesus (8:1–15). This is followed by the commendation of the delegates who will receive the Corinthians' gift and ensure that everything is handled properly (8:16–24). Next Paul appeals to the Corinthians to avoid the disgrace of failing to keep their promise in this matter (9:1–5). Finally he sets out the rewards of generosity, both to the donors themselves and to the whole Church of God (9:6–15). Once again we notice how Paul is able to mine spiritual treasure from a rather mundane matter, as he shows that Christian giving is a response to the grace of our Lord Jesus Christ, who became poor so that we might become rich, and a way of thanking God for his gift beyond words, the gift of his own Son (8:9; 9:15)

THE OUTCOME OF 2 CORINTHIANS

If we are right about the relationship of the two main parts of 2 Corinthians, Paul's letters were successful. The first brought the church to its senses and the second cemented the relationship. At any rate, Paul was able to winter there after writing this letter (Acts 20:3), and the Corinthians contributed to the collection (Rom. 15:26). So peace was restored. These letters are frequently hard to understand and we may feel remote from the disagreement they deal with, but no letter does more to reveal the apostle as a man of like nature with ourselves—hurt, angry, concerned to justify himself, but also capable of forgiveness, tenderness and self-knowledge. Above all, the lessons Paul learnt about the meaning of Christian suffering, the character of Christian ministry and the motives of Christian giving are of permanent importance. 2 Corinthians, like its author, is a jar of clay, but it contains great treasure!

CHAPTER 12

PAUL'S STORY: ROME

THE STORY BEHIND ROMANS

Dear Paul,

Hope you are well now and that things have settled down at Corinth. We thought you'd like some news from Rome. Things are much quieter here, politically speaking, now that we have a new emperor. We've been able to return and set up the leather business without hindrance. The church is growing too. There are so many groups meeting in houses in different parts of the capital that it's a job keeping them all together, especially as some are Jewish and very conservative while others are Gentile and rather free in their ways. It's hard to get them all under one roof because the conservatives insist on vegetarian meals to be sure of not contracting defilement, and some of the more liberal brothers make a point of demanding pork chops! We had quite an argument in our own home the other night when we met to share the Supper, and half the Jewish folk walked out.

I really think you should come and see us now that things are sorted out in the East. You've often talked of doing so but you never show up. Failing that, please write us a letter that we can read out at our meeting and pass on to the other groups, so that we can enjoy the salvation we all hold in common rather than focusing on controversial matters the whole time.

All the members send their love.

Grace and peace from
Aquila and Priscilla

The letter of course is imaginary, but the situation it describes is not. For a start, Priscilla and Aquila really were in Rome when Paul wrote this letter, because he sends them greetings (16:3–4). They had had to leave Rome earlier when Emperor Claudius expelled the Jews from Rome, and we last met them in Ephesus (Acts 18:2, 26). Now they have been able to return to Rome, probably because, with the accession of a new emperor, Claudius' decree had lapsed, permitting Jews (including Jewish Christians) to return.

What sort of church would they have found on their return? Almost certainly a divided church. Rome was a big city and the Jewish community met in several different synagogues, as we know from archaeological evidence. It is likely that the Christian house churches would have been similarly scattered. The long list of greetings with which Paul ends this letter tends to support this idea (16:3–16). More seriously, the churches would tend to divide along ethnic lines, Jewish Christians versus Gentile Christians. We know that this was a problem because Paul devotes a chapter and a half to it at the end of his letter (14:1—15:13), urging the two sides to accept one another and form one church, Jews and Gentiles together praising God. The formation of such churches had been Paul's great concern from the start, and in this letter he brings to bear all the arguments he has honed in debate with more conservative Jewish opponents.

If the church's story helps to explain why Paul has written as he has, so does his own story, as we learn it from this letter (15:14–33). Paul is at a major crossroads in his life. He has finished his work in the eastern Mediterranean (15:19). From Jerusalem round to Illyricum on the Adriatic coast (modern Croatia) he has planted churches in significant urban centres and sees no scope for further work in that region. He is now looking for a new mission field, and Spain beckons (15:23–24). But Spain is a long way away, very much 'the ends of the earth' to a Jew from Tarsus, and Paul is going to need help. If only the church in Rome will provide a base for the new mission and send him out with their blessing and support, as Antioch had done in the east! If the church is to do this, it will not only need to be united, it will need to trust Paul and agree with his stance on the acceptance of Gentiles on the basis of faith alone. So Paul gives them this long and careful defence of his gospel.

Before coming to Rome, however, he is off to Jerusalem again, taking with him the great collection and a delegation from the contributing churches (15:25–26), and he is expecting trouble (15:31). From long experience, Paul knows that he is the object of considerable suspicion, if not outright hostility, in Jerusalem, and it is likely that he sees this collection as more than a charitable gift. If the church in Jerusalem accepts the gift, it will signify their acceptance of Paul's mission and the churches that have sprung from it. The visit, then, is important to Paul, and it is very likely that in this letter he is rehearsing the arguments that he will also use, if necessary, in debate with critics in the Jerusalem church.

All of this will have been in Paul's mind as he sat down to write Romans—the needs of the divided church in Rome (whether or not he had received a letter from Priscilla and Aquila telling him about it), his own need of a base for the Spanish mission, and his forthcoming journey to Jerusalem where he hopes to establish a lasting peace. In a sense, we could say that the story behind Romans is the whole story of Paul's life to date, so it is not wrong to see this letter as Paul's last will and testament.

THE MESSAGE OF ROMANS

Romans is a long and complex letter, so it will be helpful to have an outline of its contents. Romans develops the slogan Paul announced in Galatians: 'All one in Christ Jesus' (Gal. 3:28). After a brief introduction (1:1–17), the main part of the letter can be divided into the following four sections.

* We are all one in sin   1:18—3:20
* We are all one in grace   3:21—8:39
* We are all one in God's great plan   9:1—11:36
* We need to be all one in our life together   12:1—15:13

The argument of the letter is complete at this point, and the rest deals with Paul's plans and greetings.

The church in Rome was not founded by Paul and he has not been there, so he begins by introducing himself and establishing common ground in the gospel. The gospel he preaches is the gospel they too believe. It is a message from God. It is in accordance with the Scriptures. It is a message about Jesus, Son of David and Son of God. It is addressed to the whole world and calls people to 'the obedience that comes from faith' (1:1–7). After speaking of his longing to come to Rome and his reasons for doing so, Paul states the theme of his letter in words that are so important they are worth quoting in full:

For I am not ashamed of the gospel; it is the power of God for salvation to everyone who has faith, to the Jew first and also to the Greek. For in it the righteousness of God is revealed through faith for faith; as it is written, 'The one who is righteous will live by faith.'
ROMANS 1:16–17 (NRSV)

The key thought here is that the gospel mediates God's saving power to everyone on the same terms, regardless of their ethnic origin. The phrase 'to the Jew first and also to the Greek' tolls like a bell through the opening chapters of Romans (2:9–10; see also 3:29). God's saving power is also described as his 'righteousness'. This is a legal metaphor well-known from the Old Testament (Is. 46:13; 51:5). God is being likened to a judge who upholds the cause of the weak. As such, he comes to the rescue of his people, those who trust in him, by rescuing them from the power of sin and death. The 'righteousness' of God is another way of speaking of his faithfulness. (By translating these words as 'a righteousness from God', as in 1:17, the NIV shows that it understands Paul rather differently. 'Righteousness' is then not so much the character and activity of the judge as the verdict that the successful litigant receives. He is declared to be 'in the right'. So understood, 'righteousness' is another way of speaking of God's forgiveness.)

This righteousness of God is revealed 'through faith for faith' (1:17, NRSV). This might simply be a way of saying 'by faith from first to last' (and so the NIV takes it), but it is more likely that Paul is deliberately using 'faith' in two different senses. The same Greek word (*pistis*) can mean either 'faith' or 'faithfulness' (as we saw in Galatians 2:20: see page 142), and Paul several times speaks of the 'faith of Jesus Christ', which a growing number of scholars understand as meaning Christ's faithfulness in being obedient to God to the point of death. If this is right, Paul is saying that the righteousness of God (his saving power) is revealed through the faithfulness of Christ (his death on the cross) and is appropriated by the faith of his people (or possibly that the righteousness of God is revealed through the faithfulness of Christ with the goal of producing faithfulness in his people). The same ambiguity is present in the words from Habakkuk 2:4 that Paul goes on to quote: 'The one who is righteous will live by faith / faithfulness' (1:17, NRSV). But will the righteous find life through their own faith or through God's faithfulness—or both?

WE ARE ALL ONE IN SIN (ROMANS 1:18—3:20)

In this section, Paul is not seeking to prove that each individual is a sinner, and that they must come to Jesus to have their sins forgiven. He is arguing that Jews and Gentiles are *equally* sinners, so that all must come to God on the same terms. The argument goes as follows:

Step 1   We know that God judges sinners (1:18–32). The purpose of this section is not to prove that the whole world is sinful but that the sinful world lies under the dreadful judgment of God (v. 18), and so deserves death (v. 32). Paul would expect his Jewish critics to agree with this.

Step 2   God is impartial (2:1–11). This too would be readily agreed by Jewish hearers.

Step 3   Gentiles are not all bad (2:12–16). As a matter of simple observation, many Gentiles lead upright lives and there is much to admire in the ethical systems of other religions. God will take notice of that, won't he?

Step 4   On the other hand, Jews do not always behave admirably (2:17–24). Regrettably, people who have God's law do not always keep it, and when they don't, other people are quick to point this out.

Step 5   If God is impartial, it will be no use pleading that you are one of the chosen people (as evidenced by circumcision), will it (2:25–29)?

Step 6   Possession of the law is a great privilege (3:1–2), but it provides no immunity from prosecution (3:9). The conclusion is clear: Jews and Gentiles are all one in sin. All are under its power and subject to judgment. In another key statement, Paul says, 'For "no human being will be justified in his sight" by deeds prescribed by the law, for through the law comes the knowledge of sin' (3:20, NRSV).

The word 'justified' is another word borrowed from the world of the law-court. A person who is justified wins their case, and the judge pronounces in their favour. Applied to God's relationship to human beings, it means that God declares that they belong to him as his people, and the question in dispute between Paul and his critics is, 'On what basis can people of other nations belong to the people of God?' The critics say that it must be by doing what the law says, especially in the matter of circumcision and other marks of the covenant, but Paul says that the same law that prescribes the requirements you do keep also condemns you for the requirements you don't keep. There must be some other way for God to gather a people for himself drawn from every nation. There is! Read on!

WE ARE ALL ONE IN GRACE (ROMANS 3:21—8:39)

In this section, Paul first explains how God's grace operates (3:21—4:25) and then goes on to explore the benefits that grace conveys (5:1—8:39). You may want to approach them as two separate sections.

How God's grace operates (3:21—4:25)

Something radically new has happened. God has found a new way to show his faithfulness and saving power—in other words, his right-eousness. Once again, while this could refer to the right relationship with God that the believer receives, it is more likely that Paul is talk-ing about the faithfulness and saving power that God displays. God has broken into the circle of sin and alienation in which we were imprisoned and gathered a people for himself. How has he done this? Not through having everyone observe the requirements traditionally laid on Jewish people, although firmly in accordance with the Scriptures, properly understood. God has acted through Christ, whom he sent into the world as a sin offering to cancel our sins by means of his death. By his faithfulness to God all the way to the cross, Jesus has made freedom and life possible for all who will put their faith in him, so that all can come to God on the same basis. In this way, God can forgive people their sins without being untrue to himself. He displays his righteousness not, as might be expected, by condemning the guilty, but by showing mercy. Meanwhile, those who have sinned (Jews and Gentiles alike) find themselves, against all expectation, justified—that is, they are declared to be God's people. As a result, no one can boast, either of their achievements or their ethnic origins and religious tradition. All must acknowledge their debt to God's mercy (3:21–26).

It may help to understand this very dense paragraph if we look at a pair of parables in Luke's Gospel. Luke's portrait of Jesus is heavily influenced by the understanding of the gospel that he learnt from Paul. The first of these stories, the parable of the unjust judge (Luke 18:1–8), shows us what the words 'justification' and 'righteousness' mean in their normal court-room setting. Two parties stand before the judge, the widow and her adversary, and the judge must 'justify' one or the other. The widow cries out for justice. For a long time the judge ignores her plea, but eventually her persistence wears him down and he grants her request—that is, he justifies her and she leaves court having won her case.

In the second parable (Luke 18:9–14), two men stand before God, a Pharisee and a customs officer, seeking acceptance with God. The Pharisee makes a list of laws and traditions that he has observed, while the customs officer cries out for mercy. As we all know, it was the customs officer whose prayer God accepted, but notice the word used to express this acceptance. This man went down to his house *justified*, rather than the other. The word 'justified' binds the two stories together and invites us to see the similarity and difference between them. The widow and the customs officer were both justified, but whereas the judge justified the widow by giving her justice, God justified the customs officer by showing him mercy. When applied to God, 'justification' is a metaphor, a picture borrowed from another world of discourse. Just as a judge finds for one party against another, so God declares someone to belong to him, just as long ago he declared Abraham to be his on the strength of his faith alone (Gen. 15:6). In the next chapter of Luke's Gospel, an actual tax collector, Zacchaeus, is similarly justified (although the word is not used) when Jesus accepts him as a member of the covenant people by declaring him to be a 'son of Abraham' (Luke 19:9).

Finally, we should notice how these two stories help to explain the different meanings of the term 'righteousness'. In the first story, the judge (eventually) displayed his righteousness (or justice) by upholding the rights of the widow, and the widow received justice (or righteousness); but the righteousness that the judge displayed and the righteousness that the widow received are not the same thing. In the same way, in the other parable, God shows his righteousness paradoxically by showing mercy to the customs officer, and the customs officer received a paradoxical righteousness from God in the form of mercy; but the righteousness that the customs officer received is not the same as the righteousness that God displayed.

Back in Romans, if we speak of 'the righteousness *of* God', we are thinking of the activity of God in showing mercy and gathering a people for himself. If we speak of 'a righteousness *from* God', we are thinking of the mercy and right relationship with God that those who trust in him receive.[1]

Paul rounds off his argument with a series of questions and answers (3:27—4:3). I imagine him drawing one of his assistants—Timothy, say—into dialogue with him at this point:

Paul: What room is left for human pride?

Timothy: It is excluded.

Paul: On what principle? On that of observing the law?

Timothy: No, but on that of faith. For we reckon that a person is accepted by God through faith and not by religious observance.

Paul: Or else God would be God of the Jews only. But is he not God of the Gentiles too?

Timohty: Certainly he is God of the Gentiles too, since there is only one God, and he will accept the Jews through faith and non-Jews through faith.

Paul: Does this mean that we are using faith to undermine the law?

Timothy: Not at all. We are actually upholding the law!

Paul: What, then, are we to say about Abraham, the father of our race?

Timothy: If Abraham was justified by anything he did, then he has grounds for pride.

Paul: But not before God! For what does Scripture say? 'Abraham put his faith in God and that faith was counted to him as righteousness.'

In the rest of chapter 4, Paul will show that justification by faith is not a new doctrine that makes nonsense of the Old Testament revelation. On the contrary, as the story of Abraham shows, it is how God has always worked.

The benefits that God's grace conveys (5:1—8:39)

From the point of view of his argument with his conservative Jewish critics, Paul could have moved straight from the end of chapter 4 to the beginning of chapter 9. This is where the question of God's faithfulness to his Old Testament promises is taken up again and answered. Before that, however, he takes time to spell out the benefits that God bestows on those who trust in his Son Jesus Christ. The first of these is peace with God (5:1), later described as 'reconciliation' (5:10–11). This gives us access to God now, but we also have the hope that one day we shall share the glory of God himself (5:2–3). If you ask how we know this, Paul says that we know it because God has shown how much he loves us by sending Christ to die for our sins, a point to which he returns at the end of this section (8:31–39). This makes Jesus a second Adam, in that Adam's sin brought death into the world and Jesus' act of obedience has brought eternal life for all who belong to him (5:12–21).

It has been convincingly shown that the role of the second Adam was the role to which God called Abraham and his descendants, the people of Israel.[2] When Israel proved unable to fulfil their mission to be the light of the world and the healing of the nations, Jesus came as Israel's king and representative to carry their sins and the sins of the whole world, so as to gather a new Israel and, through them, a new humanity. The story of Jesus thus brings a happy ending to the story of Israel and the story of Adam (see the Prologue, pages 16–17). As children of Adam, human beings are subject to sin and death, but Paul will go on to show that 'there is now no condemnation for those who are in Christ Jesus' (8:1), since they are set free from the power of both sin and death. Before he does so, though, he feels the need to clear up some possible misunderstandings.

'Shall we go on sinning, so that grace may increase?' (6:1). In other words, is all this talk of grace a bit easy? What about God's moral demands? Or doesn't it matter what we do, because grace will cover it? It is important to see who is asking the question. It is sometimes suggested that it is being asked by new converts who are tempted to take advantage of God's grace so as to live immoral lives. This seems unlikely. New converts are not usually so cynical. It is much more likely that the question is being asked sarcastically by the conservative Jewish critics for whom it is obvious that the law is a barrier against sin, and that if people are allowed to join the Church without observing the law all sorts of wickedness will result.

Paul's answer is to point to the decisive and costly nature of Christian conversion. It is not a light thing to become a Christian in a society where other gods and lords hold sway. It means dying to a whole way of life, losing one's very identity within that society and gaining another identity as a member of Christ. It is the end of one life and the beginning of another, like leaving a country where one no longer feels at home and seeking asylum and citizenship in another country. There is no possibility of return and the rewards and penalties of the old society no longer exercise any influence. The moment when this crossover becomes public and irreversible is baptism. Those who are baptized into Christ Jesus may very well find that they have been baptized into his death, or at least his sufferings—crucified with Christ, in fact. The rite of baptism thus becomes the funeral service for the person we used to be—constituted, as we all are, by all our relationships to others—but at the same time a gateway into a new life, a new family and a new set of values and standards. When Christ died and rose again, he passed for ever beyond the power of human authorities to tempt him or threaten him, and the new convert, united to him by faith and baptism, is called and enabled to live a new life.

That is Paul's answer to those who think that grace is all too easy.

They have simply failed to reckon with the cost and decisiveness of conversion. But Paul knows that it is not automatic. Sin is not impossible for believers, and the new converts need to be urged to live in the light of the step they have taken and allow themselves to be socialized in the ways of the country of which they have become citizens. So he returns to the question, 'Shall we sin because we are not under law but under grace?' (6:15), and answers in terms of a different picture—that of a slave with a new master. The claim of a master on a slave in the ancient world was total, and a slave transferred from the ownership of one master to another would have neither leisure not inclination to go on serving the master he had left behind. The new Christians were formerly slaves of sin; they must now live as slaves of righteousness (Paul would not be comfortable speaking of Christians as slaves of God, since in 8:15 he will want to say that we are not slaves but sons and daughters), and it is important that they do, since persistent sin leads ultimately to death, while the path to eternal life leads through increasing holiness of life. As Paul has reminded the Jews, he now reminds the Christians, 'God will give to each person according to what he has done' (2:6), and 'the wages of sin is death' (6:23).

Believers *must* lead holy lives, but the great thing is that they now *can*, precisely because they are no longer 'under law, but under grace' (6:14). Paul knew from his own bitter experience that being 'under the law', as an observant Jew, provided no guarantee of a life pleasing to God. After all, it was out of devotion to the law that Paul and others had rejected Jesus and persecuted his followers. The law had actually aroused sinful passions rather than controlling them, so that he says 'we bore fruit for death' (7:5). But now, just as baptism had meant, for many of Paul's readers, dying to the old life in paganism, with its immoral practices, so for Paul himself it had meant dying to his old life in Judaism. Like a woman whose first husband has died, Paul is now able to embark on a new commitment, and one with infinitely greater potential for holy living, for the way of grace is the way of the Spirit (7:6).

At this point we expect Paul to tell us about life in the Spirit (as he does in chapter 8), but first he has to clear up another misunderstanding, and one of his own making. He has said such negative things about the law that we might be forgiven for thinking that the law and sin are the same thing. After all, he has spoken of dying to sin and dying to law, and of being set free from sin and set free from law. Yet the law is God's law, given by God to Israel for the sake of the whole world. How, then, can it have such disastrous effects? The problem, he tells us, lies not with the law but with human nature. The word Paul uses is literally 'flesh', which should not be translated 'sinful nature' (as if we had any other nature), but 'human nature', or what human beings are apart from the grace of God. The law is like a high-performance motor car. In itself, it is a magnificent machine, but in the hands of a bad driver it is lethal. The fault is not in the engineering but in the driver's handling of himself and his vehicle. The driver is not killed by the car but by his own impatience and lack of consideration for others, yet the powerful car makes it possible for him to have a worse accident than if he were riding a bicycle.

Can the wretched driver not see where the problem lies? Indeed he can! But he finds himself powerless to do anything about it. He will readily agree with you on the need for proper care and the correct handling of himself and his car, but once behind the wheel, all the old instincts assert themselves. So it is, Paul says, with human beings and religion, including even the highest religion known to humanity, namely the law of Moses. (This, in my view, settles the question of whose struggles Paul is describing in Romans 7. Despite the present tense, they are not the struggles of Paul as he now is, filled with the Spirit, but the struggles of Paul as he was, and as many of his Jewish contemporaries still are, trying to please God by the light of the law alone. What interest could Paul possibly have in telling us at this point in the argument how tough he finds life as a *Christian*?)

Now, at last, Paul is free to do what he has been wanting to do since the end of chapter 5—to tell us about the new life that Jesus has made possible by his act of obedience. He says, 'There is therefore now no condemnation for those who are in Christ Jesus. For the law of the Spirit of life in Christ Jesus has set you free from the law of sin and of death' (Rom. 8:1–2).

Formerly, we were under the control ('the law') of sin and death. That is to say, we sinned compulsively and we died deservedly. But now, in Christ Jesus, we are under the control of the Spirit, and that means righteousness and life. The whole chapter can be seen as an explanation of what it means to be set free from the law of sin and death: verses 1–17 are (mainly) about being set free from the power of sin, and verses 18–39 explain how we are set free from the power of death.

Sin is a power. All people, Jews and Gentiles alike, can be said to be 'under' it (3:9). It is an occupying power taking control of the springs of thought and action within each person (7:23), and the law is powerless to do anything about it (8:3). But now God has acted, and in two ways. First, he has sent his Son into the world to lead a perfect human life and to offer himself as a sin offering on behalf of the whole world, and in this way he has broken open the prison of past guilt. Second, he has sent his Spirit to live in those who believe, to enable them to fulfil the original purpose of God that was expressed in the law. So now we have a choice, and for the first time it is a real choice. We can choose to go on following the promptings of our human nature, or we can allow ourselves to be led by the Spirit so as to live lives pleasing to God. To go on living in the old way leads ultimately to death—the disintegration of the personality in this world and the next—whereas to live according to the Spirit leads to our becoming more fully alive in this world with the hope of being raised up to share God's glorious life in the future. The Spirit makes us sons and daughters of God, and as such we have the duty of obeying him, the privilege of addressing him, and the expectation of inheriting all he has to give (8:15–17).

Death is a power, and the whole creation lies in its grip. But God has already broken the power of death by raising Jesus from the dead, and it is his plan that the shock waves of that event should spread outwards to embrace more and more people through their faith in Jesus until, ultimately, the whole of creation will be swallowed up by life. However, that is for the future. It is a matter of hope. Meanwhile, the creation groans in frustration and pain, and we ourselves groan over our continued physical weakness and mortality, longing for God to set our whole being free (8:22–23). We are in an interim state, progressively set free from the power of sin, but still visibly subject to the law of death. So we groan, but we do not groan alone! The Spirit groans in us and for us, praying that God's will may be done in us and by us, until all his purpose for us is complete (8:26–27). This means that although we continue to suffer—and, as God's people in a hostile world, we may suffer more than most—our sufferings have no power to separate us from the love of God, since they are actually the tools God uses to make us more like his Son (8:29). Paul concludes this long section on the benefits that God's grace bestows with a triumphant shout of praise (8:31–39).

WE ARE ALL ONE IN GOD'S GREAT PLAN
(ROMANS 9:1—11:36)

Yet how can the gospel be true when so many people do not believe it? Especially, how can it be true when so many of God's historic people, Israel, do not believe it? This is the problem that presses sharply on Paul in these next chapters and we shall understand his dilemma better if we think of our own situation in the contemporary world. How can the gospel be true when so many of the world's peoples live and die in the religion within which they were born, even after two thousand years of the Church's witness and the heroic efforts of missionaries to convert them? Especially, how can it be true when so many people in countries with a long Christian history have already abandoned it or are in the process of doing so? They have had a preacher, they have heard, and they *no longer* believe! This state of affairs presents a serious challenge to faith and it should cause us the same 'great sorrow and unceasing anguish' as Paul says he feels in his heart as he contemplates the unbelief of his fellow countrymen and women (9:1–2).

Many readers have felt these chapters to be something of a digression, dealing as they do with the place of the Jewish people in God's great plan, but we may be sure that Paul did not see it like that. In many ways, they are the point to which the whole argument has been moving and the heart of the matter. Paul has said that he is not ashamed of the gospel, and nothing is more likely to cause people to be ashamed of the gospel (or any other belief system) than the sense that it lacks plausibility with a majority of their contemporaries. To be accepted as true, the gospel must reveal the righteousness of God (1:17), his faithfulness to his covenant, and explain how it comes about that at the present time the Gentiles are inside the Father's house while the Jewish people, for the most part, find themselves outside. Accordingly, these chapters are not basically about 'predestination'. They are about the righteousness of God. The credibility of the gospel and the honour of God himself are at stake. How can the gospel be true if so many of the chosen people have rejected it? How can God be true to his promises if it means rejecting most of his people? If we can see how Paul met this challenge to the faith in his day, we may be able to see how similar arguments can provide an answer to the challenge to the plausibility of the gospel in ours.

The argument unfolds in response to two questions: 'Has God's word failed?' (9:6) and, 'Has God rejected his people?' (11:1). It proceeds as follows:

Step 1   It depends what you mean by Israel (9:6–29). Israel is not to be identified with the entirety of a particular nation. In every generation, Israel is a chosen people, God choosing to work through some and not through others—Isaac but not Ishmael, Jacob but not Esau. This is a great mystery, but there is nothing new about it. Moreover, God can use even those who oppose him, to bring about a greater good, as the example of Pharaoh shows. No Pharaoh, no exodus! The great Potter knows what he is doing, and is not defeated by the intransigence of his materials.

Step 2   It is Israel, not God, who has failed (9:30—10:21). In every generation it is possible for people to miss God's path through unbelief. In this case, a majority of the Jewish people have missed God's way through a misplaced zeal for the law. The law, as a system of religion, was given by God to preserve Israel until the coming of their Messiah, but now that the Messiah has come, its work is over. The Scriptures from Moses onward make plain that God's salvation would one day be available to all peoples, free of national or cultural restrictions; and now, with the coming of Christ, that time has come.

Step 3   The present state of exclusion is not, in any case, total (11:1–10). We should not exaggerate the Jewish rejection of the gospel. Paul himself is a Jewish believer, and there are plenty more like him.

Step 4   God has not finished with us yet (11:11–36). The God who
used Pharaoh's intransigence to bring his people out of
Egypt and make them a nation is quite capable of using the
present unbelief to bring into being a greater Israel than
anything we have yet seen. And this is happening! Rejection
by the Jews has led to the gospel being taken to the Gentiles,
but this is not the end of the matter. When the Jews see
Gentiles streaming into the Church, then, like the elder
brother in Jesus' parable, they will want to come and join the
party—or they will if Gentile arrogance does not impede the
Father's purpose. Working through the ebb and flow of
human response, God's mercy will be seen to be wider and
stronger than can be grasped by finite human minds.

If the great future glimpsed by Paul has so far failed to arrive, this may
be because his warning to the Gentile Christians was not heeded. The
Church's treatment of the Jews for most of its history has made it as
difficult for Jews to join the Church as once the attitude of law-
observant Jews threatened to make it for the Gentiles to do so. But
Paul's argument leads to a more hopeful reflection, for the Church's
decline in countries where it had flourished for centuries has coin-
cided with the great missionary expansion of the Church, so that now
a majority of Christians live in countries that, a hundred or two
hundred years ago, had never heard the gospel. Paul would see this as
reason to hope for the eventual recovery of those nations that appear
at present to be lapsing into apostasy. And if God's purposes can be
served by human opposition and intransigence, so as to bring about
something 'more than all we ask or imagine' (Eph. 3:20), may they
not be served by the continued rejection of the gospel by those who
live by the other great religions of the world?

WE ALL NEED TO BE ONE IN OUR LIFE TOGETHER
(ROMANS 12:1—15:13)

If Paul's exposition of God's plan is accepted, the practical outcome
will be a united Church. It is this that holds together the seemingly
scattered thoughts of this final section of the letter. The basis of unity

is personal surrender to God, leading to a renewed mind (12:1–3) This in turn will lead to mutual esteem, which is the way that unity will be achieved, each person making his or her own contribution to the common life and valuing the contributions of others (not least those of Jews and Gentiles, although this is not mentioned) (12:4–13).

This is then applied to two urgent problems. The first is that of living in a hostile world, both with neighbours who make trouble and with a government that is unsympathetic at best. The Christian community is to live at peace with the former and show respect for the latter, living by the rule of love until Jesus comes again (12:14—13:14). The second problem is that of living with Christian diversity. Paul devotes a chapter and a half to this and makes it the final main topic of the letter, which shows that it is no afterthought. The problem is put in terms of the need for the weak and the strong to accept one another, but it is plain that these terms refer respectively to Jewish and Gentile Christians. The 'weak' eat only vegetables, presumably because, like Daniel, they fear defilement from meat offered to idols; they consider one day more sacred than another—a reference to the Sabbath—and they sit in judgment on those who think differently. By contrast, the 'strong' have no such scruples. They eat meat without asking questions, as Paul had recommended in Corinth (1 Cor. 10:23); they consider all days alike and they despise those of more tender conscience—the situation described in our imaginary letter from Aquila and Priscilla. Paul urges mutual acceptance and respect for one another's positions, but he is not simply neutral on the issue. He identifies himself with the 'strong' (15:1), whose point of view he shares. 'All food is clean' (14:20), 'but if anyone regards something as unclean, then for him it is unclean' (14:14). Observance of the law is thus made a matter of private conscience, not universal obligation; but Paul tells them that it is more important to be loving than right, following the example of Jesus (15:3, 8). The bottom line is, 'Accept one another, then, just as Christ accepted you' (15:7). If they do that, the Scriptures will be fulfilled and God will have one people, Jews and Gentiles together praising him with one voice.

THE OUTCOME OF ROMANS

Paul's plans never materialized, or not in the way he hoped. He did go to Jerusalem, of course, but the prayer of Romans 15:31 was not answered. Paul was not saved from the unbelievers in Judea, but was arrested and tried as a troublemaker. We have no positive evidence that the church in Jerusalem accepted his collection, and if they stood by him in his various trials, Acts is notably silent on the point. He did get to Rome in the end, but arrived as a prisoner.

The details of Paul's last years are obscure. An early tradition says that he reached Spain, but there is no record of his achieving anything there. Some people think that he was acquitted or released after two years and enjoyed a further period of active work in the east before being arrested again, imprisoned and executed. As we shall see in the next chapter, though, this does not seem very probable.

Romans was probably the last letter Paul wrote of which we have any knowledge. If so, it makes a fitting monument to his life and work, and as such it has always been seen and revered by the Church. Its influence has been immense. Time and again, significant movements of renewal and reform in the Church have been sparked by someone reading Romans. Romans was instrumental in the conversion of Augustine in the fifth century. Its effect on Martin Luther in the 16th century, Wesley in the 18th and Barth in the 20th changed the course of Christian history. And in a moving interview on the BBC's *Songs of Praise* programme, the actor David Suchet told how it was his decision to read Romans in a hotel bedroom that led to his finding a living Christian faith—a reminder that Romans is still changing lives today.

Of course, each generation hears Romans speaking to its own particular problems. Luther turned to Romans in search of a gracious God who would relieve the pain of a guilty conscience and the burden of trying to earn one's salvation through good works. Barth found in Romans the answer to his disillusionment with human-centred liberal theology. Neither of these was exactly the problem faced by Paul, who was more concerned with how Gentiles could join the Church than with how he could be sure of going to heaven. Yet there was a family likeness between Luther's problem and Paul's, and the answers Paul came up with were found to speak equally powerfully to the concerns of another time and place. It is a mark of the greatness of Romans that when we take the trouble to find out what it meant when it was first penned, it will speak afresh to the needs of our generation. It is perhaps no accident that our ecumenical age has rediscovered that Paul's overriding concern was the unity of the Church.

CHAPTER 13

THE STORY CONTINUES:
THE PASTORAL LETTERS

The Pastoral Letters are different from the other letters that bear Paul's name. Even someone reading the letters in English will feel that the language is different, and the statistics bear this out. Of the 848 different words used in the Pastoral Letters (excluding proper names), 306 are not found in the other Pauline letters, and these include some of the key words of these letters, such as 'godliness' to describe the Christian life and 'appearing' to refer to the first and second comings of Christ. Words common in Paul's other letters are rare here (for example, 'justification'), while words frequently used in the Pastoral Letters are rare in the other letters (for example, 'saviour' and 'teaching').

The style is also different. It is much less lively, lacking the cut-and-thrust of argument so characteristic of Paul's usual style. We sense that the writer is putting forward traditional material rather than formulating fresh ideas, and he employs vague generalizations with reference to those he attacks, so that it is often hard for the reader to know what it is they were teaching. Although the letters are addressed to people who were Paul's close associates for many years, they seem rather impersonal and tell them things that such people might be expected to know. Once again, the differences are a matter of fact, acknowledged by almost everybody, but the story that explains these facts is a matter of dispute.

THE STORY BEHIND THE PASTORAL LETTERS

There are alternative stories behind the Pastoral Letters, each of them supported by significant scholars. Let us call them story A and story B.

STORY A

Since the personal and historical details mentioned in the Pastoral Letters cannot easily be fitted into the story of Paul as we know it from Acts, it is proposed that these letters were written during a period after the story in Acts has finished. According to Acts, when Paul reached Rome he spent two whole years in his own rented house, but what happened next we are not told. According to story A, Paul was released from this imprisonment, either because he was acquitted or because the case was abandoned for lack of evidence. He then travelled to Crete with Titus and engaged in an evangelistic campaign, resulting in the formation of new churches in the cities of that island.

Before the work could be finished, he was forced to leave Crete and travel to Ephesus, where false teaching was threatening the church. Paul excommunicated the ringleaders (1 Tim. 1:19–20), and then travelled on to Nicopolis in Macedonia. From there he wrote to Titus in Crete summoning him to Nicopolis (Titus 3:12), and to Timothy in Ephesus telling him to remain until Paul himself returned (1 Tim. 3:14). He probably never reached Ephesus, however. Instead he was arrested, perhaps in Troas, which is why he was compelled to leave his cloak and books behind, and from there taken to Rome. From prison in Rome he wrote a final letter to Timothy (2 Timothy), urging Timothy to visit him in Rome before winter, but clearly expecting the end.

This story just about hangs together, but faces a number of problems. Although there is evidence from later church tradition that Paul was released and went to Spain, as he intended, it says nothing about his going back to the east. Paul himself said that he had no room for further work 'from Jerusalem all the way round to Illyricum' (Rom. 15:19). Why, then, would he undertake an evangelistic campaign in Crete? If Paul was released at the end of two years, why does Luke not tell us, since it would be greatly in his interest to do so? It is easier to see why he might choose not to talk about Paul's execution. Assuming that Paul was released, why would he be rearrested, and if rearrested, why taken to Rome again? Even if these questions can be answered satisfactorily, we are still left wondering why Paul has adopted such a different style and chosen to express himself in this way to close associates.

STORY B

Paul was not released from the prison at the end of the two years. He lost his appeal and was executed. The great apostle was now dead. Who would carry on his work and continue his teaching in the churches of the Pauline mission? The answer proposed is that his closest co-workers, including Timothy and Titus and probably Luke as well, composed these letters to legitimate Timothy and Titus as Paul's successors and ensure that his voice continued to be heard in the churches he had founded. They probably wrote 2 Timothy first. It is the most personal of the Pastoral Letters and provides the sort of deathbed 'last words of Paul' that Paul himself had been unable to speak. (The many incidental details, especially in 4:9–22, are perhaps taken from a genuine letter of Paul to Timothy, though not necessarily written from Rome.) They then wrote the letter to Titus, either to give backing to a real mission of Titus in Crete or as a blueprint for the sort of teaching that newly established churches would need. Finally, they wrote 1 Timothy, a more elaborate version of the instructions given in Titus, suitable for a more developed church like that of Ephesus.

This story avoids the historical improbabilities of story A. It explains the change of vocabulary and style if, in fact, the letters were actually written by somebody else.[1] It also explains why the letters are relatively impersonal. They were really written to be heard by the churches, not by close friends of Paul as individuals. They deal with recurrent threats to the churches, but not with specific problems like those dealt with in 1 Corinthians, for example, which is why it is hard to identify the 'opponents'.

A variant on this story proposes that the letters were written some thirty years after Paul's death, but this is surely unlikely. There is nothing in the teaching given or opposed that does not fit the time of Paul's death, while the need for such letters is much more obvious in the immediate aftermath of that tragic event than a generation later. By that time, Timothy and Titus themselves would have been dead, which would make nonsense of the clear intention to bolster their authority. The relatively undeveloped church order presupposed by the letters fits much better at the end of Paul's life than thirty years later.

The real question story B must face is whether *by the standards of the time* the writing of such letters would have been seen as fraudulent. This is a big subject. We know that it was *not* considered acceptable in the second century, when the church was beginning to define its canon of Scripture. So if someone, thirty years on, had claimed to have 'discovered' hitherto unpublished letters of Paul, that would have been seen as fraudulent. My proposal, by contrast, is that everybody in the Pauline churches knew of Paul's tragic death and that these letters were written as part of the grieving process and to enable the Pauline mission to continue.[2]

THE MESSAGE OF 2 TIMOTHY

In fiction, the hero dies uttering some profound or witty saying, or he gathers friends and family around the bed and gives them parting instructions—and then he dies. In reality, it doesn't often happen this way. Whether we end our days sedated in a hospital ward or, like Paul, brutally done to death in a prison cell, there is usually no time to prepare, no strength or opportunity to speak and no one gathered to listen. But when a great man or woman dies, we feel that they ought to have something important to say—they ought to have ended their life with a bang rather than a whimper. The Jews felt this too, and in the intertestamental period there was a fashion for writing farewell speeches, also known as 'testaments', in which Old Testament characters on their deathbed predict the troubles that will follow their death and call on those who come after them to imitate their faith.

Although written in the form of a letter, 2 Timothy can be understood as such a farewell speech, presenting what Paul would have said as he bravely faced the end, if anybody had been present to listen to him. His friends had two purposes in writing it—first to safeguard

Paul's own reputation and second to encourage Christians to follow in his footsteps. Paul was a controversial figure during his lifetime, and he did not cease to be so after his death. His opponents will have been quick to seize on his ignominious death to portray him as a failure. The letter portrays him as a martyr and aims to give courage to those who can expect to meet a similar fate.

Accordingly, the first section of the letter (1:3—2:13) issues a call not to 'be ashamed to testify about our Lord, or ashamed of me his prisoner' (1:8). Despite being in prison, Paul is not ashamed (1:12); and the humble figure of Onesiphorus shows what it means not to be ashamed of the imprisoned apostle (1:16), like the readers of the letter to the Hebrews of whom it was said, 'Sometimes you were publicly exposed to insult and persecution; at other times you stood side by side with those who were so treated. You sympathized with those in prison...' (Heb. 10:33–34). Timothy is called to 'endure hardship with us like a good soldier of Christ Jesus' (2:3), and to 'remember Christ Jesus, raised from the dead' (2:8). The section ends with a metrical version of Paul's teaching in Romans 6 about dying and rising with Christ, confirming that being baptized into his death was always about the social cost of becoming a Christian (2:11–13). It is striking how much this section draws on themes in Romans, from the initial call not to be ashamed (Rom. 1:16), to the summary of the gospel in terms of Jesus being descended from David and raised from the dead (Rom. 1:3–4), to the idea of dying and raising with Christ. Paul's last and greatest letter was also the one most readily available to the friends who wrote this letter in Rome after his death.

The letter continues with a call for the Christian worker not to be quarrelsome (2:14–26), which also contains echoes of Romans (compare 2:14 with Rom. 14:1; and 2:20–21 with Rom. 9:21). Then there is a prediction, very typical of such farewell speeches, of a coming time of apostasy, which the readers will recognize as already upon them (3:1–9). A reminiscence of a well-known incident in the life of the apostle is made the basis of a further exhortation to faithfulness (3:10–17), and the body of the letter ends with a solemn charge based on the apostle's knowledge of his approaching death (4:1–8). The closing section presents a moving picture, no doubt closely based on recent events, of the apostle alone, cold, betrayed, but confident and unashamed.

THE MESSAGE OF TITUS AND 1 TIMOTHY

The other two Pastoral Letters are less personal. Although formally written to Titus and Timothy, they are more obviously addressed to the churches that Titus and Timothy will be overseeing.

The letter to Titus falls naturally into three sections, of which the first might be entitled 'Safeguarding the congregation' (1:5–16). The churches are still threatened by the false teaching of those more conservative Jewish Christians who wanted to force the Gentiles to judaize. Although the reference is vague, this is plain from the fact that the letter calls them 'the circumcision group' (1:10), speaks of 'Jewish myths' (1:14), apparently in connection with scruples about clean and unclean food, and of 'quarrels about the law' (3:9). The congregation will be kept safe by the appointment of suitable leaders, people of good character who 'hold firmly to the trustworthy message as it has been taught' (1:5–9).

The second section might be entitled 'Safeguarding the Christian household' (2:1–15). The health of society as a whole was widely seen to depend on the health of its constituent households, so the extended family was a matter of great importance in the ancient world, not just to itself but to its neighbours. Christian households would have been viewed with suspicion by outsiders quick to point the finger at any irregularity, so we find several of the later New Testament writings giving attention to this and showing how the gospel does not break down the traditional structures of society but injects a new spirit into them. So, in Titus, 'sound doctrine' has something to say about the behaviour of older and younger men, older and younger women, and slaves, and this is seen to be grounded in the grace of God as it has been made known in the first appearing of Christ (in his incarnation and death) and will be completed in the second appearing of Christ (when he comes as judge).

The third section might be entitled 'Safeguarding the reputation of the Church in society' (3:1–15). Its theme is 'doing good'. Christians must be 'ready to do whatever is good' (3:1, 8, 14), and this too is grounded in the gospel. God's kindness and love have 'appeared' in Jesus, and Christians have become part of that story by baptism, and have been justified by his grace. Good deeds do not earn salvation, but they are the proper fruit of it, and this is expressed in one of the 'faithful sayings' so characteristic of these letters: 'those who have trusted in God must be careful to devote themselves to doing what is good, things that everyone counts fine and profitable' (3:8, my translation).[3]

Two things stand out in this short letter. There is no attempt to boost the dignity or status of Titus. He is to appoint elders, but he himself is given no title beyond that of being Paul's true son—and that is enough. His authority resides in his relationship to the absent apostle, and not in any title of office that he might be tempted to claim. Equally notable is the writer's confidence that the gospel itself has the power to safeguard the Church and produce 'a people that are [God's] very own, eager to do what is good' (2:14). That is why he gives us the two gospel summaries (2:11–14; 3:3–7) that take up such a large proportion of this letter.

1 Timothy can be seen to contain a fuller version of the teaching found in Titus, either because it was written later or because it was directed to a larger and more complex church at Ephesus. There is the same pressing challenge from conservative Jewish Christians who are insisting that Gentile converts observe the law (1:3–11; 4:1–5), to be met, we may suppose, by insisting on the worldwide, saving purpose of the one God (2:1–7). However, the majority of the letter falls under the rubric contained in 3:15, that 'you will know how people ought to conduct themselves in God's household, which is the church of the living God, the pillar and foundation of the truth'. Accordingly, we have instructions for the conduct of men and women in worship (2:8–15), and a fuller account of the kind of people who should be appointed to leadership in the Church (3:1–13). The instructions on older people are greatly expanded, with rules for the care of widows and the honouring of elders who preach and teach (5:1–25). The advice to slaves is to some extent balanced by instructions and warnings to the rich (6:1–10, 17–19). Running through the letter is a strand of personal commissioning more akin to 2 Timothy than to Titus. The writer recalls Paul's conversion and on this basis calls Timothy to 'fight the good fight' (1:12—20). He gives detailed instructions on the kind of man Timothy is to be and how he is to spend his time as Paul's delegate (4:6–16), and concludes with a final charge to guard the Christian message entrusted to him (6:11–16, 20–21).

To summarize, we may say that 1 Timothy is composed of three strands—a doctrinal strand, a social and ethical strand, and a personal strand—and these are all woven together so that it is difficult to trace a coherent plot in the letter. No doubt this reflects the writer's conviction that these things cannot be separated. The health of the Church requires both sound doctrine and good order, and both require the dedication of those who seek to walk in the apostle's footsteps and carry on his work.

THE OUTCOME OF THE PASTORAL LETTERS

For all their rather humdrum tone and content, the Pastoral Letters were brilliantly successful. Together with the Acts of the Apostles, they were responsible for preserving Paul's influence and safe-guarding his reputation in the troubled years after his death, by fixing a particular portrait of Paul in the mind of the Church. He is the model convert (1 Tim. 1:12–17). He is the great apostle and teacher of the Church (1 Tim. 2:7; 2 Tim. 1:11). He is the great example for others to follow (2 Tim. 3:10–11; 4:6–8). In contrast to ascetics and other enthusiasts (2 Tim. 2:18), he is a person of balanced views, and an advocate of sensible Christianity (2 Tim. 1:7) that does not seek to overthrow the social order but rather transform it from within. In the controversies of the second century, the Pastoral Letters played an important part in detaching Paul from the Gnostic camp and cap-turing him for orthodox Christianity.

Down to the present day, the Pastoral Letters have been loved and hated but rarely ignored. One of their lasting contributions, perhaps insufficiently appreciated, is their insistence that God is the God of the whole world. He desires all people to be saved; he is the Saviour of all, especially those who believe; and as a consequence his Church must be open to all and not a secret mystery religion. This means prayer as wide as the world itself, and a proper concern for the every-day structures of society and the opinion of ordinary people.

It is in this context that the demand that women learn in silence (1 Tim. 2:11) should be understood. It is prompted by a desire that the Church should not erect unnecessary barriers to the acceptance of the faith by ordinarily thoughtful people of that time by presenting itself as some sort of mystery cult (in which, notoriously, women behaved with abandonment). Today, of course, times have changed, and the literal adherence to what the writer says would, in our society, produce exactly the negative reaction he was trying to avoid. However, the principle that we should not needlessly antagonize people—not because we want people to think well of us, but because God desires their salvation—remains valid and its implications need to be thought through afresh in every age. In this, as in other things, the Pastoral Letters are true to Paul's memory (1 Cor. 9:19–22).

Another enduring legacy of these letters is their portrait of Christian ministry. Their call to 'watch your life and doctrine closely' (1 Tim. 4:16) and to preach the word 'in season and out of season' (2 Tim. 4:2) continues to inspire preachers and pastors and all who seek to present themselves to God as one approved, 'a workman who does not need to be ashamed and who correctly handles the word of truth' (2 Tim. 2:15).

PART THREE

LIVING BY THE STORY

CHAPTER 14

APOSTOLIC LETTERS
AND SERMONS

The Hebrew Bible (unlike the Christian Old Testament) is arranged in three sections. First there is the Law, consisting of the five books of Moses and telling the story of how Israel came into existence. Then there are the Prophets—the Former Prophets consisting of Joshua to 2 Kings, and the Latter Prophets consisting of Isaiah, Jeremiah, Ezekiel and the Twelve. The remainder is called the Writings, which include the Psalms and wisdom literature and end with the books of Chronicles. By accident or design, the New Testament can be seen to have a similar arrangement. The four Gospels correspond to the Law, being foundational to all the rest, largely narrative in form, yet containing (in the Sermon on the Mount) the Law as restated by Jesus. The letters of Paul, Romans to Philemon, contain the authoritative interpretation of the gospel and correspond to the Prophets (with Acts as a narrative introduction corresponding to the Former Prophets that we think of as the historical books). The remaining books, Hebrews to Revelation, correspond to the Writings, being a diverse collection of documents, probably later than the rest of the New Testament and in some sense secondary to it.

Though diverse, these writings are linked together by a number of common features. They all address communities of Christians who are in danger of falling away from their faith and who are under pressure to give it up. Sometimes the pressure comes in the form of persecution. Hebrews reminds its readers of the sufferings that attended their conversion and the bravery they showed then, as a spur to standing firm now (10:32–35). 1 Peter tells readers not to be surprised at the 'fiery ordeal that is taking place among you' (4:12, NRSV) and encourages them to stand firm 'even if now for a little while you have had to suffer various trials' (1:6, NRSV). Even James begins, 'My brothers and sisters, whenever you face trials of any kind, consider it nothing but joy' (1:2, NRSV).

Sometimes the pressure comes in the form of new teaching that creates divisions or licenses immoral behaviour. Jude perceives the Church to be under threat from 'certain intruders… who pervert the grace of our God into licentiousness and deny our only Master and Lord, Jesus Christ' (v. 4, NRSV). 2 Peter warns that 'there will be false teachers among you, who will secretly bring in destructive opinions' (2:1, NRSV), and who will say, 'Where is the promise of his coming?' (3:4, NRSV). The letters of John address a community that has been divided by those who deny that Jesus is the Christ in whom God himself has become flesh.

In each of these letters, there are signs that the readers are second-generation Christians, or, at any rate, not new believers. The readers of Hebrews are told to 'remember your leaders, who spoke the word of God to you. Consider the outcome of their way of life and imitate their faith' (13:7). These leaders are clearly no longer around, and the readers themselves are scolded for not making the spiritual progress that they should (5:11–12). Jude calls on the readers to 'contend for the faith that was once for all entrusted to the saints' (v. 3), and 2 Peter reminds them of 'the commandment of the Lord and Saviour spoken through your apostles' (3:2, NRSV). Paul's letters are now spoken of as Scripture and, as such, hard to understand (2 Pet. 3:15–16). It is true that the readers of 1 Peter are addressed as newborn infants (2:2), perhaps on the occasion of their baptism, but the church into which they are baptized seems to be well-established under the leadership of its elders (5:1ff.), as do the churches of James (5:14) and John.

Third, these letters all betray a strong interest in the implications of the faith for daily living. This is obviously true of James, which is almost entirely concerned with Christian behaviour and has no explicit doctrinal teaching at all. When Jude denounces those who have infiltrated the church with new teaching, it is because he is concerned about its moral consequences. 2 Peter restates the doctrine of the second coming to reinforce Christian living and calls on his readers to 'make every effort to support your faith with goodness' (1:5, NRSV). 1 Peter is concerned about the way Christians live in society and the impression they make on their non-Christian neighbours (2:11–17). John issues a strong call to love as the proof of true faith. 'We know that we have passed from death to life because we love one another' (1 John 3:14, NRSV). 'Little children, let us love, not in word or speech, but in truth and action' (1 John 3:18, NRSV). Even Hebrews develops its magnificent teaching about the person and work of Christ in the service of calling Christians to stand firm in their faith and not to drift away, and concludes with reminders about loving kindness, and the temptations presented by sex and money (13:1–6).

Generally speaking, these letters present little in the way of Christian doctrine, and when they do it is by way of reminder, the writers knowing that right living comes from right believing. Several of these writings, in fact—notably Hebrews, James and 1 John—have been classified as sermons or collections of sermons rather than true letters.

This third part of the New Testament is held together by no story that we can now discover. The letters of Paul gain in meaning by being related to chapters in the life of Paul as we learn it from Acts and the letters themselves. There is a story behind each of the Pauline letters consisting partly of the story of the Church and partly that of the apostle. Obviously the same was true for each of these letters also, but we no longer know what those stories were. Even where we are told something of the story of the Church—persecution, false teaching, division—we cannot usually locate the recipients on the map (1 Peter is an exception here) or assign them a date, and we know next to nothing about their authors.

Hebrews is anonymous. Tantalizing hints in the last chapter link it to the Pauline circle and some have guessed, on the strength of the description of him in Acts 18:24, that the author was Apollos, but this remains a guess. James and Jude are traditionally identified as brothers of Jesus, though neither letter makes this claim explicitly. 'James' simply calls himself a servant of Jesus Christ, and 'Jude' calls himself the brother of James. Even if the tradition is correct, it adds little to our appreciation of these letters, since we know little of the lives of these men and nothing of the circumstances in which they wrote. Two letters claim to be by Peter, but we know nothing certain about Peter's later life after he drops out of the pages of Acts. In any case, style alone suggests that the two letters are not by the same person. Since, as we have seen, both letters appear to be addressing a second- or third-generation situation, it is likely that they have been produced by the church in Rome, reworking Peter's teaching for a new day. The letters of John are also anonymous. Tradition ascribes the fourth Gospel to John. On grounds of style and content, these letters appear to be by the author of the fourth Gospel, or at least someone very close to him, and that is why the letters are called the letters of John.

The letters of this third section of the New Testament are almost impossible to date. Those who accept the traditional authorship tend to prefer an early date, somewhere in the middle of the first century; those who are impressed by the evidence that these letters address the problems of the second generation tend to place them in the years between AD70 and 90, a period of church history of which, conveniently, we know almost nothing. Some of these letters may in fact be early, earlier even than some of Paul's letters, but by virtue of their place in the canon of Scripture they are now read in the light of Paul's letters and as a supplement to them.

Whoever actually wrote these letters, they have not been collected together here as a counterweight to Paul, as if the collectors were interested in giving a voice to non-Pauline Christianity. (They may serve this purpose for historians of earliest Christianity, but that is not the reason they are here!) On the contrary, they appear now as a supplement to Paul, showing that the apostle was supported and confirmed by the rest of the Church. This is true even, or particularly, of the letter of James, which is often seen as contradicting Paul in the matter of faith and works, but is in reality only preserving Paul from distortion at the hands of those whom 2 Peter calls 'ignorant and unstable' (3:16). The writer of 2 Peter speaks for those who collected all these letters together to form the Writings section of the New Testament, when he says: 'So also our beloved brother Paul wrote to you according to the wisdom given him, speaking of this as he does in all his letters. There are some things in them hard to understand, which the ignorant and unstable twist to their own destruction, as they do the other scriptures' (3:15–16, NRSV).

Whatever the stories, now for ever lost to us, that originally lay behind them, these letters now call us with one voice to live by the story of Jesus, of which Paul was the inspired interpreter.

THE LETTER TO THE HEBREWS

THE REASON FOR HEBREWS

It was tough being a Christian in first-century Rome. Our writer reminds his readers that 'insult', 'persecution', 'prison' and 'the confiscation of your property' had followed their conversion, and they had put up with it all cheerfully enough in the first enthusiasm of their newfound faith and fellowship (10:32–34). But things had got no easier as the years went by. Disgrace, arrest and torture (13:3), if not actual martyrdom (12:4), continued intermittently, but the excitement of being a Christian had waned and faith had begun to flag. The first generation of leaders had passed away (13:7) and the Lord's coming seemed no nearer, and some of the readers had begun to think wistfully of the security and prestige they had enjoyed in their former way of life. Some of them had been Jews or adherents of the local synagogue and, while not exactly popular as such, they had enjoyed a measure of legal protection and the consolations of an ancient faith and liturgy by which, week by week, the conscience could be eased and sins forgiven. The benefits of Christianity seemed increasingly insubstantial.

It is to this pastoral situation that this written sermon is addressed. More than half of it is taken up with urgent calls to persevering faith and warnings about the terrible consequences of apostasy. The danger is not so much that they will lose their faith to superior arguments or experience a sudden crisis of unbelief, as that they will drift from their moorings and lose their faith by neglect (2:1). Like the people of Israel of old, they hear God's voice week by week but are in danger of hardening their hearts and of losing the 'rest' to which God has called them (3:7—4:11). They need to listen to God, encourage one another and take their sins and fears to Jesus in prayer (4:14–16). They have grown unreceptive and, as a result, what was once simple faith is now simply immaturity (5:11–14).

Those who refuse to advance in faith regress, and some of the severest warnings in the whole Bible are reserved for those who backslide (Heb. 6:4–8; 10:26–30). Yet no one needs to do so. God keeps faith and he can be trusted to save all who turn to him (6:9–20; 10:19–23). With the encouragement of fellow Christians (10:24–25), each one of them can follow in the steps of those great heroes of Israel's story, which is also their story (11:1–40). Above all, they should look 'to Jesus the pioneer and perfecter of our faith, who for the sake of the joy that was set before him endured the cross, disregarding its shame, and has taken his seat at the right hand of the throne of God' (12:2, NRSV). Jesus, after all, died outside the city gate, condemned to death by both religious and secular authorities. Rather than looking wistfully back to the imagined comforts of the old religion and the security of society's good opinion, they should take their stand with Jesus and find security in a city that will outlast the vicissitudes of this present age (13:12–14).

Like any good preacher, our writer is not content to scold or threaten. His exhortations are grounded in the reality of what God has done for us in Christ. His appeals characteristically begin 'Therefore…', pointing us back to truths that make obedience reasonable and possible. In Hebrews we find neither 'theology' detached from life nor appeals devoid of truth, but a subtle blend of teaching and advice that our writer describes as a 'word of exhortation' (13:22). God has spoken to us through his Son Jesus, who once shared our weakness and suffering and now shares God's glory, so that we have a great high priest who understands our problems and has dealt once for all with our sins. With his help and the assurance that he gives, we can draw near to God and live lives of courageous faith in this world. Christian living is grounded in the person and work of Christ—who he is and what he has done for us on the cross.

AN OUTLINE OF HEBREWS

The letter, or sermon as it might more accurately be called, can be seen to fall into three main sections, which can be summarized as follows:

The person of Christ, God's Son and our brother (Hebrews 1:1—5:10)

God has spoken to us through his Son, who is superior to the angels and all human, cultural traditions of which they are guardians, including the law (1:1–14). So we need to pay attention to what he has said and not become dull of hearing or hard of heart. You may wonder why, if he is superior to angels, God's Son lived on earth as a man, who suffered and died. It was to make him a faithful and merciful high priest, able to help and sympathize with those who are tempted (2:5–18), and we too need to be faithful and avail ourselves of his mercy (4:14–16).

The work of Christ, our great high priest
(Hebrews 5:11—10:39)

But, you may be wondering, how can Jesus be our high priest when the Bible already provides for a priestly system, to which Jesus did not belong? This merely shows that you haven't read the Bible with sufficient attention! You need to go deeper if you are not to remain immature or even lose your faith altogether (although there is no need for that, and God is faithful). Scripture in fact leads us to expect the coming of a superior priesthood to that of Aaron (that of Melchizedek, 7:1–28), and a better covenant than the Mosaic (8:1–13), as foreseen by Jeremiah—one that deals with sin comprehensively by changing hearts and securing forgiveness (9:11–14). Jesus, who came down to where we are, has ascended to where God is and, in the words of the Book of Common Prayer, 'made there by himself once offered a full, perfect and sufficient sacrifice, oblation and satisfaction for the sins of the whole world' (9:23—28). As a result, you need to draw near to God with faith, in the company of all God's people, remembering the faith you showed when you first became Christians (10:19–39).

The call to faith (Hebrews 11:1—13:25)

The story of Israel is full of men and women whose stories show us what faith means. It means taking God at his word, putting more confidence in the future he has planned rather than in the world we presently experience, and sticking to our commitment through thick and thin (11:1–40). Of course, the supreme example of faith is Jesus himself, who is the pioneer and perfecter of our faith (12:1–3). You must derive strength from his example and reckon seriously with belonging to the city of God (12:22). Faith needs to be worked out in obedience to God's laws (13:4–5) and in a willingness to be identified with Jesus and all his true people—outside the camp (13:13).

May God bless and keep you! (13:20–21).

THE MESSAGE OF HEBREWS

As the writer admits, there is much in this letter that is hard to explain and, like the first readers, it is to be feared that we are often dull in understanding. Angels and high priests are not subjects that we think about much, yet there is gold here if we will dig for it. In the first place, to say that Jesus is superior to the angels makes sense if we remember that in Jewish thought angels were the spiritual guardians of the various nations, including Israel, so that the law itself was thought to have been given through angels. To say that Christ is superior to angels is to exalt him above every norm of culture and tradition, and that is as relevant to us as it was to those who were tempted to return to Judaism.

Second, the writer's use of Melchizedek shows us that Scripture is made up of many voices and traditions, some perhaps speaking more directly to our age than others. As the old Puritan Robert Robinson put it, 'The Lord has yet more light and truth to break forth from his word', and we do well to ask not only what Scripture says but where it points. Third, no part of the New Testament has more to say about the reality of Jesus' human nature and experience than Hebrews. We gladly affirm that he is able to sympathize with our weakness and that he has been tested in every respect like ourselves, but are still shocked to read that, 'During the days of Jesus' life on earth, he offered up prayers and petitions with loud cries and tears to the one who could save him from death, and he was heard because of his reverent submission. Although he was a son, he *learned* obedience from what he suffered' (5:7–8, my italics).

Fourth, Hebrews offers us the most sustained reflection in the New Testament on the mystery that we call the atonement—how the death of Jesus achieves our salvation. It does so not in terms of punishment but of gift. Jesus, our representative, offers to God a perfect human obedience on our behalf so as to 'do away with sin by the sacrifice of himself' (9:26) once and for all, and for all who will by faith identify themselves with his action.

Finally, Hebrews tells us what it means to live by faith. It means taking God at his word and choosing the unseen future rather than giving in to the fears or desires aroused by the present that shouts so loudly. It means looking forward 'to the city with foundations, whose architect and builder is God' (11:10); it means choosing 'to be mistreated along with the people of God rather than to enjoy the pleasures of sin for a short time' (11:25).

THE LETTER OF JAMES

WARNING TO WORLDLY CHRISTIANS

What does it mean to live by the Story? No part of the New Testament is more concerned with this than James. But what is this document? It is hardly a letter in any ordinary sense. We learn nothing from it about the circumstances of either the author or his readers. It is rather a sermon, or collection of short sermons, prefaced by a greeting that serves to address it to the whole Church. Perhaps we should call it an open letter to Christians everywhere. With its echoes of the teaching of Jesus, James paints a picture of Christian existence marked by simplicity rather than ostentation, equality rather than hierarchy, community rather than individualism, spiritual wealth but material poverty. Unfortunately, that is no longer the kind of church to which his readers belong. Wealth has produced division and discrimination and killed off simple obedience to the call of God and the needs of the poor. The temptations of office have led some to boast of their wisdom, while others display envy and selfish ambition. The world has got into the Church, and James would call the Church back to its first love.

JAMES AND THE GOSPEL

It is obvious that James is concerned about *living*, but where does *the Story* come into it? At first sight, James seems to have little to say about Jesus, and nothing about his cross and resurrection, so that some people have even wondered whether this is really a Christian writing at all—but they are wrong to do so. James addresses us as those who 'hold the faith of our glorious Lord Jesus Christ' (2:1, NRSV). 'The faith of our Lord Jesus Christ' is either the Christian faith as believed by the Church, which in all its forms tells the story of Jesus, or it is the same faith as Jesus himself held and lived by in his earthly life as recorded in the fourfold Gospel story. By his life and teaching, Jesus pointed people to God his Father, and so does James. God 'gives generously to all without finding fault' (1:5); God promises a crown of life to those who love him (1:12); every good and perfect gift comes from him (1:17); God is our Father (1:27), utterly good (1:13), unchangingly faithful (1:17), the source of new birth (1:18). He is the friend of those who trust and obey (2:23; 4:4). He is the 'one Lawgiver and Judge' (4:12), constantly attentive to the cries of the poor (5:4), 'full of compassion and mercy' (5:11), who hears prayer, forgives sin, heals the sick and raises the dead (5:15). He is the God of Abraham (2:21), Rahab (2:25), Job (5:11) and Elijah (5:17), and also the God and Father of our Lord Jesus Christ.

Because of what he says about faith and works (2:14–26) James has often been thought to be contradicting Paul at this point—but Paul would have agreed with him. Paul comes out just as strongly against faith that is not put into practice (Rom. 2:6–11), and he is just as clear that Christians must not be conformed to this world but be transformed by the renewal of their minds (Rom. 12:2)—which is the message of James in a nutshell.

THE PLAN OF THE LETTER

James consists of a number of short sermons on a variety of topics and it is not easy to find an overall plan. However, it is noteworthy that the letter begins and ends by counselling Christians on how to respond to trouble (1:2–12; 5:13—20). At the heart of the letter is the contrast between worldly wisdom and the wisdom from above, friendship with the world and friendship with God (3:13—4:10). I suggest, then, that the whole letter has been arranged chiastically, as follows:

A   Responding to troubles   1:2–18

> B   The need for patience   1:19–27

>> C   The dangers of wealth   2:1–26

>>> D   The misuse of the tongue   3:1–12

>>>> E   True and false wisdom   3:13—4:10

>>> D'   The misuse of the tongue   4:11–12

>> C'   The dangers of wealth   4:13—5:6

> B'   The need for patience   5:7–12

A'   Responding to troubles   5:13–20

THE MESSAGE OF JAMES IN OUTLINE

We may summarize the teaching of these five strands like this.

- The beginning and end of the matter is that troubles are inevitable in this life. Christians should not be discouraged but bring everything to God in prayer, knowing that God has some good purpose in it all. We need not struggle alone with our trials, but should seek the help and prayers of the Christian community, and be ready to help others in our turn (1:2–27; 5:13–20).

- Patience is important as we wait for God to intervene to put a situation right, and angry words, whether against God or other people, will do nothing to help (1:19–27; 5:7–12).

- The great danger of wealth is worldliness. This shows itself in bowing and scraping to the rich, neglecting the needs of the poor, and in arrogant self-sufficiency. Faith must show itself in obedience to God's command to love our neighbours as ourselves (2:1–26; 4:13—5:6).

- The tongue is another source of worldliness, leading us to boast about ourselves and criticize others. Gifted speakers are often most at risk (3:1–12; 4:11–12).

- It comes down to this: the world's wisdom is marked by envy and selfish ambition, and leads to quarrels and fighting. God's wisdom is 'pure, peace-loving, considerate, submissive, full of mercy and good fruit, impartial and sincere', and leads to peace and right relationships. We can be either friends of the world or friends of God, but we cannot be both. We need a profound conversion (3:13—4:10).[1]

THE LETTER OF JUDE

Since Jude claims to be James' brother, we will take him next. Although the tone of this letter is quite different from that of James, there are points of contact. Like James, this letter is addressed not to a particular community but to all Christians (v. 1), suggesting that, whatever its origin, this material has now been edited for general circulation. Then, Jude's concern that grace should not be abused and taken as a licence to do wrong (v. 4) is similar to James' concern that faith express itself in good works. Finally, both writers end their appeal with a call to bring back those who have strayed from the path of virtue (vv. 22–23).

We know nothing of this brother of Jesus beyond the name. We know nothing of the circumstances that prompted this letter, who the recipients were, where or when they lived, or the identity of their visitors whose teaching so disturbed the writer of the letter. The arguments that Jude employs against them strike us as obscure, with references not just to Old Testament stories that we have difficulty in recalling (such as Korah's rebellion), but to ancient Jewish writings (such as Enoch) that only scholars read today.

The heart of the letter is contained in verses 3–4 and 20–21. It is an appeal to 'contend for the faith that was once for all entrusted to the saints' (v. 3). This faith is in danger of being perverted by representatives of a new movement who are teaching something different. From the way in which Jude characterizes their teaching in terms of licentiousness (v. 4) and lust (v. 18), and his appeal to the example of Sodom and Gomorrah (v. 7), it is usually held that they were teaching that Christians were free to do as they liked, especially in sexual relations. It is hard to be sure, however, since the writer is employing conventional invective against his opponents and painting them in the blackest colours. They may simply have been 'liberated' Christians relaxing traditional Jewish prohibitions, as Paul did, for example, in the matter of food offered to idols. Not everyone agreed with Paul, as the book of Revelation shows (2:14). In response, Jude calls on his readers to have nothing to do with them, but rather devote themselves to the practice of religion as they have been taught. 'Build yourselves up in your most holy faith and pray in the Holy Spirit. Keep yourselves in God's love as you wait for the mercy of our Lord Jesus Christ to bring you to eternal life' (vv. 20–21).

Once we have grasped this simple message, we may be ready to go back to the material that Jude uses to reinforce his appeal. He appeals to various stories in Scripture and other Jewish writings to show that God's judgment is real and no one is exempt from it. The people of Israel, the fallen angels, Sodom and Gomorrah all serve as examples (vv. 5–7). The false teachers display the arrogance typical of their kind, speaking scornfully of the angelic guardians of morality, using religion as an opportunity for personal enrichment and, like all rebels against God, they will perish (vv. 8–16). The apostles (now perhaps dead?) warned us of such people, and here they are (vv. 18–19)!

In its stern way, the letter of Jude reminds us of the essential link between professing the Christian faith and living the Christian life, and the disaster that will follow if these two are put asunder. Seductive movements offering 'cheap grace' are as much a part of our world as they were of his, even if we do not feel comfortable using Jude's type of invective against them. But invective is neither Jude's first word nor his last. He begins by addressing Christians as those who are 'kept safe for Jesus Christ' (v. 1, NRSV), and he ends by ascribing praise to God as the one 'who is able to keep you from falling' (v. 24). It may be necessary to 'contend for the faith' (v. 3), but the Church is in good hands!

THE FIRST LETTER OF PETER

THE REASON FOR 1 PETER

In the year AD111, the Roman governor of Bithynia in north-west Asia Minor wrote to Emperor Trajan as follows:

It is my custom, lord emperor, to refer to you all questions whereof I am in doubt. Who can better guide me when I am at a stand, or enlighten me if I am in ignorance? In investigations of Christians I have never taken part; hence I do not know what is the crime usually punished or investigated, or what allowances are made... whether punishment attaches to the mere name apart from secret crimes, or to the secret crimes connected with the name. Meantime this is the course I have taken with those who were accused before me as Christians. I asked them whether they were Christians, and if they confessed, I asked them a second or third time with threats of punishment. If they kept to it, I ordered them for execution; for I held no question that whatever it was that they admitted, in any case obstinacy and unbending perversity deserved to be punished.

Before long, as is often the case, the mere fact that the charge was taken notice of made it commoner, and several distinct cases arose. An unsigned paper was presented, which gave the names of many. As for those who said they neither were nor ever had been Christians, I thought it right to let them go, since they recited a prayer to the gods at my dictation, made supplication with incense and wine to your statue... and moreover cursed Christ—things which (so it is said) those who are really Christians cannot be made to do. Others who were named by the informer said that... they had been, but had ceased to be such some years ago.

They maintained, however, that the amount of their fault or error had been this, that it was their habit on a fixed day to assemble before daylight and recite by turns a form of words to Christ as a god; and that they bound themselves by an oath, not for any crime, but not to commit theft or robbery or adultery, not to break their word, and not to deny a deposit when demanded. After this was done, their custom was to depart, and to meet again to take food, but ordinary and harmless food. On this I considered it the more necessary to find out from two maid servants who were called deaconesses, and by torments, how far this was true: but I discovered nothing else than a perverse and extravagant superstition. Therefore I adjourned the case and hastened to consult you.[2]

This letter gives a very good picture of what we mean when we talk about Christians being persecuted at the time the New Testament documents were being written. Note especially:

- There was no official, empire-wide policy of persecuting Christians. Christianity was not a crime as such, otherwise Pliny would not have needed guidance. Action by the authorities against Christians was sporadic and in response to complaints against them by others.
- Christians were unpopular, no doubt because they refused to join in the rituals and festivals that most people observed. They were suspected of crimes, including cannibalism, and might be informed against at any time by those who disliked them, especially if the local governor showed a willingness to proceed against them.
- To a large extent it was up to the local governor to act as he saw fit in the maintenance of law and order. When Pliny began to punish Christians, accusations increased.
- The governor had wide powers of punishment. People could be punished for 'persistence and unbending stubbornness', as evidenced by a refusal to recant their Christian beliefs when ordered to do so. Unless they were Roman citizens, they would have no defence against such arbitrary treatment and no redress.

1 Peter is addressed to churches in the same part of the world, including specifically Bithynia, faced with just such a situation. Peter writes:

Beloved, do not be surprised at the fiery ordeal that is taking place among you to test you, as though something strange were happening to you. But rejoice insofar as you are sharing Christ's sufferings, so that you may also be glad and shout for joy when his glory is revealed. If you are reviled for the name of Christ, you are blessed, because the spirit of glory, which is the Spirit of God, is resting on you. But let none of you suffer as a murderer, a thief, a criminal, or even as a mischief maker. Yet if any of you suffers as a Christian, do not consider it a disgrace, but glorify God because you bear this name.

1 PETER 4:12–16 (NRSV)

As in Pliny's court, the readers are suffering specifically as Christians. They are reviled for the name of Christ, probably by their neighbours, and accused of all manner of crimes. They have no defence except a clean record and a respectful manner (2:15–17; 3:15–16).

We cannot prove that 1 Peter is a response to the persecution carried out by Pliny, but the fact that it addresses churches in the same area and describes the peril facing them in the same terms makes it tempting to do so. Certainly Pliny shows the kind of thing that could happen and probably was happening to the people Peter addresses. If so, of course, there is no chance that the letter was actually written by the apostle Peter, but it seems unlikely that Peter would have been moved to address a letter to such faraway churches, with whom, so far as we know, he had no connection. Were there even churches in Bithynia by the time of his death in AD64, and would we expect him to address them in such exalted language and solemn tone? It must be more likely that this letter comes from a Roman church that is beginning to aspire to leadership of the Christian movement following the destruction of Jerusalem, and speaks in the name of its famous martyr, Peter.

AN OUTLINE OF 1 PETER

It is widely agreed that 1 Peter falls into three easily recognized sections, as follows.

Remember who you are (1 Peter 1:1—2:10)

Although in the eyes of their neighbours they are contemptible and in the eyes of the governor 'nothing other than a perverse and extravagant superstition', the Christians of these distant provinces are to know that they have been 'chosen and destined by God the Father and sanctified by the Spirit to be obedient to Jesus Christ and to be sprinkled with his blood' (1:2, NRSV). They have been given 'new birth into a living hope', and they have a great inheritance (1:3–4). In fact, they are persons of great dignity with great expectations, nothing less than the Israel of God, 'a chosen people, a royal priesthood, a holy nation, a people belonging to God' (2:9), called to do what Israel of old was called to do, to offer 'spiritual sacrifices' (2:5) and 'proclaim the mighty acts of him who called you out of darkness into his marvellous light' (2:9, NRSV). In saying this, Peter does not mean to imply that Christians have replaced the Jews as God's people but that, though formerly Gentiles ('not a people', 2:10), they have now joined faithful Jews to form one people of God founded on Jesus Christ as foundation stone, and the privileges and responsibilities of Israel are now theirs.

In the light of this, they must see their present troubles as a test of faith. They must resolve to live holy lives, not conforming to the ways of this world. God is their Father and they must honour him by their obedience. They must love one another and desire, above all else, the milk of God's word so that they become mature Christians.

Because of the emphasis on new birth (1:3; 2:2), it has sometimes been suggested that the letter particularly addresses new Christians and even that it incorporates a baptismal sermon. This is unlikely. The whole church is being addressed, elders as well as younger members, and the fiery trial affects them all. On the other hand, wise pastors will continually remind Christians of the meaning of their baptism and draw their minds back to their Christian beginnings by way of encouraging them to live by the story of Jesus today, and that is what Peter does here. The drama of baptism says all the things Peter says here by way of promise and command and is the rich treasure on which Christian preaching draws. Interestingly, in the one place where baptism is mentioned specifically (3:21), it is described as a means of salvation that is effective both as prayer and pledge—the place where God's grace and human commitment meet.

This is how you should live (1 Peter 2:11—4:11)

If the Church is Israel, then life in this present world can be likened to Israel's exile in Babylon, and that is the metaphor that controls this second part of the letter. Those who live as 'aliens and exiles' (2:11, NRSV) in a foreign country are particularly vulnerable and need to live prudently and blamelessly. They are bound to attract suspicion, so it is all the more important for them to make sure there is no substance to the allegations made against them. They are to be model citizens, subject to every human institution and honouring the emperor. This does not imply that Peter has a positive view of the Roman empire— still less that he thinks Christians may give the emperor worship, should this be demanded—simply that they should not bring trouble on themselves by wrongdoing or needless disrespect.

One particularly sensitive area is the household, where Christians cannot help attracting the attention of those around them and suspicion that they are undermining the social order. So slaves must be careful to obey their masters and, if necessary, accept punishment even when it is not deserved (2:18), knowing that they are following in the footsteps of Jesus and modelling obedience for the whole Church. Wives in Greco-Roman society were expected to follow their husband's religion. Christian women married to non-Christians will not do that, but that makes it all the more important that they show themselves to be good wives in every other way that would be expected (3:1–4). By contrast, where the husband is a Christian, the problems will be less acute, so the instruction to husbands is briefer (3:7). It is important for modern readers to note that what Peter says about marriage is designed to address the problems of mixed marriages in patriarchal societies and can no more be taken as the last word on Christian marriage than can his comments on slavery be seen as the last word on labour relations.

All Christians, however, slave or free, male or female, need to live upright lives and not get involved in arguments with neighbours or authorities. They are to cultivate a gentle manner at all times, while being ready to explain their faith (3:8–16). This is commended in Scripture, and is also the example set by Jesus—and Jesus, be it noted, did not only suffer and die; he rose in triumph, guaranteeing ultimate victory to his people over all authorities and empires and the evil spiritual forces that stand behind them. Christians too should remember that they were united in their baptism both with Christ's suffering and his resurrection, and should keep their consciences clear. They should separate themselves from the dissolute ways of their neighbours and instead throw themselves into the life and worship of the Christian fellowship, using whatever gifts they have for the common good (4:3, 10). There are a number of clear echoes of Paul's letter to the Romans here (4:10–11) and elsewhere in the letter (1:14; 2:13–14; 4:7).

Facing the present crisis (1 Peter 4:12—5:11)

How, then, should the Christians of Bithynia and other places respond to this outbreak of slanderous accusations and the harsh sentences meted out by the courts? They should see it as quite normal, as something they were led to expect (4:12). Provided it is for the name of Christ, such suffering is actually an honour, a sharing in Christ's sufferings and proof that the Spirit of God is resting on them. All such crises foreshadow the great day of judgment and bring it nearer, but God the creator of all things and judge of all people can be trusted to look after his own. There is a special responsibility resting on the elders of the church to act like good shepherds at this time of danger and to model the Christian response, and the church needs to honour and support its leaders (5:2–5). Unlike his contemporary, Ignatius, Peter does not call on the church to gather round its bishop, but, in the tradition of the Roman church of this early period (as witnessed to by 1 Clement), to accept the authority of their elders. Finally, they should obey God, resist the devil's accusations, and be sure that the God who called them will also 'restore, support, strengthen and establish' them (5:10, NRSV).

THE MESSAGE OF 1 PETER

At the heart of everything this letter has to say is the story of Jesus. Jesus indeed is the foundation stone not just of the Church but of the whole edifice of Christian theology (2:4).

- He was destined by God before the foundation of the world (1:20).
- He was foretold by the prophets (1:10–12).
- He lived a life of humility and non-retaliation (2:23).
- He suffered violence for the sake of God's will (2:21).
- He died, and his death has ransomed us (1:18), healed us (2:24) and reconciled us to God (3:18). Like the servant of the Lord in Isaiah, he died in our place, the just for the unjust.
- But God raised him from the dead (1:3; 3:18).
- Risen from the dead, he has proclaimed his victory over the principalities and powers and imprisoned them (3:19), and now he sits at the right hand of God with the powers subject to him (3:22).
- From there he will be revealed as judge and saviour (1:7, 13; 4:13).

This story provides Peter and his audience with two great benefits. The first is an example (2:21; 4:1). The idea of Jesus as an example is surprisingly rare in the New Testament letters, but it is central to Peter's response to persecution threatening the church. Jesus left us an inspiring example, which doesn't only show us what to do; it shows us that it can be done.

The second benefit is hope. Christians are born again to a living hope (1:3). They have a hope that is set on God (1:21). When put on trial, they are to give an account of the hope that is in them (3:15). Christian women are the daughters of those holy women of old who hoped in God (3:5). The present world is full of trouble and suffering for those who want to obey God, but they are sustained in their troubles by the hope of an inheritance that is imperishable, undefiled and unfading (1:4), and if it is kept safe for us, we shall be kept safe for it by one who is the 'shepherd and overseer' of our souls (2:25).

THE SECOND LETTER OF PETER

THE REASON FOR 2 PETER

Although the letter presents itself as the last words of the apostle Peter (1:1, 12–15), there is not much doubt that it was written long after his death. Such 'testaments' attributed to great men of an earlier age were a recognized literary form, through which they, although dead, were held to speak to the needs of the present. The letter looks back to the apostles as those who belonged to an earlier generation but whose words are still powerful. The style and language both point to a Hellenistic rather than a Palestinian origin, even more than in the case of 1 Peter. Also, of course, if we are right to see 1 Peter as a response to Pliny's persecution in AD111, this letter, which calls itself the second letter (3:1), must be even later. Like the earlier letter, it most probably comes from the leadership of the Roman church.

Once again the faith is under attack, but this time from within, not from outside. 'False teachers' have arisen with 'destructive opinions' (2:1, NRSV), and they have had a good response. Time has passed and with it the first one or two generations of Christian leaders, and still the Lord has not come to judge the wicked and reward the faithful. Some influential teachers are calling for a rethink, and some of them appear to be ready to give up faith in God altogether. From this letter we get a pretty clear idea of some of their slogans. In particular they are saying:

- The idea of Christ's coming again is a myth (1:16).
- The prophets were just presenting their own ideas (1:20).
- God sleeps on and judges no one (2:3).
- The promised Christ never comes (3:4).

Perhaps the writer was stirred by Jude's call 'to contend for the faith once delivered to the saints' (Jude v. 3). He certainly knew the letter and made use of some of its more unusual phrases in constructing his own polemic against the new theology (2:4—3:4).

THE PLAN OF 2 PETER

The writer begins with a restatement of the gospel according to Peter. God has done all that is needed to bring us from death to life, from the corruption of this world to a share in the life of God himself. In response, we need to grow in our faith, advancing in goodness, knowledge, self-control, endurance, godliness, mutual affection and love. In this way we shall make God's promises our own and experience their truth for ourselves. This is the message that Peter has left us and what he would say to us if he were still here and able to remind us of what he taught (1:3–15).

The author then deals with the objections that are being raised to this faith. In the first place, it rests on the eyewitness testimony of those who were with Jesus, and who saw him transfigured in heavenly glory. The witness of the apostles confirms the message of the prophets, and the prophets did not just make it all up. On the contrary, they were inspired by the Holy Spirit and their warnings are to be taken with the utmost seriousness (1:16–21). These teachers will bring on themselves the very judgment they scoff at, and this is no idle threat, as the Scriptures show. God judged the fallen angels; God brought the flood on the sinful world; God destroyed Sodom and Gomorrah, and only Lot was saved. Will he not also judge these people with their immoral lifestyle and arrogant rejection of God's word—and all the more because they have known the truth and rejected it (2:1–22)? The warnings of the prophets have now been decisively reinforced by the 'command given by our Lord and Saviour through your apostles' (3:2). God who made the world can unmake it. He did it before and he will do it again. If he seems to be taking his time, you need to remember that God is outside time as we know it. If he delays, it is because he is giving people time to repent. But as Jesus said, the day of the Lord will come like a thief in the night, and this world will be burned up (3:1–10).

This being so, we need to wait patiently for God to bring about his promise of a new heavens and a new earth, where righteousness is at home, and live as those who will also feel at home in such a world. We should ignore all suggestions that it will never happen, or that it has happened already in some spiritual sense, or that it doesn't matter how we live because God will forgive us anyway. Instead, we should do everything we can to lead lives of holiness in response to God's call—in a word, to 'grow in grace and knowledge of our Lord and Saviour Jesus Christ' (3:18).

This plan can be set out in chiastic form as follows.

A   1:3–15: the gospel according to Peter

    B   1:16–19: it rests on the eyewitness testimony of the *apostles*, which confirms…

        C   1:20–21: …the inspired message of the *prophets*

        C'   2:1–22: the *prophets* witness to the reality of judgment (vv. 1–10), which these people richly deserve (vv. 11–22)

    B'   3:1–10: the *apostles'* teaching reinforces this and assures us that the Lord will come to bring this world to an end

A'   3:11–18: renewed call to believe and obey the gospel according to Peter

THE MESSAGE OF 2 PETER

Notice how up-to-date it all seems. The arguments against the faith have not advanced much in the last two thousand years, although they have intensified with time. If people in Peter's day could say, 'Where is the promise of his coming?' how much more can we? It is still not easy to demonstrate the reality of God's judgment from history or current affairs. The arguments that Peter advances have not changed either. We still have to remember that God is outside time, so all ages are equally present to him. It is still plausible to guess that, if God exists and if the world is not consumed, that is a sign of God's patience and mercy, not of his impotence or indifference. When pressed for evidence, we, like Peter, point back to the story of Jesus, and though we were not 'with him on the sacred mountain' (1:18), we live by the testimony of those who were, and 'feel the promise is not vain that morn shall tearless be'.[3]

THE LETTERS OF JOHN

From time to time, astronomers find themselves looking at a new body in the heavens, and asking, 'What is it? How was it formed? How does it relate to what we know already?' This group of letters raises similar questions. What is the document we know as the first letter of John? It doesn't look much like a letter. And why are the other two very small letters here at all? What is their relationship to 1 John, and what is the relationship of the group to the Gospel of John and to the rest of the New Testament? Why were these letters written, and what were they written *against*? As with most of the letters in this part of the New Testament, these questions can only be answered by the use of a fair amount of conjecture, but here are the conjectures that I think make most sense of these letters as we have them.

First, the three letters all belong together, being written by the same person, at the same time and to the same church situation. 3 John is to be seen as a 'covering letter' to Gaius, a leader of the section of the church still loyal to the gospel as John teaches it; and 2 John as a 'covering letter' to the congregation, introducing the sermon contained in 1 John.[4] This suggestion has the great merit of answering two of our questions: Why are 2 and 3 John here at all, and why does 1 John lack all the features of a letter, especially its opening and closing? If they were not originally attached to 1 John, it is hard to see why 2 and 3 John would ever have been preserved, given their brevity and content. 2 John contains little that is not found in 1 John, and 3 John on its own lacks any clear message for the Church at large. Taken closely with 1 John, 3 John provides the greetings and personal details familiar to us from other New Testament letters, while 1 John is seen to be another example of Christian preaching like Hebrews or James, which also lack some of the conventional features of letters.

It may be argued that whereas 1 John is about Christology and ethics, 3 John is about personal differences or perhaps church order. Diotrephes may be objectionable, but he is no heretic. But if Gaius has 1 John, he does not need to have its content repeated. What he needs is a word of reassurance that the Elder thinks highly of him and recognizes his commitment to the truth (which is not further defined, being set out in 1 John). Part of that reassurance takes the form of an attack on Diotrephes, who, we suppose, is a leader of the breakaway faction. Rather than focusing on his doctrinal position, which Gaius knows all too well and which will be dealt with in 1 John, the Elder impugns his motives and charges him with arrogant behaviour and with wanting to run his own show—a very typical accusation when a church splits and, sadly, often true!

Second, it is plain from 1 and 2 John that the church has split and that a sizeable part has broken away (1 John 2:18–19; 4:1; 2 John 7). John calls the dissidents 'antichrists', 'liars' and 'false prophets'. Who were they and what did they teach? In his sermon, John keeps returning to three ideas—right belief about Jesus, obedience to God's commandments and loving relationships within the family of faith— but it is probably a mistake to think that everything John asserts, his opponents denied, or vice versa. The real issue is the person of Jesus. The opponents deny that Jesus is the Christ (1 John 2:22; 5:1) or the Son of God (5:5). They deny that Jesus Christ has come in the flesh (1 John 4:2; 2 John 7), or that he 'came by water and blood' (1 John 5:6). At the climax of the sermon, John designates his own side as those who 'are in him who is true—even in his Son Jesus Christ', and concludes, 'He is the true God and eternal life' (5:20).

All sorts of shadowy heretical groups have been measured for these garments, but the people they fit best are surely Jews, or Jewish Christians who are unhappy about the growing tendency to equate Jesus with God. As such, they deny that Jesus is the Christ, at least as John understands the term. They deny not the humanity of Jesus but that, in the human Jesus, God has come and died for the sins of the world; and they deny that Jesus is God. They are thus the same opponents as we meet in the fourth Gospel, who deny what that Gospel and this letter are concerned to assert—the deity of Jesus.[5] If we must find a label for them, they are early Ebionites. But were they also antinomian?[6] Not necessarily. John's emphasis on the importance of right living may be a defence against accusations of antinomianism by his law-observant opponents, while his emphasis on love shows what he understands this law to imply (compare Paul in Romans 13:8–10). It is also a call for the faithful to maintain that unity in the Spirit which the dissidents have ruptured.

It is not known for certain who wrote these letters, but similarity of style has naturally led to their being attributed to the author of the fourth Gospel and, despite the doubts of many scholars, that still seems the best option. If, as we saw in Chapter 5 of this book, that Gospel was the work of at least two hands, the beloved disciple and his editor (the 'we' of John 21:24), the letters may well be the work of the editor, which would explain both the similarities that are obvious to everyone and the differences that only highly trained critics claim to detect. Belief in multiple authorship of the letters and the Gospel has fuelled talk of a 'Johannine community'—almost a separate branch of the early Church, with its own distinctive gospel. For this there is no evidence. What we do have is evidence of a Johannine *mind*, of a creative individual who expressed the story of Jesus in his own way and left the imprint of his personality on it, for the benefit of his church and the Church at large. To conclude this section with the metaphor with which we began, the letters of John should be seen as a planet with two moons, but a planet in the same solar system as the rest of the New Testament, orbiting like Paul, James, Peter and the rest around the same sun, Jesus, whom they know to be Christ and Lord.

OUTLINE OF 1 JOHN

1 John has defeated the attempts of scholars to find some neat literary or thematic plan by which the author has arranged his thoughts. Instead we find a succession of short meditations circling round three points—right belief, right doing and right relationships in the family of faith. Often the meditations are linked together by a word common to the last sentence of the previous one and the first sentence of the next.

The story to live by (1 John 1:1–4)

The Christian message is the story of how that which was from the beginning appeared on earth to human eyes. As such, it rests on the eyewitness testimony of those who heard and saw and touched. The purpose of Christ's appearing is that human beings may enjoy fellowship with God and with one another. The purpose of the letter is to retain the readers in fellowship with the writer and assure them that they thereby retain fellowship with God.

Walking in the light: link word, 'fellowship' (1 John 1:5—2:11)

What does it mean to have fellowship with God? It means to walk in his ways and do what is right. Sin breaks this fellowship, but God has acted in Jesus to repair it. So we should confess our sins so that they can be forgiven, and then recommit ourselves to obedience and to love. In this way we live in the light.

Word of reassurance: link word, 'know' (1 John 2:12–27)

You are those who know God and overcome the evil one, so do not live as the world lives. This world is passing away—in fact, this is the last hour—and this is seen by the emergence of a pernicious heresy. There are people denying that Jesus is the Christ, but you have been anointed by the Holy Spirit to know the truth. So long as you remain in this, you are quite safe.

Children of God: link word, 'remain' (1 John 2:28—3:10)

We remain in his truth when we do what is right, thus showing ourselves to be children of God. We have been born of God as his children. One day we shall see him and be visibly like him; right now, our status as his children is proved by our lives of righteousness and love.

Love one another: link word, 'love' (1 John 3:11—24)

Love is the distinguishing mark of the Christian. Love is measured by the sacrifice of Christ but is to be worked out in our sacrificial living. Such love gives us assurance of eternal life, and shows that we possess the Spirit.

The two Spirits: link word, 'Spirit' (1 John 4:1–6)

Not all teachers have the Spirit of God, however impressive they may be. The test is whether they confess that Jesus Christ has come in the flesh, as we do.

God is love: continue the theme of 'love' (1 John 4:7—5:4)

Love is the test of new birth. True love is shown by God's sending his Son into the world. It is also shown in our loving our brothers and sisters. Children of God are marked by faith that Jesus is the Christ. This faith is proved by love for other believers. Love in turn is seen in obeying God's commands, and those who thus believe and love will enjoy God's victory.

Eternal life: link word, 'victory' (1 John 5:5–18)

God's victory is eternal life, and it belongs to those who believe that Jesus is the Son of God, who came by water and the Spirit (a reference to his baptism and death on the cross). Those who have the Son have eternal life. Such people enjoy great confidence before God, especially in their prayers, and they should use it to rescue those who are going astray.

Our confidence (1 John 5:18–21)

We know who we are because we know who Jesus Christ is. He is the true God, and to claim to worship God apart from him is idolatry.

THE MESSAGE OF 1 JOHN

John's message is one of assurance in a time of confusion and strife. How can people be sure that they know God, that they are children of God, that they have eternal life? John proposes three tests.[7]

- Do they obey God's word? (2:3–6; 2:28—3:10; 5:2)
- Do they love God's people and show it in practical, sacrificial ways? (2:9–11; 3:11–24; 4:7–21)
- Do they acknowledge God's Son? (1:1–4; 2:18–23; 4:1–6; 5:5–12, 20)

Just as there is no true faith that does not show itself in love and good works, so there can be no true living that is not empowered by the story of Jesus who appeared on earth (1:2), was anointed with the Spirit (5:6), died on the cross for the sins of the world (1:7; 3:8; 4:10; 5:6), and is our advocate in heaven (2:1–2), from where he will again appear to take us to himself (3:2). This is the story that underlies John's preaching. Those who want to please God must live by it, and those who live by it must love and obey.

CHAPTER 15

THE STORY OF TWO CITIES:
THE BOOK OF REVELATION

More than any other book of the Bible, Revelation forces us to ask, 'What kind of book is this? What kind of questions will it answer?' We easily think that this book is like no other, a strange, supernatural communication to which the normal rules of interpretation hardly apply, so it may come as a shock if I begin by saying that Revelation is a *pastoral letter*. It begins like Paul's letters, 'John, to the seven churches in the province of Asia: Grace and peace to you from him who is, and who was, and who is to come' (1:4). Like all letters, it is from someone, to someone, who lives somewhere, at some time, about something and written for some purpose.

- It is *from someone*. He simply calls himself John and he is, or has recently been, on the island of Patmos, just off the coast of Asia Minor. Whether he is the apostle John or another man of the same name, and whether he also wrote the fourth Gospel and/or the letters of John is hotly disputed, but of no help in understanding the book of Revelation.

- It is *to someone, living somewhere*. John writes to the churches in seven major towns of Asia Minor. These are real places and we can find them on the map. John knows these people and the problems they face.

- It was written *at some time*. Obviously the readers knew what date it was, but we do not. It has been usual to date Revelation by reference to the persecution the churches are allegedly undergoing, placing it either in the reign of Nero (AD54–68, but especially during the persecution of AD64) or in the reign of Domitian (AD81–96). But Nero's and Domitian's persecutions were probably confined to Rome, and Revelation itself suggests that John sees the persecution as future rather than present, so this may be of little help in dating the letter. AD95 is still the majority verdict, but it could well be ten or fifteen years earlier.[1]

- It is *about something* that is going to happen soon. Although this has traditionally been thought to be the second coming and the end of the world, it is much more likely to be a time of fierce persecution that John expects when the idolatrous claims of the Roman empire force Christians to choose which king they will honour and to which city they will belong.[2]

- It is written *for some purpose*. That purpose is not to provide the readers with a timetable for the future, but to warn them of the perils they will soon face and to strengthen their resolve to resist. Like Hebrews or 1 Peter, Revelation is a *pastoral* letter, a 'word of exhortation' (Heb. 13:22). Remembering this will help to keep our feet on the ground. John is not likely to be writing to his friends about something they could not possibly know anything about— like the Pope or the European Community, for example!

Revelation also calls itself a prophecy (1:3), but here we must be careful. Prophets in the Bible are not those who predict future events like fortune-tellers, but those who are granted special insight into the meaning of the times in which they live, who are allowed to go behind the scenes and bring God's point of view on the affairs of their own time. The story of the prophet Micaiah ben Imlah makes the point (1 Kings 22:1–28). Micaiah is reluctantly summoned by the wicked king Ahab to advise him on the wisdom of going to war against the Arameans. He tells the king that he has had a vision of the Lord in council, as a result of which he foretells utter disaster for the king if he goes to war—and this is exactly what happens. Micaiah predicts the future, certainly, but it is not the future of the world but the immediate future of the kingdom of Ahab, and it is a future conditional on Ahab's response. If he heeds the warning, he will avoid the disaster. In the same way, Jeremiah claimed to have stood in the council of the Lord, as a result of which he predicted that Jerusalem would be destroyed if its inhabitants did not change their foreign policy (Jer. 23:18).

John fits this pattern perfectly. He is summoned to the control room at Supreme Headquarters (4:1) to see the churches' battle from the point of view of the Supreme Commander.[3] As a result, he is able to give the churches of Asia insight into the true meaning of the times in which they live and warn them of the danger of compromise.

We talk of John's readers, but it would be more accurate to speak of John's *hearers*. The book of Revelation, like all the New Testament letters, was heard by the congregation rather than read. We need to picture a small group of earnest folk crowded into a smallish room lit with oil lamps while someone reads aloud from the scroll that has arrived from John. What would they have made of it? They would probably have been less puzzled than we are, because they were familiar with the symbols John uses, and knew the code, so to speak. As well as being a letter and a prophecy, John's book has been written in the form of an apocalypse, a kind of writing well-known at the time, in which God's purposes for the world are made known by the use of vivid symbolism. It may be helpful to think of *Pilgrim's Progress*, in which spiritual lessons are taught by means of the report of a dream, where many fantastic things take place which the readers can immediately identify as standing for realities in their own world. An apocalypse is rather like the report of a dream: events that happen in the dream stand for events in the real world, but the two should never be confused. It is no good asking for the grid reference of Doubting Castle, for it does not exist outside the dream, though the condition it stands for is real enough. In the same way, it is no good going to the Natural History Museum to look for the beast that comes out of the sea in Revelation 13, though the truth it expresses is part of John's world, and perhaps ours.

John's symbols would have been familiar to his hearers and the comparison has often been made with the symbolic figures used in political cartoons today. I came across a particularly vivid example shortly after the United States declared its 'war on terrorism' in 2001. The front cover of a weekly news magazine[4] portrayed two horsemen charging at one another, the one a medieval Crusader with a red cross over his armour, the other a Saracen with turban and curved scimitar. It was left to the reader to work out what was being said, but the message seemed obvious: this is another chapter in an old conflict between east and west, Christian against Muslim. Yet closer inspection showed that the Crusader-figure was wearing Nike trainers and baseball cap, as if to say, 'Don't think this conflict is about religion; it is a clash of culture fuelled by commercial interests.' The high-flown rhetoric of the allied nations was being gently questioned and perhaps ridiculed. Notice three things. First, the picture was entirely symbolic; no one was literally riding horses, although the conflict portrayed was quite real. Second, the symbols were instantly recognizable, otherwise the cartoon would not have communicated. But third, the artist had subtly altered the symbols so that they now said something new and subversive.

John uses symbolic language in just this way. Some of his symbols have been drawn from the Old Testament and others from events in John's own time, but the point John is making will often be found in the small details by which a familiar image has been significantly altered. Thus, when John says, 'I saw a beast coming out of the sea. He had ten horns and seven heads' (13:1), the reader is supposed to know that Daniel had a very similar vision in which he saw four such monsters and that each of them represented an evil empire that oppressed God's people. John's beast has the same meaning, and there is not much doubt which empire he has in mind. But to make it even clearer, he says, 'One of the heads of the beast seemed to have had a fatal wound, but the fatal wound had been healed' (13:3). That was never part of the traditional symbolism, but it doesn't only contribute to the identification, it adds a further twist. John's readers lived under the most splendid and ruthless empire the world has ever seen, ruling over the entire Mediterranean world, but in AD68 the whole edifice had nearly come crashing down. Four generals in succession seized the throne in a series of military coups before Vespasian (AD69–79) restored order. Most people were very glad of the peace, stability and prosperity Rome brought, and were very happy to accord divine honours to the emperor (13:4), but for John it was a blood-thirsty monster, a demonic regime demanding idolatrous worship, ready to liquidate all who worshipped God rather than Caesar. Yet, despite its terrifying power, Rome had been wounded once, and would one day be destroyed. Before that day, John knew, the Christians faced a tough time in preserving their integrity (13:10).

What kind of book is this? It is a pastoral letter, containing a prophecy, expressed as an apocalypse. What kind of questions will it answer? Not so much 'When will the world end?' as 'How should Christians live in a hostile world as they pray for God's kingdom to come?' Understanding the book of Revelation then turns out to be not so different from understanding any other book of the Bible. We have to enter into the situation of the first readers and ask what it meant to them. Just as we shall understand 1 Corinthians better if we know something about Paul, Corinth and the Corinthian church, so we shall understand Revelation better if we know something of the problems faced by Christians in the Roman empire at the end of the first century. Revelation will be found relevant in the same way as 1 Corinthians, too. As we read, we shall see that their times were much like our times, their churches much like ours; and above all, their God is our God, who still calls us to be steadfast in the face of the temptation to compromise with the idolatrous claims of the dominant culture.

AN OUTLINE OF REVELATION

THE RISEN CHRIST CALLS HIS CHURCH TO ORDER
(REVELATION 1:1—3:22)

Revelation opens with a vision of Christ in glory in the midst of seven golden lampstands. We learn that the lampstands represent the seven churches (1:20), which we guess represent the Church as a whole, because their function is to give light in the darkness of the pagan cities where they are set. This is an old picture of the people of God (Zech. 4), made new in Jesus, who says to his disciples, 'You are the light of the world' (Matt. 5:14). The Church is to shine by its endurance and faithfulness (Rev. 1:9), by its love (2:4–5) and by its proclamation of the good news. If it fails to do this, it loses the right to be called a Church (2:5).

But the churches are under threat. John writes to warn them of imminent danger (1:1), and calls them to do battle and to overcome in the same way as Jesus overcame (3:21). The danger is twofold—persecution from without and compromise from within, and the two are linked. The demand for emperor worship puts the Church and the empire on a collision course, and refusal to worship will lead to persecution, if it has not done so already. So far, only one man has actually been killed (2:13), but trouble is expected (2:10). It is often supposed that John himself was a prisoner (1:9), but this is not very likely. There is no evidence that Patmos was a prison camp, and only very well-to-do aristocrats were punished by being exiled to islands. John was on Patmos 'because of the word of God' (1:9), but whether he had gone to Patmos to spread the word, or to receive the word, or had been sent there as a punishment for preaching the word, is not clear. Meanwhile, there are Christian leaders and teachers advocating compromise (2:6, 14, 20). John charges them with immorality, but it is unlikely that they were sexually promiscuous. More probably, their adultery was spiritual adultery and they were teaching that the Church's uncompromising stance was unnecessarily strict. Very likely, some of the Christians belonged to trade guilds where participation in religious ceremonies was a condition of being able to do business at all. To those who wanted to 'get on', John's teaching must have seemed unrealistic.

We may well sympathize with the churches' dilemma. Just as they were faced by the problems of moving the faith from rural Galilee to the sophisticated world of Ephesus or Rome, so we face the problem of trying to live out an ancient faith in a modern world. When is adaptation apostasy? When is faithfulness irrelevance? When does a church submit to government regulations, even though it means not doing what we believe to be right? When does a church do what is right, even though it means breaking the law?

The purpose of the seven letters, however, is not merely to blame but to encourage. Christ is the conqueror, he holds the stars (meaning the angels of the churches) in his right hand and he will keep his churches safe. He moves among the lampstands and he knows all about them—what they do (2:2), what they suffer (2:9), where they live (2:13), what their strength is (3:8), what they hide (3:1, 15). Like the God of the exodus, he has heard and seen and will come to them (2:5, 16; 3:3, 20; compare Ex. 3:7–8). This is not his final coming at the last day, but a localized coming in judgment or blessing within the historical process and conditional on their response to his word. It is a coming that will be realized even in the fires of persecution that will break over the churches and find out their weak spots. He is at the very door (3:20)! This may be terrifying, but every letter promises victory and reward. Even the worst are promised that they will reign with Christ (3:21). The rewards are 'out of this world', but the earning of them is very much in this world as the churches listen to what the Spirit is saying and identify with Jesus in his faithful witness.

THE BREAKING OF THE SEALS (REVELATION 4:1—8:1)

John is taken behind the scenes to see how the battle looks from the viewpoint of heaven, like a journalist admitted to the control room at Supreme Headquarters. The purpose is not to satisfy our curiosity but to help us make sense of our world. The first thing John sees is a throne, and it is not vacant. Despite appearances, our God is reigning over the whole world. The rainbow tells us that he reigns mercifully (remember Noah?); the thunders tell us that he reigns justly (remember Sinai?); the sea of glass tells us that he reigns victoriously (the sea is an ancient symbol of evil, but now it lies calm and beautiful at the feet of God). God reigns, but he doesn't reign alone. John sees 24 other thrones, on which sit the elders who represent the people of God, and the whole people of God and the whole created universe unite to give God praise and glory (4:1–11).

But John is in tears! There is a scroll in the right hand of God, containing the revelation of God's goodness and the plan of God for his creation, and it is sealed. No one can read it. God's will is every- where contradicted. God's glory and grace are everywhere obscured. God may be king in name, but his will is barred by all the sorrows of the world that are the result of human sin. How can God be king when these ancient evils stalk the earth? How can we believe in a God of love when people suffer as they do? The answer, of course, is Jesus. Jesus who is the mighty lion of God is also Jesus the slain lamb of God. He has taken away the sin of the world and ransomed men and women for God, and now he shares his reign and his priestly work with them, and they in turn worship him as God and praise him for the salvation he has brought (5:1–14).

Now we are in a position to understand the opening of the seven seals. They are not a vision of the future. They are a description of the present world that we know so well, ills as old as the earth itself. It is not that they are to *happen* one after the other in our world, but John *sees* them one after the other as they pass before his gaze in the other world to which he has been summoned. They are not a catalogue of judgments hurled on the earth by a vengeful God, but the things that stand against God and block the knowledge of his power and love. They are not, in fact, so much sent by God as summoned by creation itself to come and bow their knee before the lamb who has defeated them by his death on the cross. Military conquest (6:2), the grim reality of war that makes it possible (6:4), the poverty that results from it (6:6), death in all its hideous forms that accompanies it (6:8), the persecution of the righteous (6:9–11), and even hell itself (6:12–17): these are the seals that prevent the will of God from being seen and done. The judgment of God is set forth in traditional images, but if God can win only by destroying the world, he has lost. So wrath and hell are seals too, along with sin and death, but Jesus has overcome them. Broken by the cross, they are now paraded before John and before the eyes of God's people as the defeated foes they are (6:1–17).

The full realization of that victory is still future, so far as this world is concerned, and meanwhile generations of God's people come and go, but they are not lost. God is saving a people for himself, through all the pains and troubles of this world, and the vision of the 144,000 tells us that in the end not one will be missing (7:1–8). But this is no remnant, no exclusive club. On the contrary, it is a great crowd that no one can number. They come from the whole wide world, and celebrate salvation through Christ, not just for themselves but for the whole of creation. They have suffered, as all believers suffer, but they have kept faith, and now they are set free from pain, sin and death. Their sins are forgiven, their questions answered, their hurts healed and their regrets are no more. The meaning of this vision is that one day every knee will bow and every tear be wiped away (7:9–17). After that, there is no more to be said (8:1)!

THE SOUNDING OF THE TRUMPETS
(REVELATION 8:2—11:19)

The first thing to notice about this complex vision is that it begins with the prayers of the Church (8:3–5) and ends with the praise of God's people (11:16–18). God's people pray, as their Lord has taught them, 'May your kingdom come', and everything that happens in the vision is part of God's answer to that prayer. At the end of the vision, God's kingdom does come (11:15). When that happens, rebellion will be crushed, servants will be rewarded, destroyers will be destroyed and God's people will give thanks. But how will God answer this prayer?

Seals obscure; trumpets warn. The next sequence of pictures presents the same sorts of evil that have obscured the truth of God's loving reign, but this time portrays them as trumpets (8:6—9:21). God warns people through the pains of creation. As C.S. Lewis said, 'Pain is God's megaphone to rouse a deaf world.'[5] The first four trumpets belong together, speaking of disaster on land and sea, in the rivers and in the heavens—the whole created universe that is the environment of rebel humanity. This does not speak of the end of the world: only a third is destroyed. Nor should we take these visions literally as a prediction of coming events. John is rather saying that the natural environment itself is out of joint. Natural disasters of every kind lie in wait for humankind—drought, storm, earthquake—and when people ask why, John says that they are warnings. God is warning us in exactly the same way as he warned Pharaoh in the exodus story, which the vision echoes. Just as Pharaoh said, 'Who is the Lord, that I should obey him?' (Ex. 5:2), so rebel humanity has been saying this to God, and God has created an environment that reminds us of the insecurity of our tenure. Describing the pains of the world in exodus language also tells God's faithful people that through it all their redemption is drawing near.

The next trumpet speaks of the torments of sin that fall specifically on those who do not obey God (9:1–12). They are not something to be experienced after death, but characterize life on earth. They arise from the abyss, that great symbol of rebellion against God, an infernal reservoir of evil to which our sins contribute—as if to say that the evil that we do does not evaporate into nothing, but returns to haunt our consciences and plague our descendants. The plague released by the next trumpet is described in terms of the invasion of alien hordes (9:13–19). The Roman empire lived in constant fear of such invaders from the east, much as we live in fear of nuclear war, and John draws on this fear to describe the horrors of death—something forever beyond humanity's power to tame, something of which we must go in fear all our days. But John says that this will not be enough. Despite all this, people do not repent (9:20–21). Pain may prepare the way for repentance, but it will not usually accomplish it. Something else is needed.

In the next two chapters, we find that that 'something' is provided by the preaching of the gospel and the witness of the suffering Church. First, God stays his hand (10:1–7). We see a mighty angel clothed with the attributes of God himself, the thunder of judgment rolls and we expect God's judgment to fall on the impenitent, but the angel hushes it. God will accomplish his purpose, but not that way. Instead, God sends forth his gospel (10:8–11). The angel has a little scroll in his hand, recalling the great scroll of chapter 5. That scroll contained the loving plan of God for his world, to be put into effect by the death of the Lamb; this scroll also contains the gospel, but this time it is to be put into effect by the witness of the Church. In other words, the witness of the Church is a sort of 'junior version' of the work of the Lamb—lesser in dignity, but of exactly the same shape and purpose. That is why the scroll is bittersweet. It is sweet because it is the message of God's redeeming love. It is bitter because it will be accomplished only by the sufferings of the Church, as the next chapter makes plain (11:1–14).

The Church is first represented by the temple, which is partly to be protected (measured), and partly exposed to suffering; kept safe in its innermost self, yet exposed to the hostility of the world. Then we see the people of God under the guise of two olive trees. The picture is drawn from Zechariah, where the trees represent the king and the high priest. Here they represent the people whom Jesus has made 'kings and priests to God' (1:6), and who have the task of prophesying— that is, of preaching God's message to the world. Like their Lord, they are first anointed with power, then killed, and finally vindicated and raised to heaven. And now at last, people in great numbers turn to God in awe and give him the glory due to him, and the way is clear for the last trumpet to sound, and to sound with the news not that

God destroyed the world, but that the kingdoms of this world have become the kingdom of our Lord and of his Christ. God has won the world to himself not by the exercise of naked power, but by the blood of the Lamb and the witness of his Church.

THE STORY BEHIND HISTORY (REVELATION 12:1—15:4)

If we have not noticed it already, the book of Revelation is the report of a series of visions, and these visions all cover much the same ground, if from a different point of view. The kingdom of God comes as the climax to each of them (7:9–17; 11:15–19; 15:3–4; 19:1–4; 21:1–4). This means that just because John says, 'I *saw* this, and then this, and then that', we should be very unwise to understand him to mean, '*First* this will happen, and *then* this and *then* that.' The sequence of events in John's dream is no sure guide to any supposed sequence of events in our world, beyond the fact that both will end with the establishment of God's kingdom. So the visions we come to now are not to be thought of as happening after the sounding of the trumpets, but concurrently with it, pointing us to the age-old struggle between good and evil that lies behind the Church's battle for the truth.

The first vision is a drama in three acts (12:1–17). The *dramatis personae* are the woman, who represents the ancient people of God; her son, who is the Christ (12:5); her other children, who are the faithful Christians; and the dragon, alias the satan, or accuser. Act I takes place on earth. The woman gives birth to a child. The dragon tries to destroy the child, but succeeds only in bringing about his enthronement. The woman finds refuge in the desert, away from the sinful city, for a time determined by God.

Act II takes place in heaven, which is the counterpart of earth. In the heavenly courtroom, which corresponds to the earthly battlefield, the satan loses his case against God and his people and is driven from the courtroom (12:9) because of the death of Christ on the cross (12:10–11). John's Gospel has Jesus utter the same idea: 'Now is the judgment of this world; now the ruler of this world will be driven out. And I, when I am lifted up from the earth, will draw all people to myself' (John 12:31–2, NRSV).

Act III takes place back on earth. The dragon renews his attack on the woman with a stream of propaganda (since it comes from his mouth), but unsuccessfully. So he attacks her children instead. And the message in all this? The victory of Christ on the cross ensures the eternal security of the Church, even though for the moment its children must suffer for their faith.

In the next vision, the enemies of the people of God are depicted as savage monsters. There is first the monster from the deep (13:1–10). To understand this, you need to know some biblical background and also something of the world of John's day. Long ago, at a time of great crisis for the faithful, the prophet Daniel had described the tyrannical empires that had oppressed God's people as savage monsters coming up out of the sea. There were four such monsters, and the fourth was the most terrible. Daniel probably had in mind the Greek empire, and Antiochus Epiphanes in particular, who in 168BC tried to destroy the Jewish faith, but John sees the role of this monster fulfilled by someone else. John and his readers lived, as we know, in a world dominated by Rome, which most people saw as magnificent and the source of world salvation, but which John sees as a cruel and blasphemous monster. In AD68, on the death of Nero, the Roman empire had been rocked to its foundations, but had recovered, and we are probably right to see a reference to this in 13:3. In this vision, the evil empire is seen as the tool of the old dragon, who whistles it up out of the sea, where all evil things come from. The horns and heads symbolize its power and cruelty, while the blasphemous names refer to its demand that people pay to it the honour that belongs to God alone.

The rule of the monster from the deep is made all the more terrible by the addition of a second monster, the monster from the land (13:11–18). Later John will call this monster a false prophet, and here describes it in religious terms. This monster makes 'the earth and its inhabitants worship the first beast' (13:12). It is, in fact, the state religion, the cult of Caesar, which sought to promote the unity of the diverse peoples of the empire by getting them to express their loyalty by burning incense at the statue of the emperor. It could even pass itself off as a Christian option (the monster looks quite a lamb, 13:11), and as we have seen, there were those in the churches who were taken in by it (2:14).

Those who refuse to worship Caesar are punished either with death (13:15) or economic sanctions (13:16–17). The number of the monster, 666, has long puzzled readers (though it was probably quite clear to John's hearers). It is probably a traditional reference to Nero Caesar, who, it was rumoured, had never died and would return to Rome to wreak his revenge—but notice the pastoral purpose of all this! It is not just religious sci-fi, nor wild political diatribe. It is a call for endurance and faith on the part of the saints (13:10), who need to know their enemy in order to withstand him.

What can God put in the field against such enemies and their supporters? In contrast to the empire of the great monster, God's kingdom is the kingdom of the Lamb, and his army is an army of martyrs (14:1–5). They oppose the blasphemies of the monster by presenting an eternal gospel, and call people to worship God. They proclaim that Babylon, the great city, is doomed. They warn people not to be found to have chosen the wrong side, and we are assured that such witness will not be in vain (14:6–13). The chapter ends with a double vision of the great harvest. The people of all nations will be gathered into God's house (14:13–16), and the blood of the martyrs, we learn in the next section, will fill the cup that sends the great city of Babylon reeling to its doom (14:17–20; compare 17:6). The vine is the Church, and it is the Church that suffers outside the city (Heb. 13:13). The blood of the martyrs, like the blood of the Lamb, is God's secret weapon in the fight against evil.[6] The section ends, as others have done, with a hymn of praise to God (15:1–4).

THE FALL OF BABYLON (REVELATION 15:5—19:4)

The message of this long passage was stated back in the previous chapter: 'Fallen is Babylon the Great' (14:8). John, of course, is talking about Rome (as is proven by 17:3, 9, 18). Babylon was the great oppressor of God's people in the Old Testament, and Rome's power and wealth, its idolatrous claims and murderous activity show that Babylon has risen again in John's time. It is time to warn Christians: don't be deceived by Rome's beauty, don't be dismayed by its ferocity, for the great city is doomed! With its references to plagues and to the song of Moses, chapter 15 reminds us of the exodus. Then as now, it says, God's people were oppressed; now as then God will overthrow the oppressor—but the song of Moses has become the song of the

Lamb. God will win through the blood of the Lamb and the witness of the Church.

The seven bowls of wrath are certainly final—no more warnings—but they do not speak of the destruction of the human race or the physical world. It is not the end of the world. The target is Babylon and those who choose it as their refuge. The first four bowls say that the natural order will fight against Babylon—land, sea, rivers and sky above. Just as the stars in their courses fought against Sisera (Jdg. 5:20), so in the end nature itself will turn on those who receive the gift without giving thanks to the Giver, who despoil the earth with harshness and rule it without pity or consideration (16:1–9). The evil empire will fall, as evil empires do—in this case by the failure of government, the invasion of alien hordes, and the rebellion of subject peoples—and Rome will meet its 'Waterloo' (otherwise known as 'Armageddon' or the Last Battle). As God remembered Noah for salvation (Gen. 8:1), so God will 'remember' Babylon for judgment. It is not the End; it is not the beginning of the End; but it is the end of Babylon and of everyone who is found clinging to the wreckage, whether in complacency or defiance (16:10–21).

John goes on to portray Rome as both a prostitute and a monster. As a prostitute she is fascinating. (Unless you go into the desert, away from the glamour and bustle of city life, you are likely to be taken in by her, 17:3.) She seduces the people of God, attracting to herself the love that belongs to God. Rome, or any great civilization, has this potential—wealth, grandeur, technology, but also idolatrous claims, calling for worship, uncritical loyalty and obedience to unjust laws. Martin Luther saw the Church of Rome in this role. In our own times it has been played by Hitler, by Communism and, some people would say, even by the United States. Any state, any ideology, can exercise this fascination. Many states and ideologies have done so, and Christians have been among those deceived as well among those who bravely die (17:1–6).

Rome is also a monster. As we have seen, this is an image as old as Daniel. The seven heads identify Rome as *that* monster spoken of by Daniel, but John is saying that is days are numbered. The riddle of the seven kings, five fallen, one living and one yet to come, has been used to date the book of Revelation (with no agreement among scholars as to where the sequence begins), but this cannot have been

John's intention. His hearers knew what date it was. More probably, the message is simply that Rome will fall soon. This is a message of hope and a call for courage. There are grim times ahead, but the victory belongs to the Lamb. The blood of the saints will send Babylon reeling to its doom, although the work of destruction will actually be carried out by the constituent parts of Babylon's own empire (17:7–18).

God will pass sentence on Babylon (18:1–8). When that happens, the kings of the earth and all who have been seduced by Babylon's wealth into materialism will mourn and weep (18:9–19), but God's people will rejoice (18:20—19:4). What are they to do in the meantime? They must come out of her (18:4), not literally but in heart and mind. They are not to invest in Babylon, either financially or emotionally, or else they will share the grief of those who are left desolate by her fall. If this seems over-dramatic for today's readers, especially those lucky enough to live in democratic nations under the rule of law, it is worth remembering that it is said of the monster that though it was and is to come, it presently is not (17:8). Like us, John's people were living at peace, but John says that it will not last. Discernment is always needed to see where power has led to corruption. What he says to them, he says to us and to all: keep awake!

THE LAMB AND HIS BRIDE (REVELATION 19:5—22:5)

The final section of Revelation consists of another series of visions, and once again we shall make most sense of them if we remember that they occur in the order that John sees them, not necessarily in the order in which the events they refer to happen in our world. They begin with the announcement of a wedding (19:5–10). The evil empire has gone down to destruction and those who were wedded to it are left inconsolably alone, but that is not the end or the point of it all. The true end of history is the union of God with his people. Confusingly, the people of God seem to be both the wedding guests and the Bride. Individually they are guests; corporately they form the Bride.

Here comes the Bridegroom (19:11–16)! Here he is called Faithful and True and bears the name of the Word of God, but we know him better as Jesus. He comes as a victor on a white horse, and all his friends are with him, dressed not for war but for a party (v. 14). He is the victor, but his battles are behind him. His victory has not been cheap, as his blood-stained robe shows, but by his death he trod the winepress of God's wrath for us and won a great number of people to himself. His weapon is his word, for he wins the nations by persuasion, not coercion. His triumph is not a solitary triumph, for on his head are many crowns, the victories of the martyr Church.

So where's the Bride? She does not appear until 21:1–4. Meanwhile John speaks of a last battle, a binding of Satan, a thousand-year reign of the saints, another last battle, the final judgment—and then the Bride appears. Traditionally, this has been read as a timetable of future events in our world: Christ will come; he will fight a last battle; Satan will be bound; God's people will rule on earth; there will be another last battle and a last judgment, after which the Bride will come. It is the wedding imagery that gives the lie to this. We have heard of brides being late, but this is ridiculous! It is also unbelievable. If Christ can ride out of heaven to destroy evil, what have we been waiting for? If the wicked are destroyed because they have been judged to be wicked in 19:17–21, why are they resurrected and judged again in 20:11–15? If Christ can destroy Satan, why does he lock him up and then let him out again? If the Christian dead are resurrected to rule over the earth, who do they rule over, and how, and why for only a thousand years, and do the generations die off in the meantime?

All of these absurdities arise from supposing that we have here a timetable for the future. It is better to see that what we have here is a flashback whose purpose is to tell us how it comes about that the Bridegroom is so wounded, the Bride so lovely and the guests so numerous. The Bridegroom will come to claim his Bride, but *before then all evil must be destroyed and all people judged* (19:17–21; 20:7–15). There must be a great banquet of another kind (19:17). The evil power that rules this dark world must first destroy itself. The kings, generals, mighty men, all who oppose God and persecute his people, and in the end even Satan himself, must be destroyed. We are not told how this will happen, but in the light of the rest of the book we may say that it comes about through the blood of the Lamb and the testimony of the martyr Church, through which the princes of this world lose all legitimacy, and through their own armies by which the rulers of this world destroy each other and themselves. Evil is exposed by the cross, and falls under the weight of its own internal contradictions. To change the picture from the battlefield to the law-court, there must be a Great Assize (20:11–15), when the dead will be judged, justice will be done to all and death itself will be no more. Only then will the Bridegroom come, and the Bride be found ready, and the love of God and his people consummated in eternity.

But will there be anyone left, and will there be much to celebrate? If the greatest part of the human race has been thrown into the lake of fire, and the creator can win only by destroying his world, what sort of victory is that? John's answer is that *all this will not happen until there is an age of grace*, symbolized here as a thousand years (20:1–6). During this time, Satan will be bound, the nations will be gathered into the people of God, and those who die in the Lord will live and reign with him. If we ask, 'When and how will Satan be bound?' the answer of this book up to now, as of all Christian theology, is that he was bound at the cross, at Christ's first coming. It is the birth, life, death and resurrection of Jesus, the Lamb of God, that have driven the accuser from the court and bound the 'strong man' (12:10; compare Mark 3:27; John 12:31–32), and that is why the gospel can be preached and the nations gathered in.

So if we ask, 'When do the thousand years begin?' the answer is that they began at the cross. The number, of course, is no more to be taken literally than any of the other numbers in the book of Revelation. It means 'a long time', but it is not a measure of the saints' reward, but of the sinners' time to repent. It is a sign of the breadth and length of God's mercy and love. The world will not end, and Christ will not come back, until all who repent have been gathered into God's family. If we ask, finally, 'What will happen to those believers who die in the meantime?' John's answer is that they will live and reign with Christ. Where he is, in heaven, they also will be. As he is, risen and reigning, so also will they be. As he waits (in terms of this world of space and time), so also must they (6:9–11). They are eternally secure and happy, but not until the Bridegroom comes will they be raised to meet him as his Bride. Their death is the first resurrection; their second resurrection is the marriage supper of the Lamb.

And now at last, here comes the Bride (21:1—22:5)! She is the Church of God, the new Israel, the new humanity, all those who have put their faith in the living God and kept faith with him, all those whose deeds of faith and love show them to have been true believers —a great multitude that no one can number, drawn from every nation and people. They have waited, hoped, believed, prayed and loved, and now at last they are face to face with God and enjoy the reward of faithfulness and the consummation of desire for ever. Now the dwelling of God is with his people. What was pictured in tabernacle and temple, what was inaugurated in the incarnation, what has been tasted in the believer's experience of the Spirit, is here at last, in full and for ever.

The Bride is also a city. The ancients valued their cities as the embodiment of civilization. John's readers faced the threats and seductions of the greatest city on earth, but his answer to Rome is not a rural paradise but a better city, where human aspirations are fulfilled without the pride and cruelty that so often corrupt them. The city will exclude what is evil. There will be no more sea (21:1), or death, or curse, or darkness, and no room for those who have consistently chosen the wrong side. On the other hand, it will include all that is truly human. The city has walls, and its walls rest on the teaching of the twelve apostles (not all ideas of God are equally valid, nor do all roads lead to him); but the city also has gates, and the gates are open, open to people of every nation (21:24), open to receive their achievements (21:26), open to bring healing to their wounds (22:2). Most important of all, the city comes down from heaven. Unlike Babel, it is not built by human hands or achievement—not even by Christian hands, as if the good we do contributes to the building of the kingdom of God on earth. Rather, it is the other way round: the good we do, the love we express, the wounds we heal, the communities we establish, the worship of the Church and the witness of the martyrs, through which the nations are won and the powers disarmed—all have their *origin* in this city, which through a thousand years of the Church's witness is even now breaking into our world.

CONCLUSION (REVELATION 22:6–21)

John's book does not end with the vision of the city of God but with urgent words of warning and encouragement. The time of crisis is near

(22:6). If we are right in our interpretation of this book, this is not itself the second coming or the last judgment but a time of persecution for the Church of Jesus Christ, in which the verdict of the last judgment will be anticipated in each person's decision for or against God. But of course John still looks forward to a final coming of the Lord as Judge and Saviour of the whole world, and has written this book to show what it means to live in the light of that event. The Spirit and the Bride say to us, 'Come! Come and bear your witness and stand with us.' And the worshipping Church on earth says, 'Come, Lord Jesus!'

THE MESSAGE OF REVELATION

The book of Revelation is not easy to understand, and obviously there is room for disagreement in the interpretation of many of its details. Why should we bother with it? I suggest that we may sum up its message and its contribution to Christian thought in terms of Paul's famous trio—faith, hope and love.

No book of the Bible makes it plainer that faith is a costly choice. Revelation is indeed a 'tale of two cities'. One city dominates the world, but is doomed. The other is visible only to faith, but will last for ever. One city is passing away even while it struts its stuff to general admiration. The other city is exercising its influence in the world even though it suffers violence and is widely despised. You must come out of the first city, even though for the present you cannot avoid living in it. You can belong to the second city, even though you cannot yet see it. This is a message that is relevant in every age and in all societies.

Second, despite its reputation, Revelation is a profoundly hopeful book, and that hope is as wide as the human race and embraces the created universe. It envisages that God will gather to himself a vast multitude that no one can number, drawn from every nation under heaven. It looks forward to the day when the kingdoms of this world will become the kingdom of our Lord and of his Christ. To be sure, John is no universalist. He knows that it is tragically possible for people to throw in their lot with the city of this world and to perish with it, but John knows that the lake of fire is prepared for the devil and his angels (Matt. 25:41), not for human beings unless they stubbornly choose to go that way; and his most violent language is directed at the principalities and powers that seduce humankind and the economic systems that destroy the earth and enslave its inhabitants. Yet in the end the nations are not destroyed. They walk by the light of the city of God and the kings of the earth bring their glory into it.

Finally, Revelation with its hymns of praise invites us to celebrate the victory of God, but the victory of God is the victory of love. In the most dramatic scene in the book, the all-conquering Lion of Judah turns out to be the Lamb that was slain. The Jesus who died on the cross is the true revelation of God and is worthy to receive the worship that belongs to God alone. John knows that 'God so loved the world that he gave his only begotten Son, that whoever believes in him shall not perish but have eternal life' (John 3:16). He also knows that every generation needs those who are willing to lay down their lives so that the power of evil may be broken once again in our world. Satan is conquered by the blood of the Lamb and by the testimony of the martyrs. The monster from the deep is routed by the Lamb and those who follow the Lamb wherever he goes. In this way Revelation calls us to live by the Story, the story of God's love for the world.

NOTES

Prologue: The story behind the story

1 The aim of this chapter is to show how the New Testament story arises out of the Old Testament, and to pinpoint the key Old Testament stories that explain what the earliest Christians saw in Jesus, notably the story of Abraham, the story of Moses, the story of David, the story of the exile and the Servant of the Lord, and the story of Daniel (and the Maccabees) and the Son of Man.

2 W.C. Sellar and R.J. Yeatman, *1066 and All That* (Harmondsworth: Penguin, 1960), p. 5.

3 From the hymn 'God of grace and God of glory' by H.E. Fosdick (1878–1969).

4 I owe this interpretation of Abraham to N.T. Wright, *The New Testament and the People of God* (London: SPCK, 1992), pp. 262–263. As he says, it is an ancient rabbinic understanding found in Genesis Rabbah (c. AD400).

5 G.B. Caird, *Language and Imagery of the Bible* (London: Duckworth, 1980), pp. 57–58.

6 For this interpretation of the Son of Man, see G.B. Caird and L.D. Hurst, *New Testament Theology* (Oxford: Clarendon Press, 1994), pp. 369–381.

Chapter 1: What are the Gospels?

1 The word 'gospel' originally meant 'good news' and is so used by Paul to refer to the Christian message. Mark tells us that the beginning of this good news is the story of Jesus of Nazareth (Mark 1:1). His writing became known as 'the gospel according to Mark' to distinguish it from other presentations of the gospel by, for example, Matthew or Luke. From this, 'gospel' came to mean 'a written account of Jesus' life and ministry', and these four in particular came to be known as the four Gospels. When I want to refer to the Christian message, I shall write 'gospel' in lower case letters; when I want to refer to one of these writings, I shall spell 'Gospel' with a capital letter.

2 Richard A. Burridge, *Four Gospels, One Jesus?* (London: SPCK, 1994), pp. 1–32.

3 See D.R. Catchpole, *Resurrection People* (Darton, Longman & Todd, 2000), p. 135.

4 The first version is taken from Craig Skinner, *Lamplighter and Son* (Broadman, 1984) quoting R. Thompson, *Heroes of the Baptist Church* (London, 1937). The second is from C.H. Spurgeon, *The Early Years* (London: Banner of Truth, 1962), p. 372.

5 The majority view, that Matthew and Luke have independently used 'Q', is helpfully set out by G.N. Stanton, *The Gospels and Jesus* (Oxford: Oxford University Press, 2nd ed., 2002), pp. 23–27. The view that Luke used Matthew is not easy to find in books written for the non-specialist. It is specially associated with the name of Michael D. Goulder.

6 M. Hengel, 'The Titles of the Gospels and the Gospel of Mark', *Studies in the Gospel of Mark* (London: SCM Press), 1985, pp. 64–84.

7 The authorship of the fourth Gospel is more fully discussed in Chapter 5.

8 Keith Hopkins, *A World Full of Gods: Pagans, Jews and Christians in the Roman Empire* (London: Phoenix, 1999), p. 84.

Chapter 2: Mark's story

1 So Morna D. Hooker, *The Gospel According to St Mark* (London: A. & C. Black, 1981), p. 17, to whom this chapter is indebted for many insights.

2 This understanding of Jesus' aims is set out at length in N.T. Wright, *Jesus and the Victory of God* (London: SPCK, 1996), pp. 477–539.

3 G.B. Caird, *Language and Imagery of the Bible* (London: Duckworth, 1980), p. 256.

Chapter 3: Matthew's story

1 Mark 3:13–19; 6:7–13

2 For this interpretation, see R.T. France, *Matthew* (Tyndale New Testament Commentaries, Leicester: IVP, 1985), pp. 333–336.

3 Despite its attraction for modern people, the idea that Christ can be encountered in the persons of the poor and needy is unlikely to have been what Matthew meant. For Matthew, as for the New Testament writers generally, Christ is encountered in the persons of faithful disciples of Jesus, who would very likely be poor, imprisoned and so on (10:42), rather than in the poor as such. See further G.N. Stanton, *A Gospel for a New People* (Edinburgh: T. & T. Clark, 1992), pp. 207–31.

4 'The final passage in the Gospel of Matthew is like a large terminal railway station in which many lines converge.' U. Luz, *The Theology of Matthew* (Cambridge: Cambridge University Press, 1995), p. 5.

Chapter 4: Luke's story

1 B.E. Beck, *Christian Character in the Gospel of Luke* (London: Epworth, 1989), p. 131. 'Luke has fashioned the Pharisees… so that they embody those faults to which he believes his Christian readers are prone.'

2 E. Franklin, *Luke: Interpreter of Paul, Critic of Matthew* (Sheffield: Sheffield Academic Press, 1994)

3 N.T. Wright, *Jesus and the Victory of God* (London: SPCK, 1996), p. 570.

4 Beck, *Christian Character*, pp. 130–144

5 Wright, *Jesus and the Victory*, pp 632–639; L.T. Johnson, *Luke* (Sacra Pagina, Collegeville, Minnesota: 1991), pp. 288–295.

Chapter 5: John's story

1 R. Bauckham, 'John for Readers of Mark' in R. Bauckham (ed.), *The Gospels for All Christians* (Edinburgh: T. & T. Clark, 1998), pp. 147–171.

2 I owe this suggestion to David Catchpole, *Resurrection People* (Darton, Longman and Todd, 2000), p. 166, who cites an illuminating parallel in 1 Macc. 2:65.

3 Gail O'Day, 'John' in L.E. Keck and others (eds), *The New Interpreter's Bible*, IX, (New York: Abingdon, 1995), pp. 507–509; Richard A. Burridge, *Four Gospels, One Jesus?* (London: SPCK, 1994), p. 137.

4 G.R. Beasley-Murray, *John* (Word Bible Comentaries, Waco, Texas: Word), p. 12.

5 O'Day, 'John', p. 591.

6 N.T. Wright, *The Crown and the Fire* (London: SPCK, 1992), p. 29.

7 Beasley-Murray, *John*, p. 192.

8 G.B. Caird, *Language and Imagery of the Bible* (London: Duckworth, 1980), p. 47.

9 O'Day, 'John', p. 832.

Chapter 6: Luke's story: The Acts of the Apostles

1 Thucydides, *History of the Peloponnesian War*, 1.22.1

2 For this point and the perspective of this section as a whole, see L.T. Johnson, *The Acts of the Apostles* (Sacra Pagina 5, Collegeville, Minnesota: Liturgical Press, 1992), pp. 135–138.

3 Jacob Jervell, *The Theology of the Acts of the Apostles* (Cambridge: Cambridge University Press, 1996), pp. 82–94.

Chapter 7: Paul's story: Galatia

1 This interpretation is a minority position among scholars, but is gaining in popularity. We shall meet it again in Romans. See R. Hays, 'Galatians', in L.E. Keck and others (eds), *New Interpreter's Bible*, Vol. XI (New York: Abingdon, 2000), pp. 239–240.

Chapter 8: Paul's story: Thessalonica

1 An exception is C.A. Wanamaker, *The Epistle to the Thessalonians: A Commentary on the Greek Text* (NICGT, Grand Rapids: Eerdmans, 1990).

Chapter 9: Paul's story: Corinth (1)

1 S.J. Hafemann, 'Corinthians' in G.F. Hawthorne, R.P. Martin and D.G. Reid (eds), *Dictionary of Paul and his Letters* (Downers Grove. Il., 1993), p. 173.

2 For this interpretation of these chapters, see G.D. Fee, *The First Epistle to the Corinthians* (Grand Rapids: Eerdmans, 1987).

3 Verse 19 is difficult. I believe it should be translated, 'You insist on social distinctions so as to make plain who are the elite.' The word *dokimoi* has nothing to do with God's approval. It is the title by which the rich referred to themselves. Compare the use of the term 'the quality' in Victorian England. See R.A. Campbell, 'Does Paul Acquiesce in Divisions at the Lord's Supper?', *Novum Testamentum* 33 (1991), pp. 61–70.

4 See, for example, his treatment of food offered to idols, chs. 8—10.

5 A later hand has added verses 34–35 under the impression that women are a threat to such order, but this was not Paul's view (11:5). The verses are found in different places in different manuscripts, a sure sign that they are a later addition.

Chapter 10: Paul's story: Ephesus

1 Philemon 9, 13; Col. 4:3, 18; Phil. 1:13; Eph. 6:20.

2 B.M. Rapske, 'Prison, Prisoner' in C.A. Evans and S.E. Porter (eds), *Dictionary of New Testament Background* (Leicester: InterVarsity Press, 2000), pp. 827–830.

3 M.D. Hooker, *From Adam to Christ: Essays on Paul* (Cambridge: Cambridge University Press, 1990), pp. 121–136. N.T. Wright, *Colossians and Philemon* (TNTC; Leicester: IVP, 1986).

4 Wright, *Colossians*, p. 99.

5 A.T. Lincoln, *Ephesians* (Dallas, Texas: Word, 1990), p. xxxvi.

6 'Praise, my soul, the king of heaven' by H.F. Lyte (1793–1847).

7 L.J. Kreitzer, *Ephesians* (London: Epworth, 1997), p. 200.

Chapter 11: Paul's story: Corinth (2)

1 For the identification of the offender in 2 Corinthians 2 with the incestuous man in 1 Corinthians 5, see C.G. Kruse, *2 Corinthians* (Leicester: IVP, 1987), pp. 41–45.

2 On the meaning of 'the righteousness of God' here, see N.T. Wright, *What St. Paul Really Said* (Oxford: Lion, 1997), p. 104.

Chapter 12: Paul's story: Rome

1 The different meanings of 'righteousness' are helpfully explained by N.T. Wright, *What St Paul Really Said* (Oxford: Lion, 1997), pp. 100–103.

2 N.T. Wright, *The Climax of the Covenant* (Edinburgh: T. & T. Clark, 1991), pp. 18–40.

Chapter 13: The story continues: The Pastoral Letters

1 Some scholars have tried to account for these by suggesting that Paul was using a different secretary. Certainly Paul dictated his letters to a secretary (Rom. 16:23), but a secretary who departed so widely from his master's voice is a new

author, and there is no reason to think that Paul gave anyone the liberty of composing letters in his name.

2 Accordingly, my position differs both from the traditional view that Paul wrote the letters himself, and also from the usual critical view that they are to be dated to the end of the first century. It is similar to that put forward by Professor Marshall in I.H. Marshall with P.H. Towner, *A Critical and Exegetical Commentary on the Pastoral Epistles* (ICC; Edinburgh: T. & T. Clark, 1999).

3 The 'faithful saying' is usually identified with verses 3–7. I think this is a mistake. A comparison with the other 'faithful sayings' shows that this is far too long to be a memorable maxim. I believe that the 'saying' always *follows* the words used to draw attention to it. See R.A. Campbell, 'Identifying the Faithful Sayings in the Pastoral Epistles', *JSNT* 54, 1994, pp. 73–86.

Chapter 14: Apostolic letters and sermons

1 For the view that friendship with God is at the heart of James' vision of the Christian life, see L.T. Johnson, 'James' in *New Interpreter's Bible*, XII (New York: Abingdon, 1998), pp. 181–182.

2 Pliny, *Ep.* X.96, taken from *A New Eusebius*, (ed.) J. Stevenson (London: SPCK, 1957 [revd. ed. W.H.C. Frend, 1987]), pp. 18–19.

3 From George Matheson's hymn, 'O Love that wilt not let me go'.

4 I owe this suggestion to Luke T. Johnson, *The Writings of the New Testament* (London: SCM Press, 1986), p. 503–4.

5 For the view that the opponents are Jews or Jewish Christians, see T. Griffith, *Keep Yourselves from Idols* (Sheffield: JSOT, 2002).

6 So J.R.W. Stott, *The Epistles of John* (TNTC; London: Tyndale Press, 1964), adopting the idea of R. Law, *The Tests of Life* (Edinburgh: T. & T. Clark, 1909).

Chapter 15: The story of two cities: the book of Revelation

1 A.J.P. Garrow, *Revelation* (London: Routledge, 1997), pp. 66–79. He argues for a date in the reign of Titus, AD79–81.

2 G.B. Caird, *The Revelation of St John the Divine* (London: A. & C. Black, 1966)

3 Caird, *Revelation*, pp. 60–61.

4 *The Week*, October 2001 (Dennis Publishing Ltd., UK).

5 C.S. Lewis, *The Problem of Pain* (London: Collins, 1957), p. 81.

6 The Ebionites were Jewish Christians who refected the divinity of Christ (among other things). 'Antinomian' is a term given to people who believe that God's grace excuses them from keeping God's law.

7 As often in this chapter, I follow Caird's interpretation of the grape harvest of 14:17–20.

Guidelines is a unique Bible reading resource that offers four months of in-depth study written by leading scholars. Contributors are drawn from around the world, as well as the UK, and represent a stimulating and thought-provoking breadth of Christian tradition.

Instead of the usual dated daily readings, *Guidelines* provides weekly units, broken into at least six sections, plus an introduction giving context for the passage, and a final section of points for thought and prayer. On any day you can read as many or as few sections as you wish, to fit in with work or home routine. As well as a copy of *Guidelines*, you will need a Bible. Each contributor also suggests books for further study.

Guidelines is edited by Dr Katharine Dell, Senior Lecturer in the Faculty of Divinity at Cambridge University and Director of Studies in Theology at St Catharine's College, and Dr Jeremy Duff, Tutor in New Testament at Wycliffe Hall and a member of the Theology Faculty of Oxfor University.

GUIDELINES SUBSCRIPTIONS

❏ I would like to give a gift subscription
   (please complete both name and address sections below)
❏ I would like to take out a subscription myself
   (complete name and address details only once)

This completed coupon should be sent with appropriate payment to BRF. Alternatively, please write to us quoting your name, address, the subscription you would like for either yourself or a friend (with their name and address), the start date and credit card number, expiry date and signature if paying by credit card.

Gift subscription name _____

Gift subscription address _____

_____ Postcode _____

Please send to the above, beginning with the next January/May/September* issue.
(* *delete as applicable*)

(please tick box)	UK	SURFACE	AIR MAIL
GUIDELINES	❏ £11.40	❏ £12.75	❏ £15.00
GUIDELINES 3-year sub	❏ £28.95		

Please complete the payment details below and send your coupon, with appropriate payment to: **BRF, First Floor, Elsfield Hall, 15–17 Elsfield Way, Oxford OX2 8FG**

Your name _____

Your address _____

_____ Postcode _____

Total enclosed £ _____ (cheques should be made payable to 'BRF')

Payment by cheque ❏ postal order ❏ Visa ❏ Mastercard ❏ Switch ❏

Card number: ☐☐☐☐ ☐☐☐☐ ☐☐☐☐ ☐☐☐☐

Expiry date of card: ☐☐☐☐ Issue number (Switch): ☐☐☐☐

Signature (essential if paying by credit/Switch card) _____

NB: BRF notes are also available from your local Christian bookshop. **BRF is a Registered Charity**

brf

Resourcing your spiritual journey

through...

- Bible reading notes
- Books for Advent & Lent
- Books for Bible study and prayer
- Books to resource those working with under 11s in school, church and at home

- Quiet days and retreats
- Training for primary teachers and children's leaders
- Godly Play
- Barnabas Live

For more information, visit the **brf** website at **www.brf.org.uk**